135

Padma Vibhushan Mahasweta Devi, *Indian social activist and writer* releasing **"Behind Closed Doors"** in presence of **Ms Rinki Bhattacharya,** *author* at an event held in Oxford Book Stores, Kolkata.

Prof Susie Tharu, *Professor Emeritus, Cultural Studies Department, English and Foreign Languages University, Hyderabad* releasing **"Behind Closed Doors"** in presence of **Ms Rinki Bhattacharya,** *author* at an event held in Hyderabad

Can you beat that?

Writer, columnist and documentary filmmaker Rinki Bhattacharya has edited an anthology on domestic violence. She should know. She's been there

Satish Nandgaonkar interviews the ex-wife of late director Basu Bhattacharya

Twenty years is a long time to wait for catharsis. But cathartic is how Rinki Bhattacharya describes the experience of awaiting the release of her new book — and her volcanic act of angst — on domestic violence next week. "With this book, I want to give it (her past) a decent burial," says a much-mellowed Bhattacharya — writer, columnist and documentary filmmaker. For after 18 years of physical and verbal abuse from her husband, and 20 years after she first spoke about it in an explosive interview — bringing domestic violence out of the closet — she is ready to lay her ghosts to rest.

The former wife of filmmaker Basu Bhattacharya was among the first high-profile women to speak out about domestic abuse. Her account was carried in a 1984 interview with senior journalist Madhu Kishwar in *Manushi*. The interview brought to the fore the ugly side of Bhattacharya, one of ace director Bimal Roy's promising associates and maker of sensitive films such as the National Award-winning *Teesri Kasam*, and the trilogy, *Anubhav, Avishkar* and *Grihapravesh.*

Rinki Bhattacharya has now edited an anthology on domestic violence, *Behind Closed Doors — Domestic Violence in India* (Sage Publications, Rs 295) which explores the various complex facets of what is called "the silent crime". The 234-page book includes interviews with women victims of domestic violence in different parts of the country, apart from analytical articles by her youngest daughter Anwesha Arya, and academics and writers such as Sobha Venkatesh Ghosh, Kalindi Mazumdar and Shirin Kudchedkar.

For Bhattacharya, the book is a culmination of a personal war against domestic violence which began soon after her marriage. One of Bimal Roy's three daughters, Rinki was born in Calcutta in a joint family. Her family moved to Mumbai when she was nine years old after Bombay Talkies hired Roy to direct a film. Rinki first met Basu Bhattacharya when he was assisting her father for the film, *Parakh*. She was 17, and completely bowled over by Bhattacharya. So much so that she eloped with him four years later.

"He was very charming and had a way with words. He would visit our house frequently for long chats with my mother. But my family was opposed to our affair. I left my house with just two saris when I married Basu," recalls Rinki, reclining on a sofa in her pleasantly decorated Bandra house. A painting of Bimal Roy hangs on one of the walls. A number of framed posters of Roy's women-centric films like Bandini and Sujata adorn the walls sharing space with his classic, *Do Bigha Zameen.*

Now 62, and a grandmother, Rinki speaks about her experience of domestic violence without bitterness. "It began soon after my marriage. My son Aditya was three months old and was very ill. Basu stepped out of the house to buy medicine, and for seven hours there was no sign of this man. I was crying, thinking something that happened to him. He came back at 9 pm with no medicine," she recalls. The shocked mother asked her husband where he had been and he

erupted. "He began screaming at me. That was perhaps the beginning of the abusive behaviour."

As Bhattacharya coped with the changes in her life — moving from a liberal well-to-do family

MOVING ON: Rinki Bhattacharya at her Bandra home.
Photo: Gajanan Dudhalkar

into a one-room *chawl* and becoming a wife and mother — she began to discover a parallel face of her husband. There was, on the one hand, a sensitive and a creative side to the filmmaker whose films focused on strong women in search of an identity. And then there was the man who subjected his wife to frequent verbal and physical abuse.

For Bhattacharya, who was a part of her husband's crew — helping in scripting, costumes, set and production design — the anomaly was stark. "I think he was one of the most talented directors. Coming from his background, what he achieved was great. But, excessive abusiveness existed like a parallel stream in him," she says.

Rinki Bhattacharya put up with physical beatings till 1982. One day, 22 years ago, when she was writing an article in her room in their Bandra bungalow, Gold Mist, her husband pounded on her bedroom door, demanding that it be opened. "No doors are going to be locked in this house," he screamed. He grabbed her by her hair, pulled her into the bathroom and began lashing her with a kimono belt. Rinki's teenage son Aditya intervened and put a stop to the beating. "That was when I realised how all this was affecting my children," she says. Bhattacharya decided that she was not going to take it anymore. The next year, she filed for divorce and moved out (though it was only in 1990 that the formal divorce came through).

Why hadn't she filed for divorce earlier? "Because I had no independent source of livelihood," she replies. I was writing columns for a couple of newspapers but that was not sufficient for survival. Besides, filing for divorce is a trauma. Family members would tell me to give marriage another try and I was hesitant to go to court."

"When I realised that this was not my life, I decided to talk about it. Talking works like therapy," she asserts. She started going to the Women's Centre to discuss what was till then a guilty secret. "I got so much support from the centre that I joined as a volunteer there," she says.

Those were difficult days, for many refused to believe her. But Bhattacharya tends to recall the support that she got from different quarters — from psychiatrist-turned-actor Mohan Agashe, filmmaker Satyajit Ray and actor Smita Patil. "Dr Agashe gave me tips on how to deal with Basu's anger. Manikda wrote me a sympathetic letter after he read the *Manushi* interview. Smita Patil publicly refused to share any forum with Basu," she recalls.

As she emerged out of her own shadow, she began to collect books on domestic violence, increase her involvement with the Women's Centre and help other women in distress with a helpline for battered women. "Women are in constant denial. Many women think suffering is their fate and they internalise it. Unless the victim tries to reach out herself, we cannot help," she says.

Bhattacharya has also produced a documentary — titled *Chaar Diwari* (Within Four Walls) — that record the testimonies of domestic violence survivors, exploring its psychological impact on women and children, the lack of legal recourse for women and the societal attitude of regarding it more a "personal affair" than a social problem.

The book has been within her for long years. The idea first came to her in 1984 when she began collecting personal stories of women victims of domestic abuse. *Behind Closed Doors* contains the raw testimonies of 17 such women. They range from the story of Neela, whose husband dictated everything from which lipstick she should wear to how the food should be served clockwise on a plate, to Hansa who converted to Islam to legalise her bigamous marriage. "But I don't want just battered women to read this book. We have to try to explain the social structure and contextualise the violence. We have data collected from the JJ Hospital to show the extent of domestic violence. I have not used academic language, to make the book more accessible to women," she says.

Bhattacharya also believes that it is important to see men who abuse as victims. "You have to look at the abuser in a social context. Basu came from a family where women had never gone to school and wore a *ghungat.* When he met someone who was city-bred and more sophisticated, he didn't how to deal with it. I have nothing against Basu. The poor man has suffered in his own way," she says.

After her husband's death six years ago and the marriage of all three of her children, Bhattacharya has moved out of the bungalow they shared for two decades, and now lives by herself in a flat in Bandra. With the publication of this book, she wants to move away from domestic violence and explore other issues. She is now compiling a book on eminent women who share their experiences of motherhood. Kamala Das, Shashi Deshpande, Mallika Sarabhai, Neela Bhagwat are some of the women who will feature in her new project.

"It is out of my system now. The book has cleared my mind for other work," she stresses. The catharsis is complete.

Opening doors

The malaise of domestic violence cuts across class barriers. Rinki Bhattacharya has demolished more than just the myth of domestic bliss with her book, "Behind Closed Doors". USHA RAMAN speaks to the author lifting the veil of darkness.

AFTER MORE than 20 years of listening to women share their experiences of domestic violence, after collecting many "powerful, moving stories" from victims who needed to share and find belief, and after making her own way out of an abusive relationship, Rinki Bhattacharya decided that a book needed to be written to break the myths about the "silent crime" of domestic violence.

Rinki Roy Bhattacharya, ex-wife of the late Basu Bhattacharya and daughter of noted filmmaker Bimal Roy, knows how to wield the power of the written word. Through a regular column in Mumbai's Mid-Day newspaper, she repeatedly dealt with the issue of violence against women.

Documenting domestic violence

"But the media has its limits. There's only so much you can do through a column in a newspaper," she says. "So I started collecting the stories, documenting everything I heard and saw about domestic violence." It was in the mid-1980s that the idea of putting these stories into a book came to her. She sent in her manuscript to a well-known publisher, who initially reacted favourably.

Author Rinki Bhattacharya... some light on shrouded deeds.
Photo: K. Ramesh Babu.

Many months later, they changed their minds and returned her document, "totally mutilated". "But I'm a documentarist at heart, so I kept at it, writing and recording," she says.

And almost two decades later, Sage Publications decided to publish these oral histories in an edited volume titled "Behind Closed Doors" dealing with domestic violence in India. "The book is in a sense a sequel to a film I made in the 1990s," says Rinki. "There's been an overwhelming response to it across academic segments." The narratives of battered women are interspersed in the book with essays by scholars and activists, combining journalistic

and academic approaches. "While there is no longer that silence or disbelief that once surrounded the issue, there is still very little support for women who face violence within the home," she says. "There is still so much sanctity attached to marriage."

Statistics bear that out. A cross-cultural study conducted in 2002 by a U.S.-based research group in collaboration with Indian researchers found that two out of every five women in India remain silent about abuse because of shame and family honour. India had one of the highest rates of domestic violence in the world, with and estimated 45 per cent of Indian women reporting some form of abuse. Of the women reporting violence, 50 per cent were kicked, beaten or hit when pregnant. About 74.8 per cent of the women who reported violence have attempted to commit suicide.

Dispelling myths

The book, she hopes, will dispel some of the "myths" about domestic violence and empower more women to break the silence. "Many women think violence is something that happens only among the working class," she says. "So there's a lot of denial that women in upper classes go through before they see that they too are victims." When talking to poorer women, Rinki found that even they thought that women in well-to-do families would never have to deal with domestic violence. But with education and wealth also comes isolation, and women rarely connect what is happening to them with the notion of crime. In addition, "educated" women also feel a greater sense of shame that keeps them from "coming out".

Moreover, there is little social support for victims of domestic violence. In Rinki's film, "Char Diwari", one woman recounts how no one in her Mumbai chawl responded to her screams because they all thought it was a `gharelu mamla'.

Long way to go

"We've definitely made progress over the 20-odd years that I have been working in the area, but we are still not geared up to provide a good safety net for the majority of abused women," notes Rinki. Groups such as Nirmala Niketan and Nari Kendra in Mumbai, Sakshi in Delhi, Vimochana in Bangalore and Asmita in Hyderabad have made a difference to some women. Police are more sensitive, the special Crimes Against Women (CAW) cells have helped to some extent. But not enough. "Where is the visibility for such issues in the public environment?" asks Rinki. Rinki feels that we need to educate women more about the possibility of such violence. "I was really pleased when a woman picked up my book, telling me she wanted her young daughters to read it and understand that this could happen to anyone," says Rinki.

20 June 2004

THE TIMES OF INDIA

A Voice against Violence

Her face is an autumn composition, the golden brown eyes only hint at the pain once endured. Even as her book, *Behind Closed Doors - Domestic Violence in India*, painstakingly put together over two decades, was launched last week at Mumbai's Crossword Book Store by Union minister Sunil Dutt, with readings by Dr Shirin Kudchekar, Mahabanoo Mody-Kotwal and others; the primary feeling was one of relief. A catharsis of sorts had taken place.

It is a coming of age for Rinki Bhattacharya - zealous activist, writer and filmmaker, daughter of the illustrious Bimal Roy, and victim of domestic violence. Nothing in her carefree childhood had prepared her for the physically and verbally abusive relationship that she entered into with the late filmmaker Basu Bhattacharya, who was once an assistant director on the sets of her father's film *Parakh*.

Wife and mother of three children, who got into the habit of locking herself in an inner room, to pore over a diary that her trembling fingers could not write in, Rinki found herself curiously paralysed when it came to protecting herself, or taking proactive steps. Consequently, she stayed trapped in the situation for nearly 20 years...

It was only when her young son Aditya rushed in to protect his mother from being brutalised, that the path ahead suddenly became suffused with light. The seeds of rebellion were planted in that moment. "Most women justify domestic violence in their minds, seeing themselves as less than 'perfect' wives" she says quietly, "They remain in abusive relationships for decades without knowing how to cope, or how to escape. There's also the question of 'family honour', and the undeniable fact that wife-beating in our country has social sanction!"

She adds, "Women in situations like these desperately need protection from injury, food, shelter and advice. I was no different from these women..." Except that Rinki Bhattacharya was a fighter. Over the next 15 years, through her columns, her documentary film *Char Diwari* which recorded testimonies of survivors and examined the psychological impact of violence on children, through the crisis hotline she founded, Rinki has chipped away steadily at society's regressive attitudes that leave women with so little choice.

Her book, aptly dedicated to '*women trapped in abusive relationships... and those of us who escaped...*', has 17 chilling narratives, culled from a host of case studies, about women linked by a common thread of suffering, some of whom take positive action. The stories range from the one about Hansa whose foetus was damaged by her husband sitting on her stomach and beating her up, to the inspiring one about Sarla whose parents, unlike many other Indian parents, stood firmly by their daughter in her survival struggle, and helped her become independent.

The book, besides chronicling these records, is also an invaluable source of information for students and scholars of social work and gender studies. The chapters on 'Police Attitudes and Women' by Kalindi Mazumdar and 'Devi: The Disempowered Goddess' by Anwesha Arya (Rinki's daughter), are powerful and moving.

In its barest essence, the book is a voice that resonates with clarity in a muffled, vulnerable universe.

(Mini Chandran-Kurian)

8 June 2004

JOURNALISM OF COURAGE

Wailing Wives

If you were a man, you felt miserable there. The launch of Rinki Bhattacharya's acclaimed book Behind Closed Doors: Domestic Violence in India at Crossword, Kemps Corner on Saturday brought out some unpleasant truths.

As theatre persons-Mahabanoo Mody Kotwal, Jayanti Bhatia and Sagar Arya – read poignant tales of battered wives (Aruna, Karuna...), the predominantly women audience cursed the wife beaters. "Two decades ago I suffered this violence. I asked 17 others women who had gone through this hell to share their experiences," informed an emotionally-charged Bhattacharya. "This is not an enjoyable, but a compulsive reading."

Union Sports and youth affairs minister, Sunil Dutt, looking younger in jeans and blue shirt, made the mood lighter. Dutt, who had once stalked Maharani Gayatri Devi in Delhi for hours "because she the most beautiful women I had ever seen", counselled women: "Be self-reliant so that you can kick out the man if he tortures you. That's what I told my daughter too."

the pioneer

4 June 2004

Out in the open

Shakespeare certainly did not have the Indian domestic-violence scenario in mind while working on his *Taming of the Shrew*. Also he perhaps hadn't even anticipated that the wife-beating would see more criminal versions in centuries to come. Only to make feminists roar in defense and compile books worldwide.

And had he read Rinki Bhattacharya's *Behind Closed Doors, Domestic Violence in India*, he would have surely sobbed. A book, little about short-cut divorce cases and more about the continuing abused relationships and painful escapes in India.

Heavy in authenticity, with papers and excerpts from "dependable and reliable women activist," as Bhattacharya puts it, this book has been strategically packaged. It comes from the top-rung of women-rights activists, whose works have found space here in chapters and anecdotes — a result of decades of direct dealing with domestic-violence victims. Theories, arguments and observations are wrongly Indian. But one cannot claim that Bhattacharya's motive is to pose domestic violence as a global phenomenon.

Bedrooms, drawing rooms and police stations have been peeped into the studied daringly, in detail. The lower and middle-class have served as founder of the book's full-baked arguments. Contributions from names like Kalindi Mazumdar, Sobha Venkatesh Ghosh, Malvika Karlekar and Madhu Kishwar assure that the book can become a handbook for anti-patriarchal high-head-edness prevalent in the Indian society.

Says Bhattacharya, "The idea behind compiling the works of these experts is to provide a rather comprehensive study of the domestic-violence problem. Like others contributing this book, I have also been involved with domestic-violence victims for several years. There are various dimensions to the problem in our country, depending on social, political and domestic factors. The book makes these known, and louder."

While other taken the burden of posing as researchers, Bhattacharya herself has settled down with some direct narratives from victims. "Only a few from among the 500 women" she spoke with. The book has done good to the Indian female by mentioning that even the customary slaps and kicks are violence. Ironically, most of the narratives however defy this agenda of its activists.

Says Bhattacharya, "Whichever section of society they belong to, women face the worst when they lodge a First Information Report (FIR). High time they care for legal awareness, at least the Indian Penal Code (IPC) and Property Rights."

The book loaded with socio-political demography violence venues — the *chardiwari* being one — has many characters to it. Where on one hand it would be a favourite with debaters, it has strong properties to make "silent" victims open up. With several Hindustani *naari* characters, the book will be of interest to foreigners too.

Something like the "evolution" of the Indian women from Durga or Kali, or the female mentioned in Manusmriti , might irritate mature Indian readers. But it will be liked by those who know little about the problem background.

Fortunately the book doesn't really engage in loud male bashing. Women instigating domestic violence on women are troubled with glaring attention. Even the former Government has been criticized for its "faulty" Bills and Amendments. Bhattacharya reverts, "How about some women-shining now?"

Hindustan Times

20 June 2004

About the hell that is marriage

Rema Nagarajan

YOU'VE HEARD it often enough. Domestic violence cuts across all classes. In *Behind Closed Doors—Domestic Violence in India* it's the narratives of women who were battered by the men they loved that are compelling. It is depressing but unputdownable. Or it could just be the vile curiosity of the next-door-aunty-type in me.

There are a couple of chapters before and after the narratives giving an extensive analysis of the problem and providing sociological explanations on everything from the phenomenon of "unwanted" female children to measures being attempted to tackle the problem. While these are interesting, nothing brings home the point better than the narratives. For those with stars in their eyes about love and marriage this is a must. It gives crucial and commonsense pointers about never keeping a joint account with all the money within easy access of the man; spending all your salary on the family while he stashes away his or transfers all the property to his name; or making a joint investment in his name. Sounds cynical? Read about those who found out the hard way and you won't shrug this advice off easily.

The book has it all — rape within a marriage, manipulation using children, branding of a woman as insane. The college lecturers, womens' rights activist, maids, the ones who converted to Islam to marry the already married man they loved, a woman rejected by her husband when she was in her 60s after being married for 42 years—they are all there. Most found peace and dignity only after getting out of the relationship.

Author opens doors on domestic violence

On the eve of the launch of her book Behind Closed Doors: Domestic Violence in India, activist Rinki Bhattacharya throws light upon this crucial, yet neglected, issue.

You've pointed out in the introduction that violence against women inside the home is not unique to Indian culture. But how do you think it's different in India, vis-à-vis other country?

Domestic violence victims are linked by factors of commonness rather than difference. These women feel isolated, they've been brainwashed into believing that they're responsible for the violence inflicted on them. They're likely to keep mum about it and suffer alone, form a deep sense of shame.

Do you stand by the legal definition of domestic violence in India (section s498 of the Indian Panel Code), which centres around cruelty, or do you think it excludes bigger problem areas then it includes?

I stand by the law, but it is an outdated law. The fact is that the law which should have been implemented by now is hanging in a state of suspension because it's very controvercial.

There is no law regarding marital rape either. As far as lows for violence against women are concerned, do you think there is a reluctance on part of the Indian government to lobby for or implement them?

Who will lobby for a law on these issues when society is in denial? Also, the system is too complicated. Even with laws, women would prefer to keep quite about such violence. They face so much brutality in court and at the hands of their families and the police. Domestic violence is seen as a non-issue, a ghar ka mamla at best.

How, according to you, can domestic violence against women be curbed?

It can't be stopped. Women have to seek help themselves. Let's not underestimate the resources women have to live a dignified life, be it education or sheer strength of character. Also, grassroot changes must take place as far as attitudes to women and the girl child are concerned. Honour killings, which is an extreme form of domestic violence, are now more common in India than they were previously. Clearly, that is not a good sign.

You have been a victim of domestic violence yourself. Has writing this book been a cathartic experience?

Yes, definitely. I think this is something I just had to do, and now I feel I can move onto other kinds of writing, maybe fiction.

The book does not touch upon male victims of domestic violence. Comment.

It's because men are not victims of such violence. There is a book being written by a man who believes that it is only men who suffer from domestic violence, but I don't believe that. If men are victims of domestic violence, it's a negligible number of men. Also, men are not victims of continuous, long and repeated domestic violence, like women are.

Behind Closed Doors: Domestic Violence in India

Edited by Rinki Bhattacharya
SAGE, pp 232
Rs 295

Speaking out on abuse

The play *Katy* lack the sharpness of its literacy version in Rinki Bhattacharya's book *Behind Closed Doors: Domestic Violence in India,* but nevertheless manages to convey the message

One of the most eminent critics in the city, Shanta Gokhale will separate the best from the banal on Mumbai's culturescape each week

Sitting in the Indian Merchants Chamber auditorium on Sunday morning, listening to Katy's story unfold on the small, functional stage, I was a child again, overhearing a dear aunt sob on my mother's shoulder, "I can't take the beating any more".

Years later at age 10, putting that despairing cry together with the badly bruised arm she has tried so hard to hide under her *pallu*, I came to the horrified conclusion that the jolly man I fondly called uncle Uddi, was not so jolly at home; that uncles in specious apartments in Cumballa Hill beat their wives just as brutally as Gopal in his hut across the road.

Katy is one of 17 first-person narrative of physically abused women in Rinki Bhattacharya's book, *Behind Closed Doors: Domestic Violence in India*. Unlike the remaining 16, it is not the story of an abused wife but an abused live-in partner. So the reason why Majlis had chosen this rather unrepresentative story to inaugurate its celebration of 16 years of making justice accessible to woman, wasn't immediately obvious.

Directed by Sheeba Chhada and enacted by Puja, *Katy* fell a little short as theatre. The trouble lay with the text. Written as a personal narrative meant to be read, t meandered nostalgically through the narrator's childhood, home environment and happy first relationship with a married man, before coming to the second relationship that had turned abusive.

Lacking the sharpness of a text written for the stage, it hung loose and sagged in parts, despite the director's and actor's best efforts.

But once the audience began asking questions, it became clear why Flavia Agnes, head of Majlis's legal cell, had chosen *Katy* over the other stories in Bhattacharya's book for this event. In the auditorium sat young women lawyers from Majlis's District Lawyer's Initiative. Their question revealed a subtle bias against Katy. Where was the problem in a live-in relationship, they asked. With no children, owning a flat, financially independent and unshackled by the sanctity of marriage, wasn't Katy in a position to

Flavia Agnes chose the play Katy to inaugurate Majlis's sixteenth anniversary celebrations

throw out her abuse any time she chose? Why did she tolerate eight years of abuse before doing it?

Stepping into the space created by these doubts, Flavia questioned the mindset that lay behind them. An abused woman is an abused woman, she said. Who are we to judge? Katy's story offered her the opportunity to broaden the audience's viewpoint to include all women. Doing this was important, for Majlis believes that offering emotional support to abused women is as much part of a lawyer's work as providing legal aid.

Meanwhile, a middle-aged woman in the

row in front of me was offering a quicker solution to the problem than the legal process. "She should have hit the man back," she muttered. "These buggers are cowards. Give them a pasting and they fall in line."

I thought of Champa in Vijay Tendulkar's *Sakharam Binder*. She walks out on her sexually abusive husband and thrashes the daylights out of him when he comes grovelling back. What a *hungama* that pasting had causes. Ban the play, the moralists had screamed. But the law had stood by the play and it went on to become a hit!

There are very few Champas in real life, more Katys. Financially independent and professionally successful though she is, Katy is as psychologically paralysed as a dependent wife would be in an abusive marriage. It takes a women years to realise that she has done nothing to deserve abuse; that when her tormentor apologises after each violent episode, promising that it will never happen again, she must not believe him, because it WILL happen, again and again. Even after the woman comes to a full understanding of her situation, she needs more time to find the will to act. The day she does, she frees herself from within. She is now ready to take charge of her life.

Rights violations behind 'closed doors'

For the ones who think of discrimination against women as an imaginary exercise, the book 'Behind Closed Doors' woven around domestic violence in India, edited by Rinki Bhattacharya, and published by SAGE Publications India (Pvt) Ltd, is ample proof.

The stress, strain, agony and strife women go through in their day to day lives is evidence in the narratives presented in the book where women themselves speak out their innermost private lives putting 'masculinity' to shame – seemingly a situation which finds it's parallel in Sri Lanka – the only difference being that the Lankan women goes through similar trauma – truly behind closed doors, sheerly out of fear, shame and prestige loss.

Significantly among the women that were harassed as clearly indicated in the book, were those that tied the nuptial knots with sons of educated and well to do parents who themselves collaborated with their sons in harassing their wives.

Interestingly, a book of this nature cannot be reviewed without reference to the local domestic scene. Noteworthy is the marked increase in Sri Lanka's divorce statistics, unlike earlier. But that's it. Nothing goes beyond. No victim of violence speaks of the scars left behind and if she does its just one rare instance. So a book of the like of 'Behind Closed Doors' cannot be even dreamt of in our country. Dowry monies, land, women's intellect and male prejudices are among a whole host of what invited men into harassing their women

– a clear proof of what the status quo is in relation to women's place in society.

The nerve – wracking experiences if seventeen Indian women – all of whom have dared socio/cultural barriers in coming out and confessing the horrendous crimes inflicted on them, is exemplary and

Behind Closed Doors
Domestic Violence in India
Edited by Rinki Bhattacharya

to be noted by women outside India as well.

The intensely patriarchal system one could observe as being mainly instrumental in gender crimes.

The devaluation, subordination and mistreatment of women, their brutal

and barbaric control, a male dominated socialization process laying much, emphasis on patriarchal values, facilitates and fortifies what is now termed as silent crime. Sad but interesting are the varied myths and stereotypes that justify women deserving subordination and inferior status. The narratives also bring out – the very high degree of patience and tolerance on the part of women who even choose to deny the existence of violence – so evidence in them not even reporting such to the relevant authorities.

Nevertheless the profiles reveal the vast magnitude of emotional strength embedded in such women as they pluck enough courage and fortitude to put back their lives' broken pieces and fight to venture out into destinies unknown. Though numerous international conventions are ratified, all such still await entry into the domestic legal framework of many countries. Violence against women has thus found social licensing as it were as they go through the ordeal with none to listen to their tales of woe.

Noteworthy are the measures taken by Indian women to fight such brutality and horror. For instance, HELP is ready at hand – a hotline for women in distress.

This apart, many social workers and women's groups dedicated to the cause of their kind places India ahead of other countries that are yet to reach that milespost in fighting for women victims of violence.

⊛SAGE 𝕮𝖑𝖆𝖘𝖘𝖎𝖈𝖘

Over the years SAGE has published books that can truly be called classics.

SAGE Classics is a carefully selected list that every discerning reader will want to possess, re-read and enjoy for a long time. These are now priced lower than the original, but is the same version published earlier. SAGE's commitment to quality remains unchanged.

Watch out for more titles in this series.

Other SAGE Classics:

Adoption in India: Policies and Experiences
Vinita Bhargava

Janani—Mothers, Daughters, Motherhood
Edited by Rinki Bhattacharya

Kashmir: Roots of Conflict, Paths to Peace
Sumantra Bose

War and Diplomacy in Kashmir, 1947-48
C. Dasgupta

A Space of Her Own: Personal Narratives of Twelve Women
Edited by Leela Gulati and Jasodhara Bagchi

Mentoring: A Practitioner's Guide to Touching Lives
Sunil Unny Guptan

Buddhism in India: Challenging Brahmanism and Caste
Gail Omvedt

Operation Black Thunder: An Eyewitness Account of Terrorism in Punjab
Sarab Jit Singh

Behind Closed Doors

BEHIND CLOSED DOORS

Domestic Violence in India

Edited by Rinki Bhattacharya

www.sagepublications.com
Los Angeles • London • New Delhi • Singapore • Washington DC

First published in 2004
This edition published in 2013 by

 SAGE Publications India Pvt Ltd
B1/I-1 Mohan Cooperative Industrial Area
Mathura Road, New Delhi 110 044, India
www.sagepub.in

SAGE Publications Inc
2455 Teller Road
Thousand Oaks, California 91320, USA

SAGE Publications Ltd
1 Oliver's Yard, 55 City Road
London EC1Y 1SP, United Kingdom

SAGE Publications Asia-Pacific Pte Ltd
33 Pekin Street
#02-01 Far East Square
Singapore 048763

Published by Vivek Mehra for SAGE Publications India Pvt Ltd, Typeset in 10/12 pt Baskerville Book at C&M Digitals (P) Ltd, Chennai and printed at De-Unique. New Delhi.

Library of Congress Cataloging-in-Publication Data Available

ISBN: 978-81-321-1026-2 (PB)

The SAGE Team: Jai S. Prasad, Radha Dev Raj and Santosh Rawat

...to women trapped in abusive relationships...
...and those of us who escaped...

For Ahmedi

The pale yellow of the evening sky
Marked with crimson wounds
Shows up here and there
As clots of blue;
The sad sobs of the breeze
Like a sigh of despair.
There, thro' the door, he walks out;
And once again, it grows dark.

As everyday, that day too,
In the garden, flowers bloom;
They stand and wait
For something new to happen.

Another noon—lunch, snacks, tea.

Yes it looks like the day before; but
today is not yesterday.

Evening falls, and the sun
Shows up, a burning blister;
The breeze utters a sigh—
Like a doll of wood, there,
He lies on the cot; and then,
Thro' the door, she walks out (on him).
Once again, as always, it grows dark.

Mamta G Sagar
(Translated from Kannada by Chitra and the poet).

Contents

Foreword

I am glad to contribute these few lines to a book that furthers the cause of oppressed women. The profiles meticulously written up after long and sympathetic interviews are revealing in several respects. The extent of wife–battering among all social classes and the fact that it does extend to all classes may shock many readers, although those engaged in actively working for battered women are well aware of it. One realizes that among the working classes it is almost routine so the wife expects no better and does not attempt a break till the ill–treatment becomes utterly inhuman. Only now is it beginning to be known how prevalent abuse is in the middle-class even where both husband and wife are educated.

The value of such a book lies in its ability to encourage other women who share the same plight to resist or break away. Such readers will find how widespread is a problem which they may have thought was exclusively their own. Other readers will be spurred to assist and support. Is it not noteworthy that no profile ends with reform or change in the husband? What conclusion does one draw from this? As the introduction points out, the disparagement and downgrading of women is an essential aspect of the patriarchal system. Violence would seem to be the inevitable outcome of patriarchal values and relationships.

Hence, while redress of abuse as it takes place is undoubtedly necessary, a much more fundamental change in our age–old system alone can ensure women liberation from brutality. The fight of many of the women interviewed is not yet over. Reading their stories of suffering and courage one comes to share the editor's concern and admiration when the silenced at last come to speak.

Shirin Kudchedkar

Acknowledgements

I have many friends to thank in writing this book—Amy Laly, Asha Damle, Dhiruben Patel, Supriya, Sumita and Sonal to name a few. They believed in my work and nurtured me with constant encouragement.

I am grateful to Shirin Kudchedkar for writing her eloquent foreword. And I am profoundly grateful to Anwesha Arya, Chhaya Dey, Kalindi Muzumdar, Mamta G. Sagar and Sobha Venkatesh Ghosh for their contributions. These writers provide crucial evidence on a much misunderstood and trivialized social problem, accepted even today as a "matter of women's fate." A serious problem known simply as *Domestic Violence*.

I was extremely fortunate that Anne, Jacinta, and Velu had time to help with the manuscript.

Most of all, I am indebted to the women who shared the journey of their lives, from indignity to empowerment and by sharing, affirmed faith in the dignity of human life.

Lastly, I acknowledge my sincere gratitude to Sage India for bringing the book to life.

Rinki Bhattacharya

Introduction
Rinki Bhattacharya

Let me not be sad because I am born a woman
In this world; many saints suffer in this way.

JANABAI
(ca. 1298–1350)

The narratives in this volume focus on one issue—domestic violence. Within these individual stories one discovers a range of socio-economic dynamics that affect women's development, particularly in the context of Indian society. These life stories, on one hand, are about loss and betrayal. On the other, they are sagas of immense courage that challenge accepted cultural ideals of womanhood and question conforming to female destiny. Each tragic testimonial reveals both overt and covert violence against women. It needs to be pointed out that the root of women's oppression is an outcome of their social status. One might even argue, it is a result of their *absence* of status (see Anwesha Arya and Sobha V. Ghosh in this volume).

Home and the World

Gender crimes are *not* a recent phenomena. Crimes against women have been committed since antiquity. Violence to wives, the central concern here, is found in all societies and across all economic and age groups. Any traditional custom that places women in subordinate positions within society or in the family has the potential to turn violent. The putative sacredness of a traditional marriage, rigid ideas of conjugality, and patriarchal traditions of family structure take precedence over concerns for women or children. It has been observed that whenever male authority is threatened, the lives of women, and children become redundant, and are considered dispensable.

Prejudice towards women is entrenched in Indian culture. But by no means is this unique to India. Prejudice towards women is common in other societies. Women are devalued, subordinated, and mistreated daily. Crimes against women occur every single day around the world with forensic precision. According to the October 2002 World Health Organization Report on Violence and Health, it is estimated that interpersonal violence results in the death of one person every minute somewhere across the world. Malavika Karlekar adds:

> An alarming finding of the latest (1993) *World Development Report* pointed out that globally rape and domestic violence account for about 5 percent of the total disease burden amongst women in the age group of 15–44. Over here disease covers physical as well as non-physical ailments. It need hardly be pointed out that these figures possibly represent only a fraction of actual violence-induced physical and somatic disorders (Karlekar, 1998: 51).

Police records in India reveal that a woman is raped every 34 minutes, molested every 26 minutes, kidnapped every 43 minutes, and killed every 93 minutes. At the 1993 India Canada International Conference on Violence, Vice Chancellor, S.N.D.T. University, Suma Chitnis explained:

> There are many ways in which women suffer and are made to suffer. In behavioral terms, violence against women ranges from simple suppression to abuse, aggression, exploitation and severe oppression. We know it as female infanticide, the abortion of female foctus, the neglect and under-nourishment of girl child, denial of education to girls, rape, pre-puberty marriage, wife beating, the harassment of a bride leading to her suicide or murder. Each of these is more awesome than comparable of even greater pain of fear experienced in other contexts. For instance, childbirth can be extremely painful,

but one does not refer to the pain of childbirth as violence, no matter how severe it is. The fear of death, in a situation of terminal illness, can be extremely terrifying, but one does not refer to as violence (Chitnis, 1998: 11).

On one pretext or another, female children are unwanted or treated as burdens by their parents. An old Tamil saying for instance, compares girl children to "plants growing in a neighbor's courtyard." Dowry for a girl's marriage has been the most strenuous argument to denounce female children. Indian language proverbs caution us about the terrible outcome should daughters be born. Indian linguistic traditions echo with anti-daughter sentiments. Popular as these persuasive proverbs and idioms are, their impact on the construction of feminine identity is immense. In their separate chapters, Anwesha Arya and Sobha Venkatesh Ghosh elaborate on this particular aspect of women's socialization.

The gender of a child plays a significant role in its socializing process. Male children are permitted far greater economic and social mobility. Indulged, pampered, little boys seem to get away with misconduct, get away virtually, with anything. Girls on the other hand are taught to emulate characters from the Hindu mythology (see Arya). Female characters like Sita and Savitri from the two famous Indian epics, *Ramayana* and the *Mahabharata* are held out as role models for daughters. Female children are strictly tutored from infancy to conform to dress and behavior codes, make personal sacrifices, to be obedient, tolerant, and virtuous.

The birth of a daughter which was not a source of anxiety during the *vedic* period, in post-*vedic* phase, becomes a source of disaster to the father. Thus it was said the birth of a son is bliss incarnate, while that of a daughter is the root of family misery (Desai and Krishnaraj, 1987: 34 emphasise mine).[1]

Yearning for male children is a cultural preference across the class divide. This applies to India and its geographical neighbors. There is a popular Nepalese saying that succinctly reflects male preference: "Let it be late, but let it be a son." Neera Desai and Maitreyi Krishnaraj explain, "Women's role under the Brahminical law is to enable the male mode of descent by producing sons" (Desai and Krishnaraj, 1987: 34). Many Hindu invocation prayers to the Gods include granting of fame, wealth, and sons in their chant: *"yasham dehi, dhanam dehi, putram dehi."* This chant may be a result of interpolation by male priests. However, it clearly expresses every parent's fervent desire for male progeny in an intensely patriarchal setting. A son is perceived as the one who will legitimately carry forward the family name. Besides, sons are regarded as assets for parents in their old age. Most importantly, it is *only* the son who bears the religious obligation to perform Hindu funeral rites. These specific aspects of Hindu religion dominate an individual's life choice and determine familial goals.

> It is not poverty alone that kills baby girls. Girls born in West Bengal have a better chance of celebrating their first birthday than those born in Punjab even though the per capita income of a family in Punjab is nearly twice that of a family in West Bengal. Two other States, Haryana and Assam have very similar female infant mortality rates in spite of wide differences in per capita income (Swapna Mazumdar, 2002: 8).

The Chinese custom of foot binding crippled women for hundreds of years. In Sudan, Africa, Egypt, and the Middle East the barbaric custom of genital mutilation kill or maim young girls for life. Women are sacrificed to save family honor in the Arab states and Pakistan. Fathers, uncles, brothers, sometimes mothers or other female relatives murder women suspected of sexual misconduct by the gruesome custom of "honor killing." During the repressive Taliban rule in Afganistan, millions of women were forced into house arrest. Girls were not allowed to study, women doctors and professionals, were barred from working—or face the firing squad.

Girls are sacrificed in numerous ways. Their tragic helplessness comes into effect when a daughter has to marry. Most Indian parents would select husbands for their daughters without their consent. A parent would even justify this, with the rejoinder, "Do we have to ask the cow if it wants to eat before giving her grass?" The following report brings home the heart rending situation of daughters sharply:

> A Pakistani villager married off his 10 year old daughter to a 40 year old man to compensate for the death of a borrowed buffalo. The village council decreed that the father could

use his daughter to pay back the man and a Muslim Cleric sanctioned the wedding (*The Times of India*, 2002: 1).

Another shocking instance appeared in *Mid Day*: A six-year-old girl was strangled to death by her father at Turbhe (Maharashtra). Her mistake—she did not fetch him a glass of water (March 30, 2004).

Contract killers, dubbed "Bounty hunters", are paid vast fortunes in the U.K. to track down Asian girls and women who have fled violent homes and sought refuge in Women's Safe Housing. Committed with impunity these murders are sanctioned in the name of tradition, custom, or religion.

A blatant manifestation of gender crime peculiar to India is burning brides/wives. Dowry recurs without check or control. According to a heated television talk show with Nisha Sharma, a recent dowry victim of Delhi, on NDTV's program *HUMLOG* (broadcast 17 May 2003), 6100 women were killed in one year for dowry. Dowry demands have spread across South Asian communities. In communities where dowry was *never* demanded, in fact forbidden, amongst the Sikhs for instance, there is a persistent demand for it today. An alarming rise in Dowry related violence amongst the South Asian women of the Diaspora has been reported from U.K. and the U.S. Be it Dowry or bride price, the unfortunate victims of both are women. During wars, personal or political enmity, women are abducted, raped to punish the enemy.

Women's nutrition requirements and health are a low priority on the national health agenda as Desai and Krishnaraj observed:

> Family planning programmes are population—control oriented and do not place any emphasis on women's health, emotional and psychological welfare. They do not raise the status of women by reducing unwanted pregnancy but make them victims of experimentation and state policy (Desai and Krishnaraj, 1987: 222).

Even if we agree that women are biologically the superior sex, this does not result in elevating their social status. In a patriarchal setting women are considered inferior. There is, in fact, a silent consensus that women, irrespective of their age, remain minors, and therefore require male protection. It is logical after this assumption that men all over the world take their role of protectionists very seriously, and control women in a brutal, in fact, barbaric manner.

The Central Theme: Domestic Violence

As a journalist and media practitioner my primary concern for the last two-and-a-half decades has been the condition of *"battered* women" in the context of Domestic Violence (DV). A social problem that is known by other names like wife battery, family violence, spouse abuse, wife beating—or the more discreet phrase, *silent crime*. These various names address one and the same issue. From early 1980s I undertook to study this particular atrocity against women. I began to collect and read publications on the subject, located stories of victims in India and abroad. I watched films on the theme. Later, I became a volunteer at the Women's Centre[2] before some of us started a crises hotline, HELP[3] in 1987. In 1990 HELP was funded to produce a documentary film on Domestic Violence. I pursued my study of DV through media, simultaneously, supporting victims in every manner possible. My hope was, the study of DV would answer questions, educate and provide us a fresh insight into why so many women were condemned to suffer.

Within the women's movement, it was realized that the operative term Domestic Violence failed to describe the gamut of physical, psychological, non-physical, social, and cultural abuse of women. A comprehensive word is yet to be scripted. Until then, we continue using simplistic definitions for an extremely complex global problem.

Del Martin, observes, "Wife-beating, I soon learnt, is a complex problem that involves much more than the act itself or the personal interaction between husband and wife" (Martin, 1976: xvi). She emphasized that the roots of domestic violence lie in historical attitudes towards women, the institution of marriage. Violence of this nature is further sustained by the intricacies of criminal and civil law and delivery system of social service agencies. And blame could not be easily ascertained.

I would agree with Martin's assertion, which locates the problem in the larger societal context. In Indian families the man enjoys absolute authority, power, all privileges, and makes every decision as the undisputed "head of family." He is addressed and elevated to the position of the *annadata* (giver of grains) and *grihakarta* (household authority). The man is practically worshiped. Even in law, the "father" is assumed to be the natural guardian of his children. The fact that he may have abused his wife, and the children, does not adversely affect a man's position. Official documents, for instance, a child's birth certificate, passport, school/college admissions etc. have to bear father's endorsement. Without the father's signature, documents are rendered invalid. The privileged position of the father as natural guardian is no longer meekly accepted. In recent years there have been a few isolated attempts in the courts challenging this patriarchal assumption.

The following report mentions a novel kind of child support granted to a woman in the United Arab Emirates:

> ... the Dubai Sharjah Court last week ordered a man to pay his ex-wife Dirhams 600 (approximately Rs 8,000) a month for breastfeeding their three year old daughter for the first two years (*Mid Day*, 2003: 6).

The well known nineteenth century social reformer from Bengal, Raja Ram Mohan Roy[4] had lamented, "At marriage, the wife is recognized as half of her husband, but in conduct they are treated worse than inferior animals." Ram Mohan Roy's sympathetic observation was a reaction to prevalent social attitude demeaning women. Oft quoted Hindi proverbs, amongst other language sayings, make it quite obvious that women continue to be demeaned on a day-to-day basis. It is accepted as an act of manliness to control women at every stage of their existence (see Anwesha Arya in this volume). From childhood, girls and boys are trained to conform to a system based on patriarchal values and relationships (see Foreword). Patriarchal value system has in turn prejudiced both lawmakers and law enforcing agencies like the police (see Muzumdar in this volume).

During pre-production research for the HELP documentary film on domestic violence titled *CHAR DIWARI* (1990–91) we had interviewed the Additional Commissioner of Police (ACP) in a suburban Mumbai police station. The ACP bitterly complained that women filed false First Information Reports (FIR) against their husbands and abused the SECTION 498A (Whoever, being the husband or the relative of the husband of a women, subjects such woman to cruelty shall be punished with imprisonment for a term which may extend to three years and shall also be liable to fine) of the Indian Penal Code. However, Lawyer Flavia Agnes has argued that barely 100 cases are filed under SECTION 498A and the conviction rate under this section is negligible (see Muzumdar in this volume). "Anyone who knows the social stigma a woman faces of going public against her husband and in laws, realizes she has to be goaded beyond endurance to go to the police," observed Harish Sadani, Secretary, Men Against Domestic Violence, or MAVA, a Mumbai based group, working for raising awareness amongst men.

The same disgruntled ACP we met, advocated control of dependents. He informed us casually, that it was his duty to put his wife in place if she disobeyed him. Our request to share his forceful views in the film was turned down by the ACP. However, we convinced another high profile ACP to appear in the same documentary. The second ACP excused a man's abusive behavior on grounds of frustrations at home, work place or jealousy.

It is interesting to note that the sponsors of *CHAR DIWARI*, the Department of Women and Child, in the ministry of Social Welfare, New Delhi, refused to sanction additional funds for an English subtitled version of the film. The sponsors were of the opinion that showing the above documentary abroad would project Indian husbands and the sacred notions of marriage in a negative light.

Myths and Stereotyping

From forced marriages to maintaining a strict dress code, like covering the head or wearing a veil (see Akash in this volume) women and young girls, have conformed to sex role-stereotypes in their day to day existence. These practices proclaim and perpetuate women's subordinate status. Conforming to traditional roles has a great social legitimacy in a patriarchal system.

One of the oldest myths invented is that women are born with sealed fates. They are fated to suffer. The age-old conviction that a woman is inferior to the man in the social hierarchy has resulted in subordinating them.

Until the last decade, mental health, religious, medical and law and justice professionals accepted and perpetuated misleading stereotypes about women who remain with men who batter them. Many of those judgments were based on historical notions, more or less consistent for many centuries about the place of women in society, their capabilities (or presumed lack of them) and appropriate treatment of them by authority figures—especially husbands (Nicarthy, 1986: 9).

On one hand society reserves subordinate positions to women. On the other, myths and stereotypes are invented to legitimize *why* women deserve subordination and mistreatment. In the case of "battered women," myths abound *why* they are beaten or the *kind of women* who are beaten (see Muzumdar in this volume). These myths have no relation to women's everyday reality.

The National Health Survey findings disclosed that many victims said violence was a part of daily domestic tensions. These women even said they would make up with their spouses within a short time. There is a high degree of tolerance among women and denial of domestic violence. The myth that wife battery is *a private matter* silenced victims for centuries. Even today, thousands of women remain trapped in life threatening relationships. During the course of their marriage, women defend abusive husbands. As a result wives rarely report domestic violence. In fact they choose to deny its existence.

Family's Responses

When a woman decides to terminate her marriage—for reasons that may vary vastly—she encounters powerful resistance from within her own family. In a domestic violence case, the victim may want to leave her violent partner despite mounting opposition. Even in a life threatening situation, a woman's motives to leave the husband, are questioned in the severest manner (see Ghosh). It is relevant to mention in this context that victim's children could resort to emotional blackmail. Children from abusive homes suffer unbearable psychological pressures. They are sucked into the powerful whirlpool of violence.

A poignant case I recall in this context is of a mature housewife. After 15 years of battery and abuse, the woman was contemplating how to improve her life—even if it meant leaving her husband. When she shared her thoughts with the children, her

16-year-old daughter went into acute depression. The son, on the other hand approved her decision. When the woman finally decided to leave, her terrified daughter took an overdose of sleeping tablets. Both the daughter and son were as much victims of domestic violence as their mother. When they grow up in the harsh reality of domestic violence, the sensibilities of children are bound to get distorted (see Dey in this volume).

In many DV cases, emotional blackmail by children or family members succeed in making women reconsider "leaving" the violent husband. Socialized to believe they are mothers and home-makers first, victims procrastinate about decisions to separate—until it may be too late. Talking openly of marital matters is deemed shameful; hence women silence their fears and continue to be in the abusive marriage.

Class often determines a victim's response to domestic violence. It has been observed, that women from the upper and middle class are unprepared for domestic violence trauma. As a result they suffer from sense of isolation, shame and for years, conceal the fact that their husbands are abusive. On the other hand, working class women have few inhibitions or pretences to maintain. They are not intimidated by loss of self-esteem nor do they blame themselves for the phenomena. Living perpetually in crowded housing colonies, facing daily economic hardships, working-class women have experienced violence with their families, or witnessed it in their neighborhood.

However, women from all classes are discouraged in their decisions to leave abusive married partners. Some women may face social boycott in their lonely choice of legal separation, or divorce, and the option of becoming single in the process. Added to these existing pressures are the one-dimensional women's images churned out by the electronic media. By its glorification of marriage, idealized wifehood or motherhood, the media has successfully pinned down women into passive acceptance of their fate. Mainstream media has miserably failed to provide positive alternatives to the above stereotypes. Being bombarded by these images deter women even more from making life-choices that appear to clash with accepted ideals of traditional roles.

Certain sections of right-wing political groups like the *Shiv Sena*, a powerful political group (under the leadership of Bal Thackeray) blame atrocities on women onto women themselves. Specifically, their choice of dressing; the following news item sums it up:

The *Shiv Sena's Rajasthani* unit on Wednesday called for a 'dress code' for girl students in view of the increasing incidents of sexual abuse against them. Such incidents were increasing because of 'provocative' dresses *Rajasthan Sena* chief, Nanak Ram Thavani said (*The Times of India*, 21 November 2002: 1).

There is a tendency to ignore the complaints of battered women, if they dare to speak up. People around the victim deny the very existence of violence. If a victim protests, she will be labeled as being *masochistic, crazy*, or over reacting and being *hysterical*. Victims are regarded with disbelief, suspicion, lack of credibility. Just in case a victim is entertained, at some point she is likely to be blamed for her condition.

I agree with Ginny Nicarthy who observed "One of the most painful aspects of being beaten by the man you love is a feeling of being alone with the problem. That emotional isolation often leads to the feeling of 'I must be crazy" (Nicarthy, 1986: 3).

Of the four women interviewed in the documentary *CHAR DIWARI*, one confessed to emotional isolation. Locked up for several days without human contact, she had nothing but the four walls for company. The woman also admitted she nearly went crazy in her solitary cell.

Wife battery is unfortunately viewed as an individual woman's personal tragedy, her misfortune, or her *karma* (a word that, like *naseeb*, is used to describe one's fate or destiny). One of the earliest German documentary films on Domestic violence was by Helga Reidermaster. It was aptly titled: IS IT A MATTER OF FATE?

Helga Reidermaster's film questioned the widespread conjecture inexorably linking female fate to every form of abuse. The conjecture about women's fate, typical of Indian society, prevails in developed Western societies as the film's title clearly pointed out.

Even after authentic reports and documentation people choose to think domestic violence occurs *only among* the poor or illiterate. According to Akhila Sivadas, Executive Director of Centre for Advocacy and Research in New Delhi, "Atrocities have nothing to do with class. It is prevalent amongst both rural and privileged class." In Canada, the U.S. and U.K., for a very long time no one believed that white women or women from the affluent and elite class were battered. There was total disbelief that educated, upper-class wives were just as brutally battered as women from working class.

Facts and Figures

In general there is a notion that an insignificant number of women are abused. The following reports conclusively point out that many more women are routinely ill-treated and beaten than is actually reported. The hidden figures of domestic violence in India will never perhaps be revealed.

- Between 1967 and 1973, over 17,500 American women and children were killed by battering men.
- Nearly 60 percent of the woman killed in the U.S. die in the hands of their husbands or boy friends.
- A woman is nine times more likely to be assaulted at home than on the street (Deltufo, 1995: 6)

Indian women living in the United States have reported increasing cases of domestic abuse. In 2001, *MAITRI,* a women's NGO in San Francisco, attended to 1,500 calls while *APNA GHAR* in Chicago received 1,000 calls. Survey of Abuse in Family Environment collected data from 10,000 households in Delhi, Chennai, Bhopal Lucknow, and Tiruvananthapuram. Physical violence was 26 percent of the urban and 20 percent for the rural areas. Psychological torture was 45 and 51 percent respectively. And, this was just "tip of the ice berg" according to the authors.

In her analysis of the fiercely debated Domestic Violence Bill (*The Times of India*, 16 March 2002) Brinda Karat mentions that organizations like the All India Democratic Women's Association intervenes on an average 50,000 cases of women in distress through its justice centers in different States (see Daga in this volume).

Deltufo correctly observes "one thing you will see over and over again is how easy it is to be abused and how hard to get out once it starts to happen" (Deltufo, 1995: 8).

Men Who Batter

As there are myths and stereotypes of victims of domestic violence—a number of myths thrive about men *who* batter. These myths are dangerously misleading and inaccurate. The worse result of these myths about violent men being, they confuse their victims. It is significant to point out that batterers are portrayed with a generous degree of sympathy. For instance, a man is said to loose his self-control, be under extreme stress, provoked or frustrated as the ACP in the documentary film *CHAR DIWARI* claimed. Violent behavior in men is condoned with convenient excuses that are too many to recount.

One of the commonest excuses for violent behavior is that men turn violent after alcohol consumption. Stress, frustration, alcohol induce violent men to behave uncontrollably, and become excessively aggressive. There is another important aspect one has to bear in mind about men who batter. That in outward appearance and social interaction there is indeed no visible difference between a *batterer* and a non-batterer. Extremely successful individuals, with impressive careers—artists, doctors, suave movie icons, lawyers, politicians, are amongst wife batterers. These individuals project impeccable facades and hold esteemed social positions. Rarely are outsiders aware of the "person" behind the polite persona (see Dey in this volume).

Abusive men are not mentally ill, nor are they psychopaths. Their violence targets the wife or girl friend. They use brute violence to control their intimate female partners. Abusive men are mal-content individuals who revel in acts of cruelty. Faith McNulty, a *The New Yorker* magazine writer known for perceptive reporting who wrote *The Burning Bed* describes this kind of cruelty as "exquisitely targeted sadism" (McNulty, 1980). In her interview for *CHAR DIWARI* Flavia Agnes reminds us, "A man does not go to his office and beat the boss, nor does he beat a man on the street. He comes home and beats his wife. Why? Because there is no fear of retaliation." One of the four victims in the same documentary film, observed "... violence in not within a woman's control. Every thing in our society contributes to it."

A culture where the rhetoric of male domination has not been challenged, nor questioned, treats its female population with vile contempt. Besides when one group assumes itself to be superior, it appropriates the right to oppress others.

The Narratives

Compiling this book has been a turbulent but strangely rewarding journey for all of us concerned. For the women interviewed, their heroic resistance, and regard for human existence redeemed voicing buried memories of their tortured lives. After long hours of talking, the women would relax and regale one another with comic interludes. Their cheerfulness wiped out the gloom. These former victims were determined to regain dignity and control over their scattered lives. Aware they deserved justice, they wanted to hold nothing back during the oral history sessions. Sharing each woman's traumatic journey was often agonizing. But at the end of every saga, I urged the women to continue, and listen to the next story.

The interviews were conducted for nearly seven years— between 1984 until 1991—with several months of interruption. The women seemed grateful there was some one who cared to listen. It was inconceivable to them that their "shameful" experiences had any value. Some narratives were recorded over a period of time on tape. In case of others, I took down notes long hand. During each informal interview, we paused to share our fears our dreams with spontaneous warmth and humor. Each woman's story opened the closed doors to the problem wider, revealing fearful, familiar patterns looming behind dark shadows.

The 17 women featured in this volume belong to different regions of India. They come from the remote village, Dapoli, in Ratnagiri District (Maharashtra) to a Southern coffee plantation (Karnataka). *Gangubai* is a poor farmer's daughter from a lush rice-growing region. *Aruna* had fled from a barbaric arranged marriage to New York. *Zohra*, a refugee from the Indo–Bangladesh border worked as domestic maid. The experience of battery, abuse, and inhuman degradation is the bond between these women who have little else in common. From the women's collective experiences emerges graphic, indeed chilling images of the *crime behind closed doors*. Names and other personal details have been changed on request.

It was remarkable how each woman reposed her trust in me. At the second meeting, *Sarla* confessed about her husband's obsession with pornographic films and cheap roadside sex books. At one stage in her struggle she fervently prayed for the husband's death, thinking death was the only answer to her abominable torture. *Hansa,* was full of remorse about converting to Islam in order to legalize her bigamous marriage. Once married, the so-called legal husband vehemently opposed Hansa's pregnancy. *Ketan* had adolescent children from a previous marriage. After two abortions Hansa was silent about the third pregnancy. When Ketan learnt about it, he forced abortion by sitting on Hansa's belly. Hansa had a close brush with death. Recalling how she was pushed down the stairs during an early pregnancy, *Aruna* still shudders. Her fall resulted in a miscarriage.

Neela talks of the horrors inflicted during her second pregnancy. Especially, the night when her labor began. Husband David and his brother threw live rats and lizards at her. She was locked without food, water, and electricity. She had already lodged a number of reports (FIRs) at the local police station. She summoned the police to take her to the maternity hospital. *Neela* had suffered the additional trauma of being an abused and molested child. Pregnant women are routinely subjected to fatal injuries by partners in domestic violence cases.

Maya's story is a chilling account of organized mind control. What made it even worse was the fact that her husband Amit was her cousin brother. They grew up together, came from identical cultural milieu. In her case, as in Hansa's, the couple abused religious option by converting to Christianity. Marriage between first cousins is taboo amongst high caste Hindu Bengalis.

Amit reveled in torturing his wife. Maya was punished for listening to music. Her handbag was routinely ransacked for signs of imaginary love affairs. Amit stalked her to college and work destinations. He maligned her to senior colleagues. With the obvious result—Maya was dismissed or embarrassed.

Neela's husband controlled her fashion needs. He imposed strange rules about practically every household detail. David wanted the food to be served clockwise on the plate. He dictated the exact position of furniture and artefacts. The smallest thing triggered David's violence. It is significant to note that Neela, Tina, Jamuna and Aruna were the *second* generation of victims in their respective marital homes. There was a history of violence in the family background. Their respective mothers-in-law had been previously abused—the pattern continued.

Katy, a former colleague joined the project last. She had suffered domestic violence from her ex-boy-friend. I had no difficulty convincing Katy to share her experiences. Her story arrived via email the very next day. Katy's story was an important addition to the cluster. She highlights the abuse outside of marriage, in a man–woman partnership. This is common enough in the U.S., U.K., Europe. Her experience, like that of Gangubai and Zohra will demolish any myth that romantic relationships are a bed of roses, free of abuse. One rarely hears women speak of it. The shame and stigma attached have silenced women.

Questions may arise why I featured these particular women for *Behind Closed Doors*. The primary reason being they volunteered to speak. I was delighted when *Akash, Ganga, Bina, Deepa*, joined the project after reading my published letter in *The Indian Express* edit page (1985).

I know a number of other women who could be featured in the project. My assurance they had no cause to be ashamed of their husband's abuse yielded no results. I realized, that women were ashamed to encounter the history of abuse in their lives. Two women confessed their fear of social backlash. A few even suspected my motives. Silence is often a strategy to cope with unpleasant family history. A past such as this must be erased and life continue...speaking before a camera or for a publication was intimidating. It was pointless stirring up old memories—unless the women had agreed.

These narrative may shock you. In parts they may indeed appear excessive—even bizarre. The victims did not invent the dramatic narrations. Drama is inherent in the very situation. This is one of the chief reasons why populist Hollywood cinema churns out fictional blockbusters on the theme of domestic violence with catchy titles like LIVING WITH THE ENEMY, WAY OF THE ROSES and other melodramatic titles. However, it is splendid that the issue is out of the closet; thanks to TV channels, films, TV talk shows.

In this book, each woman privately shares a sordid secret of her intimate life. In the process of verbalizing her experiences, a victim often recovers from the burden of shame, and guilt. Most stories are narrated in the first person. I reconstructed minor parts in a few narrations.

During awareness raising campaigns on wife abuse we frequently encounter "disbelief" or "skepticism." It is my personal belief that disbelief would effectively block the process of understanding the issue of domestic violence.

Despite the ubiquity of violence against women, both within the home and in public spaces, the celebration of individual experiences has led to the emergence of alternative discourses where the truth and validity of established structures, norms and roles are called into question (Karlekar, 1998: 142).

Celebrated Cases of Domestic Violence

The first case I reported as a freelance journalist was about a Norwegian housewife *Liv* (pseudonym) from Oslo, (Bhattacharya, 1983, p. 12). For 18 years Liv had put up with unspeakable brutality from her husband *Ulf*. Several times she contemplated suicide. Her grown up children had left home. Liv had no support. In desperation, Liv bought a small bird gun, known as *Hagle*. She tucked the *Hagle* carefully into the wardrobe, thinking there was something more powerful in the house than her husband. On the fatal night, the couple had been to a friend's party. Returning back, Liv's husband accused her of flirting with other men. The minute they reached home, he pummeled her mercilessly, before forcing her to have sex. After her husband went to sleep, Liv shot him with the same *Hagle*. Within seconds Liv turned herself over to the Oslo police. The fact she informed the police went in her favor during the murder trial.

Liv's case was covered on front pages in leading Norwegian papers like the *Dagbladet*. For the first time serious attention was focused on the prevalence of domestic violence in civilized Scandinavian society. After her two year trial, Liv was acquitted in May 1983. During Liv's trial, the inevitable question was asked: why did Liv *not leave* but suffer 18 years of brutality? The Jury, composed of writers, artistes, teachers from Norway answered the question on Liv's behalf: in one voice the Jury said: "for Liv there was NO exit."

There are countless instances when women have been driven to commit murder after years of savage degradation. Many of them have been denied justice or compassionate verdicts granted to the anonymous Norwegian housewife, Liv.

Nicarthy mentions an interesting example:

In 1962 the case of a woman who wanted to sue her husband for assault damages was turned down by a Californian Supreme Court Judge because to hear the case would destroy the peace and harmony of the home, and thus would be contrary to the policy of the law (Nicarthy, 1986: 4).

Distinguished feminist scholars in Great Britain, Jalna Hanmer and Sheila Saunders, dedicate their community study of domestic violence: "to women in prison everywhere who are locked up for murdering violent men" (Hanmer and Saunders, 1984: dedication).

One of the most sensational cases in the 1970s came to be known as *The Burning Bed* (made into a film with Hollywood actress, Farah Fawcett). The case of Francine Hughes, a battered housewife from Dansville, Michigan, was published as a bestseller.

Assistant Prosecutor, Lee Atkinson of Ingham County, Michigan, was recorded to have said in Francine's case: "The best personal advice I could have given Mrs Hughes is that while I don't know the answer, the alternative is not to commit murder" (McNulty, 1980: 1). McNulty writes:

> Francine Hughes was charged with the death of her husband by fire, Mickey Hughes, in 1977. Had it occurred a decade earlier, the facts underlying the crime would probably never have been widely known, but in the seventies there was a new willingness to listen to such a story as hers. By the time she went to trial Francine's case had become a cause celebre (McNulty, 1980: author's note).

The Indian print and electronic media has reported increasing number of DV cases. "The arrest last week of Deepak Makam, the police inspector who allegedly battered his wife with a grinding stone, is another addition to the city's long list of domestic violence case. It is also amongst the few that has been reported" (*The Times of India*, 2002: 2).

Lori Heise's report analyzed Domestic Violence:

> Perhaps the most endemic form of violence to women is wife abuse. Study after study has shown that wife abuse is prevalent in all societies and crosscuts all racial, cultural, and socioeconomic lines. Studies by Stojanowska and Plata and Calderon de Clavijo reported at a 1986 meeting of experts on violence in the family sponsored by the United Nations confirm that from 90 to 98 percent spousal assault is directed at women. When women attack their husbands, it is usually in self defense (Heise, 1989: 4).

All over the world, domestic violence has claimed victims from the best amongst women—the most beautiful, gifted, wealthy, and famous—movie icons, Pop stars like Tina Turner, performing artists, musicians, painters, distinguished writers like Maya Angelou have been amongst victims of domestic violence. The print media highlighted actress Zeenat Aman's case when her adolescent son ferociously attacked her. More recently, actress Aishwariya Rai admitted being abused by her boy friend, actor Salman Khan. These stories establish the validity about the widespread prevalence of domestic violence that spares no one. Every woman is a potential victim.

Conclusion

Notwithstanding the "new willingness to listen" and a ready platform for DV victims at feminist forums, and counseling centers, I knew from the start, my work was fraught with uncertainty. There was undeniable difficulty in finding victims ready to talk about their experiences. I published letters to the editor of *The Indian Express*. Explored personal contacts like friends, neighbors, approached the Tata Institute of Social Science (TISS) Cell for Distressed Women, to reach battered women, who were willing to speak.

From the early 1980s, I worked as a volunteer along with Flavia Agnes and others at Women's center. Every week, women came with complaints of mental torture and beatings to the center. However, most of these cases were in early stages. Victims were unsure about the future course of their lives. The women who came to seek help were greatly agitated, or emotionally disoriented to talk coherently about their experience.

By 1987, some of us from the Women's movement together with a handful of individuals—lawyers, mental health professionals, doctors—decided to run a night hotline service for victims of violence. Working at HELP established beyond doubt that victims were anxious to find alternatives to their misery and suffering. Many confessed they wanted to leave (see Conclusion). At HELP, we handled close to four hundred phone complaints in 5 years. Neela and Tina are from HELP. Aruna, a family friend became my first heroine. Enthusiastic about sharing her poignant experiences, Karuna wrote her piece. Of the women featured, all but one had left their abusive husbands/partners. In her short piece

Deepa intelligently states reasons for not leaving her husband. Tina had a happy reunion with Paul. But she is one of the fortunate few to leave before the violence escalated. Kudchedkar rightly points out (see Foreword) none of the chronicles end with reform. That was not my intention. Reviewing the domestic violence documentary, *CHAR DIWARI*, cinema critic Maithili Rao had written:

> Fear and shame. Silence and suffering. These are the feelings that condition a woman to bear her lot in a society that apparently venerates her as Shakti—the energizing principle of the universe—and thinks nothing of burning her for dowry. Or selling a young girl in the marriage *bazaar*. It is easy enough to write about these with passion and crusading zeal. But to make a film about battered wives and have victims narrate their harrowing experiences is an act of political, feminist faith (Rao, 1991: 8).

All 17 heroines of *Behind Closed Doors*, and perhaps even I, affirm our political, feminist faith by breaking that deafening silence.
Believe us.

Notes

1. Suvira Jaiswal contends that society in the *Rigvedic* period was still predominantly pastoral and nomadic; it did not produce enough surplus to allow any section of society to be completely subordinated or withdrawn from the process of production. This perhaps explains the comparatively better position of women in the vedic period in terms of access to education, religious rights, freedom of movement, etc. Dr Neera Desai and Maitreyi Krishnaraj remark (p. 188) that in *Brahminical* texts a woman is considered the property of a man, and if any rights could be conferred on her, they are through the husband.

2. Womens' Centre (1982), 104B, Sunrise Apartments, Nehru Road, Vakola, Mumbai, 400055. Activities: Counselling, campaigning, legal aid, providing resources.

3. HELP Activities: telephone counseling all night, intervention, referral services.

4. Raja Ram Mohan Roy (22 May 1772–27 September 1883). Essentially a humanist and religious reformer Raja Ram Mohan Roy left his high position at the East India Company to devote his time

to the service of Indian people. Profoundly influenced by European liberalism, Ram Mohan believed that radical reform was necessary in the religion of Hinduism and in the social practices of Hindus. He devoted himself to the task of social justice—opposed the practice of *Sati*—widow burning. His efforts bore fruit. In 1829, the Governor General of Bengal, Lord Bentick, passed the *Abolition of Sati Act*. In 1828, Ram Mohan founded the *Brahmo Samaj*—known earlier as *Brahmo Sabha*. He was the first feminist in India and his book, *Brief Remarks Regarding Modern Encroachments on the Ancient Rights of Females* (1822), is a seasoned argument in favor of women's equality.

References

Ansari, Khaled. 2003 *Mid Day*, p. 6.

Bhattacharya, Rinki Roy. 1983. *The Eve's Weekly*, July 30–August 5, p. 12.

Chitnis, Suma. 1998. *Violence against Women/Women against Violence*. Delhi: Pencraft International, p. 11.

Deltufo, Alisa. 1995. *Domestic Violence for Beginners*, United States: Writers and Readers publishing, p. 6.

Desai, Neera and Krishnaraj, Maitreyi. 1987. *Women and Society in India*. Delhi: Ajanta Publications.

Hanmer and Saunders. 1984. *WELL FOUNDED FEAR*. London: Hutchinson Publishing Group.

Heise, Lori. 1989. *Response*, vol. 12, no. 1, p. 4.

Karlekar, Malavika. 1998. "Domestic Violence," *Economic and Political Weekly*, July 4–7, pp. 1742–51.

McNulty, Faith. 1980. *The Burning Bed*. New York & London: Harcourt Brace Jovanovich.

Martin, Del. 1976. *Battered Wives*. New York: Pocket Books.

Mazumdar, Swapna. 2002. "Emerging from the Shadows." *One India One People*, May vol. 5, no. 10, p. 8.

Nicarthy, Ginny. 1986. *Getting Free*, New Leaf Series, Washington: Seal Press.

Maithili. Rao, 1991. Review of CHAR DIWARI, *Sunday Observer*, October 6, "The Evil That Men Do To Women".

Srivastava, Roli. "Many Deaths in domestic violence abuse concealed as accidents," *The Times of India*, October 2002: 2.

The Times of India. 21 November 2002, p. 1.

The Times of India. 22 October 2002, p. 2.

World Health Organization. 2002. *World Health Organization Report on Violence and Health*.

Chapter One
Devi: The Disempowered Goddess
Anwesha Arya

Introduction

Within the Hindu religious tradition women are assigned a dichotomous role. Worshipped, on the one hand, as the ultimate creative principle, and controlled on the other as threats to that very creation. In most cases this is misrepresented, with an emphasis on either one or the other role. There are defensive claims that a culture which worships women can never abuse them, while women's groups scour primary texts for negative references where beating a woman is condoned. Such contradictory claims in the primary texts, have led researchers to question the "true" status of women in ancient India. It is impossible to state accurately the actual status of women in a period so far removed from our own. However, today it is widely accepted that although a strong Goddess principle persists in the Hindu religious tradition, women at the ground level share no such glorified status.

Examining the role definitions outlined for goddesses in the Hindu pantheon is crucial since it lends insights into the conceptualization of the position of women in the Hindu male mindset. Included in this volume about women in the context of domestic violence, this study may become an important contribution towards greater understanding of how deep-rooted socialization impacts upon the manifestation of violence. It is possible to argue in response to the *Manusmriti* verse "Where women are worshipped there gods rejoice"; that where goddesses are feared there they will be disempowered (Roy, 1995). This chapter highlights the spousification process of Devi and examines the negative ramifications it has on female autonomy. Although the scope of this paper is limited to the examination of only one religious tradition, it may be argued that Indian society is widely influenced by the dominant strain of institutionalized Hinduism.

Historical Antecedents and Sources

A. S. Altekar's *The Position of Women in Hindu Civilization* suggests that women in ancient India enjoyed a high status which deteriorated with time. This fall in status is blamed on the corrupting external influences of "other" cultures. At the outset it is vital to underline that Altekar's study was poised to justify the status of Indian women and Indian society to western researchers soon after Independence. The same argument is made continually to support the assertion that there is no "negative" strain in the great and golden tradition of Hinduism. Those who persist in disclaiming the inherently pluralistic nature of the primary texts and associated traditional practices are sadly unaware of the extent of the material and the period involved. It is widely accepted that the dominant culture in India follows a patriarchal strain with a few fading nuances of matriarchy. This chapter attempts to trace and understand the status of women in Indian society today as reflected in the changing role of the goddess-principle in its dominant religious tradition.

It is important to consider that at any given time in India we have a problem with uniformity. The key word here is plurality. Any realistic study of Hinduism must note and account for this influence. All the texts in question have been passed down through generations of oral tradition, recorded in writing much later. The *Manusmriti* or *Manavadharmasastra* for instance was compiled over an extended period and is "a culmination of the work of several authors" (Doniger and Smith, 1991: xviii). Often however, this treatise on paradigmatic behavior is attributed to one single author *Manu*, considered the first man; a myth reiterated by academics and others alike. Seema Sirohi hails Manu as "the godfather to Indian men," though historically fallacious, her conclusion that this work continues to inform the attitudes and actions of the Hindu male elite is quite pertinent (Sirohi, 2003: 15).

It is true that the theorists of the Hindutva brigade have become modern spokespeople for damaging patriarchal attitudes. For example, according to *Manusmriti* killing a woman is a "minor crime" (Doniger and Smith, 1991: 257). This sentiment embodies the entire ideology of the Hindu male mindset, which finally goes on to undermine female autonomy. Unfortunately, fundamentalists and other interlopers continue to claim canonical status for these texts to project an institutionalized image of the Hindu tradition. They argue that such anti-woman decrees are not shocking. The current stand on the status of the Indian woman therefore remains a major concern.

Tracing historical sources for *Devi* (Goddess) leads to non-sanskritic terminolgy implying that goddess worship may have entered the Sanskritic tradition from indigenous religious systems. In fact, linguistic infiltration in the Sanskrit texts are not rare, as we shall examine later, non-Sanskritic words like *Candika* and *Candi* (Coburn, 1986: 156) have found their way into the dominant vocabulary, as have other non-Vedic gods and goddesses. Underlining this inherent plural nature of Hinduism, we might proceed to unravel the complex and contradictory status awarded to Indian women today. It is not an easy journey.

Two distinct patterns emerge in this journey: one, the existence of an independent, almost feared entity, the independent Devi; the second, the submissive role-playing ideal wife personification, what Lynn Gatwood (1985) calls the "spouse–goddess." Julia Leslie highlights this "radical distinction" between what she calls the "(essential) woman" and the "(ideal) wife." In the traditional twofold classification of female deities as the "fierce" *Durga* or *Kali* usually portrayed as uncontrolled, destructive forces linked with sexuality, blood, and death on one hand, and as "ideal goddess–wives" who are subordinate to their husbands, and therefore unthreatening, on the other. Interestingly, it is held by the *dharmasastra* that "taming" is necessary in both the human realm as in the divine, because "…untamed female nature—with all the negative associations of female sexuality—is antisocial, elemental and dangerous…." This can only be achieved through the "controlled state of marriage" (Leslie, 1995: 320).

The married state clearly affects female autonomy adversely in most cases, whether in patrilineal or matrilineal societies. Of the five types of matrilineal societies in the world, India is home to three: the Garo; the Khasi; and the Nayar type. This, contrary to popular belief, has not positively influenced female autonomy in India. It is fallacious to equate female autonomy and matrilineality; the correlations are far more complex than what may be imagined. Marriage delineates the transfer of a woman to the kin-group of the groom in patriarchal and patrilocal groups, and even in some matriarchal groups. In most cases there is a power relation governing the relationships between families dependent on the transfer of property and child rights (see Schlegel, 1972). In examining the symbolic relationship between goddesses and women it becomes evident that we are dealing with conceptual models transmitted and controlled by an intellectual male elite (Menski, 1991: 47). The correlation between status, marriage, and sexuality is examined later in the chapter.

In her ethnographic study of these two manifestations of Indian goddesses, Gatwood critically observes their influence on women's lives in India. These ethnographic considerations will form the core of the present argument, based on Gatwood's understanding of the evident link between the Devi and lower classes of women in Hindu society, and the spouse–goddess with the higher classes of women. This chapter will examine the possible "socio-economic" reasons for such a leaning in these two diametrically opposite sections of society, while analyzing the effect this may have on their notion of identity and further, their place in society with relation to men.

Archaeological Evidence for Pre-patriarchal Societies

An issue that naturally arises in any study of goddesses is that concerning the status of women and its relationship with goddess worship. Based on the analogy of western traditions, where male deities reflect a patriarchal/male-dominated societal structure, it is usually assumed that in religions where goddesses have a prominent place, it reflects a society with a female-dominated societal structure or where the status of women is high. Simultaneously, it is often assumed that goddesses, especially powerful independent deities, affirm and promote female power, which should mirror positive consequences in the social realm.

While it is difficult to deny that societies that worship powerful independent goddesses may have positive effects on the women within those societies, as David Kinsley (1989: xi) emphasizes, it does not necessarily imply a clear relationship between goddess-centered religions and female-dominated societies. Many examples exist of patriarchal cultures where the goddess principle is central; India and Nepal are two such examples. Almost all historically recorded cultures and non-literate traditional cultures studied by anthropologists tend to be male dominated to some extent. It is therefore very difficult to find examples of goddesses who belong to a society in which there is egalitarianism between the sexes or in which males are sub-ordinate to women (Kinsley, 1989: xii).

Tempting archaeological evidence exists to support the view that in the past goddesses were central in non-patriarchal cultures. In recent years this theory has found many supporters. The primary argument is based on the discovery of an abundance of female figurines or images, assumed rightly according to Kinsley (1989: xvi) "to represent goddesses (or a Goddess)." However, a serious problem exists in the reconstruction of these cultures where goddesses were revered as central deities. Most of these societies are either dead or non-literate, or as in the case of the Indus Valley civilization, have an undeciphered script. It is further problematic to decide how conclusive such evidence is to determine the relative roles of males and females especially with reference to Hinduism. With the Hindu tradition we know of a variety of goddesses, many of whom are powerful independent deities who dominate male deities and yet India is a predominantly patriarchal society. In fact as Kinsley points out, "[h]induism seems to teach that a theology in which goddesses are important does not necessarily have to imply sexual egalitarianism. Female power, creativity and authority in the theological sphere do not necessarily imply high female status in the social sphere" (Kinsley, 1989: xvi). This is borne out by the prevalent attitudes towards women in the sphere of work and further defines power equations between the sexes.

Another important point raised by the theory of pre-patriarchal cultures is of a shift, the distinction between elite and popular religion, especially in the context of Hinduism. Briefly, the elite version of Hinduism is dominated by males (females being excluded from educational institutions and traditional *ashram*s in most cases in India until fairly recently). The texts upon which we are forced to base our picture of this religious tradition are androcentric. The elite religion tends to play down certain aspects of popular religion that emphasize non-Sanskritic elements and goddess worship represents one such element.

Placing devi in the Historical Context

Recent research on the historical and ethnographic fabric of India has unveiled "an independent, fertile, and unblushingly erotic female principle..." considered relevant mainly in rural India. In terms of textual sources for the understanding of Devi or the Hindu conceptualization of this female principle, we might look at the *Markandeya Purana*. According to Thomas Coburn, the *Devi-Mahatmaya*, is a part of the early Sanskrit *Puranas*, and was possibly composed north of the Narmada valley sometime during the fifth or sixth centuries AD. The reason why this portion of the text is valid here is, as Coburn claims, though we find various references to goddesses from the *Rigveda* onwards, this is the first time that "ultimate reality" itself is understood as being the Goddess. "The ultimate reality in the universe is here understood to be the feminine, Devi, the Goddess...[this is] the first occasion on which relentless and comprehensive articulation of such a vision is given in Sanskrit" (Coburn, 1986: 153). However, this *avataar* appears relatively unexplored compared to the "...male-controlled, religiously marginal, and morally ambiguous goddess..." widely considered as the "sole representative" of the Hindu female principle (Gatwood, 1985: 1). Gatwood draws a link between these two opposite forces and calls the first a "virtual template," upon which a later Sanskritic tradition imposed the spouse–goddess, often referred to as the Consort-Goddess (see Coburn, 1986 and Hawley et al., 1996).

Historically the existence of a mother goddess figure in pre-Aryan traditions in the sub-continent appears to corelate with characteristics associated with the independent, often violent manifestation of the independent Hindu goddess, Devi. Gatwood hypothesizes that this underwent a process of "spousification," occurring within the more widespread Sanskritization (Srinivas, 1952) of indigenous perspectives through which the second, and presently predominant spouse–goddess ideal emerged. Based on recent evidence and academic speculation, it seems likely that this aspect of the Devi as independent has changed largely due to this process of Sanskritization. This chapter examines the social and marital symbolism involved in this debate. Interestingly, two distinct geographical areas are influenced by these pre-Aryan feminine ideals to a greater degree. The goddesses worshipped in Bengal and the southern states of India display more similarity to the *Mahadevi* and Devi than elsewhere in the country. Concurrently, it was in Bengal that the women's liberation movement and emphasis on women's education (Engels, 1999: 158–60) found most parlance in the early part of the twentieth century (Engels, 1999: 10). Pertinent research suggests that women are respected to a greater degree in the southern states of India, as opposed to the intensely patriarchal northern and central states (Purthi et al., 2001). However general this statement, the note-worthy element is the correlation of the type of goddess worshipped in these communities and its influence on the predominant mindset with relation to the treatment of women.

Devi and the Spouse–Goddess: Marriage and Sexuality

The symbolic contrast between Devi and the spouse–goddess is most obvious and emerges in the critical area of Brhamanic orthodox marriage, and their differing spheres of influence. Coburn's investigation yields evidence of the conceptualization of the relationship between the Devi and various masculine divinities. He surmises that, "although Devi is understood to bear a unique relation to each particular [male] deity, this is not a 'mere' consort relation; she is *beyond being a consort to anyone*" (emphasis added) (Coburn, 1986: 154).

Therefore, we find that Devi may not always be married, and even if she is, her partner is either considered her equal or sometimes a mere helper/assistant. She is the dominant one, never subservient or inferior in any way. Devi is also seen to enter into "...unorthodox forms of marriage that allow her to function independently without censure...." Conversely the spouse–goddess must be "sacramentally married" according to *dharmic* principles. This is considered essential to her benevolent functioning. Further, "these contrasting forms of marriage parallel the marriages contracted by women at the two caste levels" (Gatwood, 1985: 4).

Both these manifestations of the feminine principle have two aspects. While the Devi reflects "the natural forces of creation and dissolution," the spouse–goddess reflects an interesting "moral duality" made up of malevolence and insipid benevolence. Devi might remain a unified deity, since both her aspects depend not on "...the presence or absence of marital control..." but on the cosmological factors governing worship addressed to her, which is not the case for the spouse–goddess. This moral duality of the spouse–goddess is divided into two distinct deities based on her positive and negative manifestation. The spouse–goddess's "inherent" malevolent side is looked upon as elemental to her original destructive nature like that of the Devi, an aspect she must harness. This harnessing process takes place through marriage. Her benevolent aspect is expressed only in her "controlled" married state, where she appears in her dharmic wifely role. Similarly for women, their unfettered side must be checked and therefore disempowered through socialization into demure, good girls who will make ideal wives. The spouse–goddess therefore mirrors the woman who carries a disempowered goddess inside.

The striking parallel of societal expectations of high caste women might be seen here. "Like the spouse–goddess the high caste woman requires close control of her potentially insatiable sexual desires, while the low caste woman mirrors Devi in remaining relatively free from such control" (Gatwood, 1985: 5). With reference to this contrast between these two goddess types a major aspect is the relation of each to her husband or partner. Gatwood illustrates both a social and cosmological aspect implied in this relationship. Devi's partner, if and when present, is considered her lover or consort. He is essentially "her co-equal or her youthful assistant." Both share this-worldly functions relating to fertility and weather etc. This gender equality extends to social interactions involved in the worship of Devi; men and women worshippers are afforded equal status. Women may hold positions of power as manifestations of shakti themselves, and therefore as appointed priestesses. This is truer of *Tantra* worship today, where women themselves embody the power of Devi. Blood is not considered impure, but as empowering.

Alternately, the spouse–goddess's husband is viewed as "her clear superior" at times even as her personal god, as is outlined in the concept of *stridharma* and the *Manusmriti* for all women. While his benevolent functions usually deal with rebirth of individual souls and perhaps even *moksha* from the cycle of rebirth, her role is limited to the well-being of the individual households that worship her. This evident gender inequality and functional disparity between the two deities, extends to the hierarchical interactions involved in their worship. Male priests define terms of worship, with women being forbidden to participate in oblations at certain times of the month. The temple is out of bounds for menstruating women, considered impure and dangerous. Several verses in the *Smriti* literature outline appropriate behavior for menstruating women. Husbands are forbidden to even sleep on the same bed as a menstruating wife (see Doniger, 1991: 78) as this will impair their intelligence and eyesight; essentially the wife has the power to damage her husband irreparably. Therefore, it follows that she must be controlled and thus disempowered.

The presence or absence of the orthodox marital imperative remains the key factor in the symbolism of a goddess. Where it is present, marriage functions as a control on a sexually threatening, benign-but-potentially-malevolent spouse–goddess, rendering her status separate and unequal to that of her husband–god. Where this imperative is absent, marriage is irrelevant to the sexually expressive, creative–destructive energies represented by Devi, who is the co-equal or slight superior of her partner, with whom she shares interchangeable roles.

Women as Financial Independents

The lives of women seem to mirror these symbolic differences between the two goddess types: low-caste women enjoy relative equality and have roles that are interchangeable with their husbands, as opposed to high caste women who generally play inferior, more gender-specific roles. There appears within a caste a definitive hierarchy of sexes dependent on purity/impurity.

These distinctions might be drawn from two primary areas, in the playing out of economic dependence and decision-making roles within these two sub-groups.

Women are intrinsically impure because the monthly menstrual cycle is considered highly polluting. However, a greater degree of importance is attached to this in higher castes, "...the difference in the levels of purity/impurity between men and women is much less among the lower castes..." (Dube and Palriwala, 1990: 9). This is essentially because low-caste women apart from dealing with "self-pollution" also have to deal with others' pollution through occupational activities like midwifery, disposal of dirt, the washing of dirty clothes and so on. Their men also have to undertake similar activities considered polluting to the higher castes, especially the burning of the dead. (see Doniger, 1991: 60). Women from lower caste groups tend to contribute substantially to the process of earning a livelihood as well as sharing these impure tasks, thus making "...the gender division less unequal..." (Dube and Palriwala, 1990: 9).

In the case of Brahman and other higher-caste men, they neither have to undertake such polluting activities, nor do they suffer the same kind of self-pollution as their women. Higher-caste women are involved in activities like childbirth and menstruation that renders them, even if temporarily, definitely polluted. As a result of this impure character, their ritual activity both in the home and in public is far more restricted. They are forbidden to take part in funeral ceremonies as a general rule, something in practice till date. They are therefore afforded a subordinate position in relation to the men in the family (Dube and Palriwala, 1990: 8–10).

Although, women from the lower classes (In the contemporary context, the term "caste" is no longer widely in use and the term "class" may be seen as a representation of income groups, which include various caste and class groups.) are not unaffected by the imposed disabilities of menstrual pollution, this is only with regard to food and worship, they continue to work and earn unhindered. This capacity to be a wage earner affords these women a more equal status in society as related to their men. However, it can also become an impediment, as discussed elsewhere in this volume. Women who earn are abused by their husbands as much as wives who are economically dependent on their husbands. The power relations governing monetary control are far more complex within an abusive relationship, and are influenced by a number of external and psychological factors unique to each particular case.

Social Autonomy, Women, and the Goddess Influence

Differences between high- and low-caste women extend from the economic to the social realm, where there is an interesting contrast in social autonomy and decision-making authority. At marriage, high-caste women are assimilated into their husband's lineage. "Women have no legal autonomy, they cannot manage extra-domestic expenses, nor may they own or sell land except where there are no sons to inherit" (Gatwood, 1985: 85). Women in the lower strata of society on the other hand, may possess a better social and economic autonomy and formal authority. Low-caste wives retain strong ties to their natal lineage, and do not always adopt their husband's kin terms. They often handle family finances as earning members themselves. Further, they engage in independent financial transactions, including money borrowing which led Harper to conclude, "family authority tends to be rather equally divided between husband and wife" in lower-class groups (as cited by Gatwood). They also enter into family legal disputes, a pattern of behavior totally unacceptable for women in higher classes. The most significant evidence is that women in this class may move unaccompanied both inside and outside the village-setting without fear of retribution.

Like the Sanskritic God and the spouse–goddess, the high caste wife is the legal, economic, and social subordinate of her husband. In fact she must virtually worship him as her first god. The high-caste conjugal pair has mutually exclusive economic roles. The lower-caste spouses share relatively equal ritual status with the Devi and her consort, insofar as they share interchangeable roles, and are more or less economic equals.

With regard to the sphere of influence of women the relevant criterion for comparison is cosmological jurisdiction. The similarities are striking, the Devi with her wide sphere of jurisdiction including both the household as well as weather, crop, and village welfare, the health of the community etc. is quite like the lower-caste woman with her "dual economic role" in life, including both domestic and extra domestic, mainly agricultural affairs. The spouse–goddess and the high-caste woman on the other hand share the parallels of being "confined to household matters." Much research in this area might yet be delved in, however not within the confines of this particular chapter.

Conclusion: Disempowering the Goddess Within

The Devi-like principle and its followers seems to have been neglected by researchers so far, possibly because in most studies of India one rarely sees any representation of the behavior or beliefs of the lower-income groups and lower castes in general. The Subaltern Studies group has examined feminist concerns, but much work needs to be done on the representation of these groups who do not always express themselves through literary traditions. The dependency, subjugation, victimization, and moral ambiguity of women in India has been overstressed. As Gatwood believes and I would agree, this representation is far truer for higher caste women.

In Gatwood's study she outlines a clear distinction between the *Brahman* and *Shudra* castes as being the dividing line in relation to female autonomy. However, as is evident especially in the present Indian context, there is a blending of the three upper castes and a coming together of the lowest caste and non-Hindus, more or less defined along economic lines. It is similar to the creation of a political power block along which tensions take place. As Gatwood points out, "while a Brahman/non-Brahman dichotomy is also evident, particularly in the area of religious practice, in the socio-economic realm Kshatriyas generally blend with Brahmans. Vaisyas are numerically few in rural areas, preferring to cluster in relatively urbanized centers [sic]. The largest segment of India's population belongs to the many Shudra and Untouchable *jatis*…"

All these factors have impacted the socialization process of both sexes, producing a unique dismissive approach toward women's rights and empowerment. Through the primary textual tradition, as well as in the oral tradition evident in sayings and children's songs, the role of the woman is underlined as inferior. As mother she is supreme, especially as the mother of a male child, but as such she continues to be considered a burden on men: father, husband and finally son (see Doniger, 1991: 115). The outreach of these intensely patriarchal values is surprising in their currency and strength as noted earlier. As evidenced by the rising cases of domestic violence, female infanticide, foeticide and bride burning, the current status of Indian, especially Hindu women is ambiguous at best. There is still a long way to go before the goddess dormant in every woman finds empowerment.

While the discussion here has outlined the symbolic reflections of two goddess types for Indian Hindu women, it has also touched upon the wider ramifications of such identification. As outlined, the stranglehold of Sanskritic values through the state-controlled institutionalized elite version of Hinduism has garbled both rural and urban attitudes to women. Bride burning is a rampant and dangerous form of domestic violence unique to Indian communities. Domestic violence subjects individuals to the loss of their personhood. They are robbed of their humanity in their own homes, which is the worst form of theft. Areas where dowry deaths, identified as the ultimate denial of status as a person, were non-existent like Nagaland (1994 two dowry deaths) and Meghalaya (1992 two deaths) now feature a regular, albeit minimal trend in bride burning (National Crimes Bureau of India). This clearly underlines the commodified status of daughters and by implication women in general. Unfortunately, the status of women and female autonomy are dependent on wider perceptions of ritual status and equality governed by a male elite. Women will remain disempowered goddesses as long as their worthiness is equated with their being classified as ideal wives.

Spousification of the Devi continues today, with an emphasis on sacramental dharmic marriage. In fact, a high proportion of marriages in India are unrecorded in civil terms; a Hindu ceremony is considered sufficiently legal. The most glaring evidence of this spousification process is found in modern physical representations of these goddesses. Kali and Durga are usually represented in all their malevolent splendor; Kali is seen stepping on Siva while Durga is killing Mahishasura. On careful scrutiny one finds that idols of these goddesses are updated with symbols of marriage. Kali is depicted with a bunch of keys at her waist, a sign of domesticity especially in Bengal. The myth of Durga highlights her creation by a pantheon of male gods like Indra, Siva, and Brahma, who unable to deal with the violent and chaotic *asuras* breathe life into an untamable goddess to kill the asura king, Mahishasura. Her myth now emphasizes her marriage to Siva. The festival linked to her, as celebrated by the Bengali community, is explained to children as Durga's visiting her maternal home on earth accompanied by her four children: Saraswati, Laxmi, Ganesha, and Kartika. Siva's photograph is hung in a corner of the puja pandal as a reminder to worshippers that she is married, and therefore benevolent though represented in the violent act of murder. Interestingly, on the final day of the puja celebrations married women join in a customary smearing of sindoor on the idol's feet and forehead to reaffirm both the goddess's and their own married state. Widows and unmarried women are not considered appropriate participants in this symbolic celebration of marriage.

Therefore, as stated in the beginning, it is widely accepted that a strong Goddess principle persists in the Hindu religious tradition despite having been subjected to Sanskritic spousification. Concurrently, women at ground level continue to have no such glorified status.

These representations of the raw and untamed goddess principle of Devi, as harnessed by domesticity, underline the current perception of the independent goddess, and likewise the independent goddess principle resident in women. Socialization has carefully disempowered the latent power traditionally linked with women by dislocating their identification with the raw and sexual goddess principle. Unfortunately, Devi continues to be disempowered at the religious level and women continue to battle for empowerment at the ground level. We continue to shovel away at the mound of patriarchy that stands in the way of our empowerment. If Indian women are able to find a route for being defined outside the sphere of marriage as individuals, not wives or mothers or daughters or sisters, there is hope.

References

Coburn, Thomas. 1986. "Consort of None, Shakti of All: The Vision of the Devi-Mahatmya," in John Stratton Hawley and Donna Marie Wulff (eds). 1982, 1986. *The Divine Consort: Radha and the Goddesses of India*. Berkley Religious Studies Series. 1982. Boston: Beacon Press. 1986, pp. 153–165.

Doniger, Wendy and Brian K. Smith. 1991. *The Laws of Manu*. trans. Wendy Doniger and Brian K. Smith. Delhi: Penguin Books.

Dube, Leela and Rajni Palriwala (eds). 1990. *Structures and Strategies: Women, Work and Family*. New Delhi, London: Sage.

Dube, Leela. 1996. "Caste and Women," in M.N. Srinivas (ed). *Caste: Its Twentieth Century Avatar*. 1996. Delhi: Penguin, pp. 1–28.

Engels, Dagmar. 1999. *Beyond Purdah? Women in Bengal 1890–1930*. SOAS Studies on South Asia. Delhi: Oxford University Press.

Gatwood, Lynn. 1985. *Devi and the Spouse-goddess: Women, Sexuality and Marriage in India*. Delhi: Manohar.

Hawley, John Stratton "Prologue," in John Stratton Hawley and Donna Marie Wulff (eds). 1996. *Devi: Goddesses of India*. Berkley: University of California Press, pp. 1–29.

King, Richard. 1999. *Orientalism and Religion: Postcolonial Theory, India and 'the mystic east'*. London and New York: Routledge.

Kinsley, David. 1986. *Hindu Goddesses: Visions of the Divine Feminine in the Hindu Religious Tradition*. Berkley: University of California Press.

———. 1989. *The Goddesses' Mirror: Visions of the Divine from East and West*. Albany: State University of New York Press.

———1996. "Kali: Blood and Death Out of Place," in John Stratton Hawley and Donna Marie Wulff (eds). 1996. *Devi: Goddesses of India*. Berkley: University of California Press.

Leslie, Julia. 1989, 1995. *The Perfect Wife: The Stridharmapaddhati of Tryambakayajvan*. trans. Julia Leslie. Oxford University South Asia Series. Oxford: Oxford University Press. Delhi: Penguin.

Menski, Werner. 1991. "Marital Expectations as Dramatised in Hindu Marriage Ritual," in Julia Leslie (ed.). 1991. *Roles and Rituals for Hindu Women*. Delhi: Motilal Banarsidas, pp. 47–65.

Mitter, Sara. S. 1995. *Dharma's Daughters: Contemporary Indian Women and Hindu Culture*. New Brunswick: Rutgers University Press.

Purthi, Raj Kumar, Romila Purthi and Rameshwari Devi (eds). 2001. *Indian Women: Present Status and Future Prospects*. Jaipur: Mangal Deep Publications.

Roy, Kumkum. 1995. "'Where Women are Worshipped, there the Gods Rejoice': The Mirage of the Ancestress of Hindu Women," in Tanika Sarkar and Urvashi Butalia (eds).1995. *Women and the Hindu Right: A Collection of Essays*. Delhi: Kali for Women.

Schlegel, Alice 1972. *Male Dominance and Female Autonomy: Domestic Authority in Matrilineal Societies*. Human Relations Area Files Inc: (HRAF) Press.

Sirohi, Seema. 2003. *Sita's Curse: Stories of Dowry Victims*. New Delhi: Harper Collins.

Srinivas, M.N. 1952. Religion and Society among the Coorgs of South India. Oxford: Clarendon Press.

Chapter Two

Contextualizing Domestic Violence: Family, Community, State

Sobha Venkatesh Ghosh

In retrospect it could be said that the New Women's Movement in India, as it has shaped itself since the 1980s, has fundamentally centred round the question of the forms of violence against women. The specific campaigns that are today read as the benchmarks of the movement—notably, those against custodial rapes, dowry murders and *sati*—brought into focus the asymmetries in gender relations that undergird our social formations, legal processes, and the very notions of citizenship rights. However, the emphasis on these "aberrant" manifestations of violence obfuscated the issue of the more banal and everyday forms of abuse that women are subjected to within the home. Flavia Agnes has consistently argued since the 1980s that by "placing dowry violence on a pedestal" in their campaigning and theorizing, Indian feminists have played into the hands of conservative agents that read gendered violence in terms of its exceptionalism rather than as the defining context of women's lives (Agnes, 1995: 109–10).

It is, therefore, not surprising that while many Western countries passed laws against domestic violence in the 1970s and 1980s, there is as yet no specific law in India pertaining to the issue, though new legislations were promptly passed in the case of custodial rapes, dowry, sati, obscenity, and procurement of minors for prostitution, by a state under pressure from feminist and democratic forces and eager to be seen as the guarantor of its citizens' rights. It is another matter that given the patriarchal and class character of the state, almost all these laws remain deeply flawed and in many cases counterproductive. However, a discussion of this is outside the scope of this chapter.

The State Discourse on Domestic Violence

In 1983 and 1986, amendments were made to the existing Criminal Law to take onboard the category of "cruelty to wives" in terms that were diffuse or incomplete in definition, difficult to implement within the procedures of criminal law, and easy to circumvent. For instance, "cruelty" was defined as the causing of "grave injury or danger to life, limb or death," thus leaving outside its ambit the mundane or non-physical forms of violence of everyday life (Agnes, 1995: 121–26). Another problem is that in the amendment domestic violence is dubiously sutured to dowry demand and harassment, with the result that often in the perception of the police and the legal machinery, a claim to cruelty cannot by definition be made unless appended to the claim to dowry harassment. It is almost as though it is only by invoking the criminality of dowry and related violence that an intervention into the sacralized space of the family can be justified.

It is only since the 1990s that domestic violence has been specifically highlighted as an endemic and pervasive reality of women's lives as well as a fundamental violation of their rights. Globally, the Vienna Congress on Human Rights (1994) and the Fourth World Conference of Women at Beijing (1995) included this issue as a critical area of concern. Apart from identifying women's abuse as a human rights issue, these also called for a crucial redefinition of what constitutes violence against women in their intimate relationships. And, indeed, there has been a radical redefinition and elaboration of the paradigm over the past few years both by international bodies and by Indian feminist forums such as the Lawyers' Collective Women's Rights Initiative (LCWRI). The LCWRI defines domestic violence as "any act, omission or conduct which is of such a nature as to harm or injure or has the potential of harming or injuring the health, safety or well-being of the person aggrieved or any child in the domestic relationship and includes physical abuse, sexual abuse, verbal and mental abuse and economic abuse" (LCWRI, 2002: 6). A study of domestic violence by the Research Centre for Women's

Studies, SNDT, Mumbai, elaborates the term as "all acts perpetrated in the private domain of the home to secure women's subordination; and which is rationalized and sanctioned by the prevailing gender ideology. It is thus seen as going beyond the legal definitions of physical assault, to include psychological and sexual violence" (Poonacha and Pandey, 1999: 1).

Taken together, these two definitions clarify domestic violence as material practice as well as the cultural–ideological context of its operation. This is not to suggest that violence in the home is uniform across different locations. There are many forms of families; they inhabit varied contexts and are subject to different pressures; they must be seen in the specificity of their constellations as affective and economic units. Nor are ideological formations dispersed uniformly across familial sites. While feminists believe that the basic character of the Indian family unit is patriarchal, they also caution that patriarchal structures and ideologies are unevenly constituted, are constantly in the process of reconstitution, and manifest differentially in shifting contexts. Further, we cannot assume a neat fit between familial structures and familial ideologies. But, more about that later.

For now, the question is, given the urgency that the issue of domestic violence has gathered, where is the Indian state in all this? Significantly, on December 11, 2001, the Government of India, through the Ministry of Human Resource Development, published and circulated a bill on domestic violence. While granting the political significance of the inclusion of the issue on the state agenda, feminists across the board have unequivocally rejected the specific proposals of the bill as it "not only falls short of our expectations and of what is required to be done, but may actually turn out to be dangerous in its implications for women who are victims of domestic violence" (LCWRI, 2002: 6). Ideologically regressive in its exorbitation of the family; placing the welfare of the family above the well-being of the victimized woman, the bill, purporting to secure the woman's rights within the home, actually carries within it the means for its own subversion (LCWRI, 2002: 21–8). If the bill were to be passed, abuse would have to be "habitual" (however that is to be determined) for it to be even recognized as violence by the law. The definition of violence itself is impressively brief and surpassingly vague—habitual assaults, cruelty of conduct, forcing the woman to lead an "immoral life," or any conduct that "otherwise injures or harms the aggrieved person." However, none of the above may constitute violence if the man was acting "for his own protection or for the protection of his or another's property" thus making available to the perpetrator of abuse the plea of self-defence! As disturbing are the omissions in the document. It has nothing to say about the woman's rights to child custody, matrimonial property or even to continue to reside in the matrimonial home. In effect, the bill offers no hope to women who are compelled to stay on in abusive relationships because of economic vulnerability, fear of losing children and the lack of support structures outside the home.

What is as interesting as the bill itself is the manner in which it was publicized, "debated" and rationalized in the media by its votaries. To underline its commitment to gender justice the BJP government at the center strategically marshalled its women members to be the spokespersons. Also highlighted was the fact that these women had been an integral part of the fashioning of the bill. The rationalizations of the bill offered by these spokespersons at different forums followed a familiar rhetoric. The starting point was without exception the sanctity of the "family" and the urgency to preserve it, for to jeopardize it would be to work against Indian culture/tradition (*bharatiya sanskriti*). Indian women themselves, it was argued, did not want marriages and families to break. Hence, the basic premise of the bill—that marriages must be preserved at any cost. The bill proposes that the woman undergo "mandatory counselling" with her abuser. As the LCWRI critique points out, given the ideology prevailing in all organs of the state and the general attitude that a woman's place is with her husband, "(s)uch counselling can only end up 'convincing' her to accept her situation of disempowerment as being normal and to continue in a violent marriage" (LCWRI, 2002: 15). However, conceded the apologists, there might be "extraordinary" circumstances when the victimized woman might need legal intervention, and the bill was intended to do just that. Questions about the silence on the woman's right to reside in the matrimonial home were answered with the apparently commonsensical observation that women who had been abused did not themselves wish to go back. In sum, the assumptions that underlay all the rationalizations were that the welfare of the family was paramount, patriliny and male control of property is the sanctioned order of things, and the Indian (read Hindu) woman places the interest of family and home above all else. Above all, violence against women is intrinsically alien to "our" culture that traditionally accords dignity and honor to its women. (That both the normative "family" and the notional "Indian Woman" with a claim to dignity invoked in this discourse is marked as "Hindu," is indubitable in the light of the deliberate violations of "other" women, such as during the terrible carnage in Gujarat that are ignored or even actively endorsed by the state.) What is significant for our discussion of the GOI bill is the specific deployment of women to justify it. Feminist scholars like Tanika Sarkar have identified the increasing cooption of women by right wing organizations. By giving women within the community a public role and apparent agency *within* structures that revalidate patriarchal arrangements these organizations ensure women's consent to gender and other inequities (Sarkar, 1991).

The dilemma that increasingly faces women's and other democratic movements has been that while they have critiqued and, indeed, confronted the state as the stabilizer of patriarchies and of class interests, they also recognize that the state may be, at same time, the last guarantor of rights and entitlements. This seems specially so in a climate where sharpening communitarian polarization heightens women's functions as symbols of the exceptionalism of the community, where new patriarchal rationales are evolved to protect the "integrity" of communities, and where economic processes such as liberalization and privatization further disempower women as economic beings and increase their vulnerability within family and community. The problem, of course, is that today we are faced with a state that itself articulates a virulently majoritarian politics, delegitimates voices of dissent, and works insidiously against women. Hindutva ideology and its claiming of special entitlements for the majoritarian community is fundamentally rooted in the assertion of religious and cultural superiority, and it is women who must pay the highest price for this exceptionalism. The Hindu woman must revalidate Hindu superiority by living out the "Hindu" domestic ideologies of sacrifice, chastity, and dutifulness. Minority communities, seeing themselves as endangered, harden their boundaries and perceive any move to intervene in their Personal Laws, especially those pertaining to women, marriage, and inheritance, as an assault. Feminists have also had to confront the fact that caste and community locations are integral to women's identities and self-definition. In fact, as Nivedita Menon points out, "many feminists argue that caste and religious community are more powerful in women's lives than gender, especially in highly polarized situations" (Menon, 1999: 11). And it is also by now clear that the women's movement has failed to provide women with a viable and more egalitarian alternative to community and the traditional family. In the event, the state, even a classist and communalized one, may be for women "the determinate horizon of struggle" for rights and justice (Sangari, 2001: xxiii).

Thus, the women's movement finds itself having to negotiate with the state on one hand and the community on the other. This is not to suggest that the two are seen as necessarily antagonistic. The relationship between the two is complex, tracing a mixed economy of collusion and conflict, and feminist initiatives are aware of the danger of playing into the hands of the one or the other. The dilemma is perhaps most sharply evident in the current debate about a Uniform Civil Code (UCC) that would govern all religious communities. Over the past decade feminists' call for the UCC has become less confident given the majoritarian community's appropriation of that demand as a way of containing "other" communities. What, then, is the most productive feminist strategy of intervention into the patriarchal practices of communities that are becoming increasingly resistant to change? While feminists continue to put pressure on the state to enact gender-just laws, several women's organizations are working to evolve community-based participatory programs to deal with issues like violence within the family.[1]

Any attempt to theorize domestic violence must, therefore, grapple with the complex intersections of family, community, and state. Further, such an exploration must also take into account a sociocultural context that is reshaping identities, and a changing political economy that in the form of liberalization/privatization/globalization is creating new ferment in class compositions and is redefining caste identities. To continue to deal with domestic violence only within the context of the family and in terms of interpersonal relationships is to ignore the fact that the boundaries of "private" and "public" are permeable. As Kumkum Sangari puts it, "In practice, 'public' and 'private' not only interpenetrate in varied and often systematic ways, but are *produced* together, connected in relations of condensation or displacement, and display different levels of articulation" (Sangari, 2001: 367).

The Family as the Site of Violence

In a study of domestic violence in the Indian context, Malavika Karlekar abstracts certain generic characteristics of the family and the "naturalization" of violence within it (Karlekar, 1988). Whether the basic family unit is joint or nuclear, it is the ground for the play of power and powerlessness along the lines of *gender* and *age*. Violence—understood not only as physical harm but also as discrimination, deprivation, denial of access to resources, intimidation, exploitation, and other means whereby economic and social inequality is perpetuated—is the tool that reproduces the inherently hierarchical structure of the family. Those most vulnerable to familial violence are children, women, and the aged. This means that an inclusive understanding of domestic violence must take into account not only inter-spousal violence but also the very real practice of child and elder abuse within the home. However, while any child is susceptible to violence, the girl-child may be the more discriminated against. A differentiation must also be made between the violence perpetrated against aged males and females. For the woman, the abuse suffered in old age might form a continuum with her experience of violence as a child in the natal home and as a wife in the conjugal home. Elder men might be seen to be disempowered by age and loss of status as they are no longer perceived as being economically "productive." As such, violence in old age signals for men the loss of the patriarchal power that they once exercised within the same familial structure. One could refer to this process as a "feminization" in status and, therefore, a greater susceptibility to abuse.[2] To this extent, all violence within the family is gendered. And, even as we isolate wife-abuse as the object of analysis it is important to keep in mind the continuum of violence of which it represents one stage.

An analysis of the power hierarchy within the conjugal home would suggest some identifiable features—a gendered division of labor, the fact that in most Indian marriages women enter as strangers into an already structured world, the creation of a permanent inequality in the relationship of the natal and conjugal homes, and overarching domestic ideologies that legislate gender status and role. Like other theorists of the family, Karlekar also makes a significant distinction between "family" and "household." The household is a physical structure, localized, and a specific constellation of emotional and economic relationships among its core members. The family is more amorphous, seen as larger kinship groupings, spread over time and space. The household, then, is "the operational unit" that "provides the ground, so to speak, for a working out of family ideologies around specific roles and expectations." Further, "inequality is embedded in oppressive structures of a family ideology committed to an age and gender hierarchy which is worked out within a household" (Karlekar, 1988: 1742).

However, as Kumkum Sangari cautions, it would be simplistic to assume that familial ideologies are mechanically reproduced in the household as a material institution. She argues that "we need to attend to the gap between familial ideologies and the family as a social entity or a concrete constellation of relationships, and resist the tendency to conflate the desired ideals of familial ideologies with the existing structure and organization of households at any historical moment" (Sangari, 2001: 376). This "gap" or disjunction may be the result of the fact that while ideologies are persistent, households are subject to structural shift because of changes in political, social or economic structures outside the family. It might, for instance, be useful to ponder how middle-class familial ideologies of the man as head and provider may be impacted by the wife's insertion into the "public" workforce. Can it be assumed that the ideologies (rooted in an asserted separation of the private and public spheres and in a sexual division of labor) are destabilized by this shift in the material economic structure of the household? Can it be further assumed that the change would win the woman agency and a freedom from gendered violence in the home? Why, then, "working" women are, and sometimes more, subject to violence?[3] Could it be that the structural changes in the household create new patriarchal anxieties that find expression in violence as a means of restoring the status quo? And, in a circular logic, that violence would be justified by the very ideology that seemed to have been destabilized, that of the supremacy of the man as head and provider.

Yet, what is also important for a feminist enquiry is the recognition that it is the very disjunction between ideologies and material structures that creates the *potentials* for women's agency. For one thing, a woman's experience of the contradictions between the ideological and material dimensions of the family might make *visible* the inequalities that are naturalized in the family. It is by now a commonplace in feminist theory that patriarchies reproduce themselves not just through coercion but also by the manufacturing of women's consent to their own subordination; in other words, by making the operations of power invisible. Most field studies of domestic violence reveal that women, having internalized patriarchal norms, often do not perceive themselves as abused unless they have suffered severe physical assault. But, the fact that patriarchies have fault lines and inherent contradictions (such as that between the ideological and economic dimensions of the family in the scenario hypothesized in the preceding paragraph) create possibilities for women's agency and resistance. It is, therefore, reasonable to expect that the experience of being economically productive or independent (because of employment or inheritance) may throw into focus for the woman the putativeness of an ideology that assumes male worth and devalues the woman as an "unproductive" being. Such a shift in consciousness may create the possibilities for resistance. This is not to suggest that the mere awareness of injustice can unproblematically translate into emancipatory action. We know that many women continue to endure violence even while recognizing its criminality because of the absence of support structures in the community at large. Individual agency is delimited by the systemic nature of patriarchal norms and practices, and feminists agree that it is only collective action that can intervene into inegalitarian structures. "Feminist agency," suggests Sangari, "consists of *organised initiatives* of women and men committed to justice within an egalitarian framework" (Sangari, 2001: 365). This is why the feminist engagement with domestic violence must function on several levels. Organizations like *Majlis* in Mumbai offer legal help to individual women. The profeminist group Men Against Violence Against Women (MAVA) makes individual interventions into abusive families in the form of counselling and mediation. *Dilasa* and *Nari Kendra* in Mumbai have set up shelters for abused women. Other organizations have focussed on involving the whole community in dealing with familial violence.[4] Alongside, forums such as the LCWRI continue to put pressure on the state to enact a truly gender-just law. This is, needless to say, only a very selective list of the numerous initiatives all over the country which, taken together, address the problem at the individual, structural, community, and state levels.

Another important issue that must inflect a feminist theorizing of domestic violence is women's complicity and active participation in the infliction of abuse on other female members of the family. The perpetrators of violence often include female affines such as the mother-in-law or sisters-in-law. The politics of the household cannot be seen simply as a struggle between oppressing men and victimized women. As the household constitutes the site for struggle over resources and power, women themselves may be inserted into a hierarchy based on age, marital status, maternal status, the ranking among daughters-in-law and so on. This differential access to power and resources would lead to a redivision of household labor among women, relationships of antagonism between them, and a re-entrenching of patriarchy as the more privileged of the female members function as the surrogate (and, often, violent) agents of male hegemony and control. While women's collectivity remains a cherished feminist ideal, the very nature of the traditional family discourages such an aligning. This is why most abused women articulate the feeling of isolation even in non-nuclear families where there are other women members.

The natal family, too, offers little support as the parents are either hesitant to intervene in the "sanctity" of the marital relationship or unwilling to take on the responsibility of a daughter who might wish to leave her husband. Flavia Agnes insists that the culpability of parents be recognized especially in cases where their daughters have been killed in dowry-related violence. Their denial of education to daughters and other resources, acceding to demands from the in-laws for dowry and subsequent gifts, refusal of inheritance to the daughter, and abdication of responsibility during the period of her torment make them complicit in her abuse. Agnes notes that parents of the dowry victim did not file cases against the in-laws during her lifetime but only upon her death and, that too, in order to avenge her death and retrieve the gifts. What is worse, "the parents were all set to marry their next daughter with an equal amount of dowry to a boy of their choice," and this itself constitutes a form of violence (Agnes, 1995: 91). Feminists now agree that the practice of dowry is not so much the cause of violence as a specific and virulent manifestation of a pervasive culture of gendered violence.

Questions of Caste, Class, Community

Even as we underscore the pervasiveness and historical persistence of violence against women, it is necessary to recognize the historical contingency of patriarchal forms and practices. Patriarchal arrangements are subject to continual reconstitution because of their fundamental implication in the historical articulation and re-articulation of class, caste, and community. Gender inequality does not function in isolation but is intricately related to other forms of social hierarchy. As Sangari puts it, "[Patriarchies] are simultaneously located in specific modes of production, in class structures and mobility, in particular forms of class–caste status and inequality, and intersected by specific forms of self-identification with custom, tradition or religion" (Sangari, 2001: 373). Such a perspective helps us to open up the family as the site of violence and to situate its politics within a larger frame. "Women's link with caste and community," Nivedita Menon reminds us, "is made through the family" (Menon, 1999: 11). Thus, rearticulations of caste, class or community identities would inflect the specific forms and intensities of (private and public) violence against women at specific historical junctures.

Such an analytical thrust equips us to explore the apparent inexplicability of the intensification of patriarchal violence during the last three decades. For instance, it helps us locate the resurgence and legitimation of the proscribed practice of *sati* in the gathering of communal energies in recent times, and the calculated assertion of "tradition" by a community eager to claim the nation for Hindus. Economic exigencies, too, play a part. Deorala, the town where Roop Kanwar was burnt, now boasts a thriving "*sati* industry." Equally, the conservative Muslim backlash during the Shah Bano case reveals the anxiety of a community that perceives itself to be in crisis and seeks to assert its integrity through an intensification of its indigenous patriarchal practices. To take another example, the spread within the middle-classes of the practice of dowry, even to communities where it did not earlier exist, calls for an analysis of new trajectories of class mobility and changing middle-class aspirations in a context of high capitalism and an ethos of consumerism. Or, the adopting of conservative middle class familial ideologies and customs by the lower castes must be read in the context of their new mobility due to economic processes and state policies such as caste-based reservations that are redefining class structures. (At an interactive session at S.N.D.T., Mumbai, in February 2003, the Dalit writer Urmila Pawar spoke of how Dalit households have increasingly begun to display the accoutrements of status such as idols of Hindu deities, the observing of religious rituals and fasts, and the wearing of *sindoor* and *mangalsutras* by the women, even when the family might be Buddhist.) A rigorous feminist analysis would need to address the apparent contradiction that the much-needed economic empowerment of families may not translate into gender empowerment, and that class mobility might be accompanied by an increased patriarchal conservatism that makes women more vulnerable to domestic violence. Some very interesting microstudies are being done by scholars who explore the complex interplay of caste, class, and economic processes and their specific implications for women. In a paper entitled "Work, Caste and Competing Masculinities: Notes from a Tamil Village," S. Anandhi, J. Jeyaranjan and Rajan Krishnan (2002) study the manners in which changes in local economy, shift in caste hierarchies, and the entry of women into the industrial workforce have modified the relationship between caste, class, and gender in a village in present-day Tamil Nadu.

Anandhi et al. locate themselves within pro-feminist masculinity studies and their work centres round the reconfiguring of masculine identities and practices within a context of specific economic and sociopolitical transformation. They trace the shifting relationships over the last two decades between the upper-caste Mudaliar community whose historical dominance in the village of Thirunur was based on their control of land and an erstwhile agricultural economy, and the Dalits who have newly acquired land and seen a relative improvement in their status. The writers trace a complex process of transition involving immigration, industrialization, changes in territorial claims and land ownership, the weakening of the agricultural economy, and the educational empowerment of the Dalits who were earlier at the total mercy of the Mudaliars as agricultural laborers. A significant aspect of the change is the induction of the majority of young educated Dalit women into the industries that have sprung up in the village and nearby. The researchers focus on the way in which masculine identities of Dalit youth are being reconfigured in this scenario. The older generation articulate their experiences of emasculation in the past when traditional caste-hierarchies were in place and when their women were prey to marauding upper-castes. The young men, on the other hand, display a hypermasculinity as old caste strictures weaken and the village class structures are reconstituted. This takes the form of conspicuous modes of consumption, drinking, raucous behavior and, often, the teasing of upper-caste women. (The dishearteningly common narrative that emerges in most studies of caste and communal antagonisms is the use of the female body as a marker of community identity.) Public displays of masculinity are accompanied by private violence against the women of the family, especially sisters who might be working and earning more than their brothers. "The use of violence by Dalit youths appears, in this context, to be a mechanism to cope with the past and prevalent insufficiency in material resources and continuing social marginality" (p. 4405). But it is not just Dalit families that have seen an exacerbation of gendered violence. New masculine anxieties within the upper castes also manifest themselves in heightened abuse of wives and daughters. "With the unmaking of upper caste masculinity in the public domain and the upper caste men's inability to exercise control over the Dalit youth, they are reworking their masculine identity by means of increased violence on 'their' women" (p. 4004). Thus, while caste-based institutionalized oppression has to some degree been challenged in Thirunur, the new norms of masculinity that are evolving are complex and it is the women, Dalit and non-Dalit, who are paying the price in the form of escalating private and public gender violence.

A great deal of important work is being produced by feminists who subject to critique ideological prescription, state, family, law, community, and the new political economy vis-á-vis the rights of women. I wish to conclude with a reference to an essay by Nandita Shah, Sujata Gothoskar, Nandita Gandhi and Amrita Chhachhi that mounts a powerful critique on the state-backed new economic policies (NEP) and the structural adjustment program (SAP) and engages with the claims of votaries of liberalization/ privatization that these will lead to a "feminization of labor" and the empowerment of women. Through meticulous research and rigorous analysis, the writers substantiate their view that the new political economy is pushing the under-classes further into poverty and women's opportunities for employment are actually shrinking. They point out that "[g]iven the existing structure of discrimination against women, the introduction of SAP via the NEP with its attendant problems of inflation, recession, restructuring of industry, fall in real wages, etc. will intensify and worsen conditions particularly for poor women" (Shah et al., 1999: 149). Actual trends on the ground have shown that with the restructuring of the industrial sector, more and more women are being pushed into survival level jobs in the vulnerable unorganized sector. Even here they might be eased out by men who have been retrenched from the industry. While poverty levels rise among both men and women, it is the women who are relatively more insecure in the workplace. The question we could ask in the specific context of domestic violence is how these trends might translate into new pressures on poor families and an increase in the vulnerability of women within them.

A theorizing of domestic violence, then, must centrally involve the identifying and analysis of old and emerging forms of vulnerabilities that debilitate women in the contemporary context. It must move beyond the merely "domestic" to address "the ambiguities and contradictions generated at the interface of different structures and relations of oppression" and their specific implications for women in a climate of growing gendered violence (Menon, 1999: 18).

Notes

1. For examples of some community based interventions across five sites in India, see Nandita Bhatla, Anuradha Rajan, "Private Concerns in Public Discourse: Women-Initiated Community Responses to Domestic Violence", *Economic and Political Weekly*, XXXVIII: 17, April 26–May 2, 1658–1664. Also see in the same volume Shramajibee Mahila Samity, "*Shalishi* in West Bengal: A Community-based Response to Domestic Violence", 1665–1673.

2. Robert Connell's influential model of the hierarchy of masculinities could also be useful deployed here to understand this process. See Robert Connell, *Masculinities*, Berkeley: University of California Press, 1995. Connell outlines four levels of masculine privilege: hegemonic, complicitous, marginalised, and subordinated. These represent a differentiated and hierarchical access to the "patriarchal dividend." Thus, it could be argued in the context of this essay that the disempowering brought about by old age might move a man from the hegemonic level to the less privileged forms of masculinity.

3. See Flavia Agnes, "Violence in the Family: Wife Beating," in Rehana Ghadially (ed.). 1988. *Women in Indian Society*. New Delhi: Sage Publications, p. 155. Agnes engages with the myths associated with wife-battering such as the one that it is poor, working class women who get beaten. She shares her findings that "women holding responsible jobs as doctors, lecturers, journalists, and models get beaten by their husbands." The only difference is that unlike poor women, "middle and upper class women are beaten behind closed doors." See also (Karlekar, 1988), where she writes that "it is not only a woman's dependence which makes her particularly vulnerable: a wife in a high-status job may be beaten more than her unemployed neighbor."

4. See note 1.

References

Agnes, Flavia. 1995. *State, Gender and the Rhetoric of Law Reform*. Mumbai: Research Centre for Women's Studies, S.N.D.T. Women's University, pp. 109–10.

Anandhi, S., J. Jeyaranjan, and Rajan Krishnan. 2002. "Work, Caste and Competing Masculinities: Notes from a Tamil Village," *Economic and Political Weekly*, (XXXVII): 43 (October, 24), pp. 4397–4406.

Ghadially, Rehana (ed.). 1988. *Women in Indian Society*. New Delhi: Sage Publications.

Karlekar, Malavika. 1998. "Domestic Violence," *Economic and Political Weekly*, (XXXIII): 27 (July 4–7).

LCWRI, 2002. *Campaign for a Civil Law on Domestic Violence, 2002: Update and Briefing Note.* New Delhi: LCWRI.

Menon, Nivedita (ed.). 1999. *Gender and Politics in India.* New Delhi: Oxford University Press.

Poonacha, Veena and Divya Pandey. 1999. *Responses to Domestic Violence in the States of Karnataka and Gujarat.* Mumbai: Research Centre for Women's Studies, S.N.D.T. Women's University.

Sangari, Kumkum. 2001. *Politics of the Possible: Essays on Gender, History, Narratives and Colonial English.* New Delhi: Tulika.

Sarkar, Tanika. 1991. "The Woman as Communal Subject: Rashtrasevika Samiti and Ram Janmabhoomi Movement," *Economic and Political Weekly*, (XXVI): 35 (August, 31).

Shah, Nandita, Sujata Gothoskar, Nandita Gandhi, and Amrita Chhachhi, "Structural Adjustment, Feminization of Labour Force and Organizational Strategies," in Nivedita Menon (ed.). 1999. *Gender and Politics in India.* New Delhi: Oxford University Press.

Chapter Three
The Narratives
Rinki Bhattacharya

Akash

Gurbir Singh, Akash Kaur's grandfather hailed from an agricultural family in Punjab. Nearly two generations back Gurbir Singh was driven out of his native village, never to return. Dramatic circumstances forced Gurbir Singh to take this decision. Akash does not remember every detail about her ancestral background but says:

"We all knew *dadaji* was an orphan. The only family he had was a brother. A large tract of farmland stood in their joint names. When he was a boy of 12 or 14 *dadaji* overheard his uncles plotting to kill him. They wanted to grab that piece of farmland. In Punjab, brother kills brother for an inch of land. Hearing about the plot, *dadaji* ran away from home. He had heard of Nanded, a pilgrimage center for Sikhs. *Guru Singhji* had breathed his last in Nanded (Nasik district). *Dadaji* first went to Nanded. From there he found his way to Aurangabad and joined the Nizam's army. My grandmother looked after the animals. This is how we settled in Aurangabad."

The violence inherent in Akash's ancestral background provides a link to her own oppression. A first person account of Akash's story follows:

I was born into a Sikh family at Aurangabad before the Independence. I don't remember the exact date or year. My father was a well-known lawyer. We were not very orthodox in our religious practice. On the contrary, the Muslim culture around us made a deep impact. The women in our family, my mother and grandmother observed *purda*.

Aurangabad was ruled by the Nizam of Hyderabad those days. Women had to wear the veil. We do not remember seeing women walking on the road or going to the market unveiled. Men did all the outdoor jobs. Women mostly stayed indoors, hidden by curtains made from strips of bamboo called *chiks*. Men did not dare venture beyond that threshold.

I was the eleventh child of my parents. My childhood was perfectly horrible. Father used to beat mother often. We had small, dark rooms, where he beat mother with sticks, or kicked her about. He did this many times in the day. I used to be in her arms. I never knew why father beat her mercilessly. These incidents resulted in my developing a hatred for men. My attitude towards my father was mixed because he beat mother. At other times I felt affection towards him. My father did not think it necessary to send me to school. As a result I had no formal education.

For a short while I was sent to an *Urdu*-medium school. The school was in the very street we lived. But I was sent without proper schoolbooks, or other materials that children normally require. I used to borrow books from my cousin or other children in the class. Due to this my studies suffered. The result was obvious, I failed the exam. My father blamed the school and also me. I was summarily removed from the school.

My elder sister was 12 years my senior and stayed home. Father put me in her charge. My sister took her duty too earnestly. Part of her duty was to beat me severely on any excuse. I hated her all my life. After beating me, my sister poured cold water all over on the raw bruises. She then dragged me down the stairs as we lived on the first floor. This torture continued until father decided to put me in a boarding school. I was so frightened in the boarding school that I was soon returned home.

In the meantime, on August 15, 1947, India became Independent. On the footsteps of Independence, police action put an end to the Hyderabad state, and the Nizam's rule. More importantly, many social changes were introduced in our lives. The *Purda* system for instance, was cast aside. About the same time, my cruel elder sister was to give her final exam. I was next in line. A tuition teacher was engaged for us both. I could not make head or tail of what the tutor was teaching. Sadly, I failed a second time. People at home, labeled me a fool and I was teased no end.

Then a second tutor came. The new tutor understood my problems and began to guide me. With her help, I was able to get through my S.S.C. exams. My cruel sister was by then in college in Poona. She insisted that I join college with her. By now I had developed a hatred for studies. I was not interested in doing the B.A. course. Much to my regret. Given a chance I would like to go back to university.

After my refusal to go to college, a Roman Catholic nun, Sister Brazil from the newly opened English convent was engaged to teach me. She understood my insecurities. Unknown to the family, Sister Brazil emotionally pressurized me to convert into the Roman Catholic faith. I was so desperate to escape the stifling atmosphere at home, that I gave in. The nun's love and affection won me over. Sister Brazil also taught me painting. I took a keen interest in my painting. When one of my cousins came to visit us from undivided Punjab, I would enjoy helping in her drawing homework.

It was only after grandmother's death that I came to Bombay with a family friend. I secured admission in the J. J. School of Arts. It was not difficult to get permission to live in Bombay. One of my sisters had moved to the city. Father placed me under her charge to complete my Arts course. Although I failed twice for want of proper guidance, I continued the J. J. School painting course.

As I mentioned earlier, I hated men. I did not take any interest in men or marriage for that matter. I was amused to be the center of attention for a couple of young Sikh boys. I ignored them. My father was least concerned about getting me married. I had become friendly with Iqbal, a classmate. When he took me to meet his family in the suburbs, Iqbal's family virtually adopted me. And I remained close to them till date. Life went on, despite failures but by this time, I had decided not to return home.

During the summer holidays, something very sad happened. My mother suddenly left home one night without telling anyone. She had a little rift with father over one of our distant relatives. She did not particularly like this man. My father, on the other hand, was very fond of the relative. It was shocking for me to see father all alone at that late stage of life—though I did not tell him so. I felt guilty about the rift. Although father beat mother, when she left, he missed her. We searched everywhere for mother. Finally, we traced her in Delhi. We took her back home. When she returned, my guilt was relieved. After that I returned to Bombay.

I confided about this incident to a room mate called Leena Patel. She advised me to forget about going back home. I agreed, and started thinking along these lines. I had failed in the fourth year painting exam. Therefore, I did a course in teacher training. Our hostel matron was helpful to me. I used to confide to her about my family problems.

After finishing my drawing teacher's course, I joined as a part-time teacher in one of the schools. A Muslim friend helped me get this job. I taught from 7 a.m. to 10 a.m. Then rushed to college at 10.30 a.m. The lectures lasted until 4.30 in the evening. This life gave me little time to think. Marriage was still out of the question.

As long as I stayed with my sister, the torture continued. She did not allow me to go out with other girls, or make friends with anyone. She shouted or insulted me before people in the dining room, and derived pleasure from this. Due to this, I turned into an introvert. Things grew from bad to worse.

There were times I wanted to end my life. When my mother visited Bombay specially to see me, I told her about these problems. Meanwhile I completed my second year Diploma from J.J. School. Soon I had a full-fledged teaching job with accommodation. At work I became friendly with a male colleague. The man who was a great talker. I always had a weakness for intellectuals, which this man appeared to be. I enjoyed his company, and we spent our leisure time together. The art school accommodation did not appeal to me for long. I shifted to a working-women's hostel where I would meet other girls. I became friendly with Shirley. Every evening she went out with her boyfriend. Many girls had boy friends. Watching them together, my loneliness became unbearable. One evening Shirley forced me to accompany her and the boy friend. I went out a little reluctantly. At the party, I met Aloke Sen. Aloke visited the hostel a few times. I saw nothing wrong in going out with him. Although I did not think of marriage, I was not shy about the opposite sex. One evening while I was out with Aloke I told him:

"I can go out with you, only if you are interested in marriage."

He twisted this sentence later, boasting I had proposed to him. I felt small and insulted. However, I had no choice but to swallow my pride. He talked so much that I hardly got a chance to say anything. During our courtship, he found out all about me specially that I had inherited property. He pretended to be rich, saying his father owned an English company—which in fact was owned by someone else.

He lied to me. Once he claimed a huge building at Churchgate was his property. He said one of his friends was staying in his flat and he could not ask the friend to vacate. I argued:

"Why cannot he vacate when the flat is yours?"

"I cannot do such a thing to my friend," was Aloke's instant retort. In reality, he was staying with his uncle, and passed off that flat as his father's. He carried on this bluff about his "rich, educated family." I believed him. By then, I was emotionally too involved with this man. I was also afraid what society or others would think. Once he decided to send me abroad. He took my passport and we went to the bank to sign documents. He brought a typed letter. I signed it, but did not read the contents. He said he had Rs 45,000 in his bank account.

After we were divorced, I went back to the same bank, and discovered Aloke had only two rupees in his bank account. I still believed him—though a rift came between us. He was demanding, dominating—never gave me a minute's rest. I had no time for myself. I think he was trying to keep an eye on me. So that I did not find out more about him. Some friends said he is very rich, and lives in the posh Flora Fountain area. Others contradicted this claim, saying he is a risky person. That it was better to leave him alone. I was involved emotionally and scared to death by the thought that what will people say?

I realize now how stupid it was to think of society, and not about what was happening to me. This kept me going with him. I took him to meet my family at Aurangabad, my father, sister. Father wanted to find out more about him. When Aloke got to know this he left town in a huff. I returned feeling quite guilty. I was torn between my loyalty to father and to Aloke.

By now Aloke had gained total control of the hostel. The hostel staff—including our warden, Mrs. D' Mello, was charmed by Aloke. The *chowkidar* was bribed to keep an eye on me.

Shirley, my best friend, behaved in a strange manner to me. There was a cold war, no one at the hostel spoke to me. Only two friends defied this. We used sign language to understand one another. I was isolated. Some of the hostel girls are in touch with me. Many have settled abroad but we write to each other.

Aloke was actually bankrupt. He relied entirely on my income. Once I went with him to a hill station Lonavala. We agreed not to have sex, for fear of conceiving. Aloke took along his friend as a "witness," in order to blackmail me. He knew, I was alone, friendless. My family did not really care. Aloke took full advantage of this situation. I introduced Aloke to Iqbal's family. They had practically adopted me. Aloke showed off to them, saying he was a rich man and owned property. I forgot to say, he always traveled in taxis.

Once during our usual outing, Aloke came out with a story about a movie in which the girl friend of the hero leaves him, because she learns he is a gambler. This was a message to me. I got the hint; Aloke gambled. That gambling was his only profession never struck me. He used to loose heavily. Suddenly he suggested we marry. And I agreed!

I was fed up of going out with him without any future. I craved for a family, and the fulfillment of motherhood. Aloke had no place to stay, even then I agreed.

We got married in January 1970. In the court, Iqbal and some friends came as witness. They bore all the expense, took pains to make it a pleasant event. I went to spend the first night at Iqbal's family home since I had no one to call my own.

I had no secrets from Aloke. He knew everything, he had my bank account number, the credit balance etc. He kept a close watch. As far as his affairs were concerned, it was the other way round. I knew nothing. He kept telling lies. Only after our marriage, Aloke disclosed we cannot have normal sex as he did not want children. I was dying to have my own family but Aloke always argued "Where shall we stay? I have no home."

I was forced to have abnormal sex. This made me depressed for days. The house ran on those Rs 400 I earned. In the 1970s, it was enough. Aloke never gave me money. He was at rummy clubs, or gambling dens all day. Once he tried to beat me up, I threatened:

"Remember I am Sikh woman—don't dare touch me, I will break your bones."

My life had turned hell. *Matka* chaps came looking for Aloke. Their knocks at the door terrified me. At times I hid all day, until dark. He never paid up so they pursued him everywhere. The mental torture drove me to psychiatrists. We married in 1970—divorced in 1973—uncontested. I discovered the real reason for Aloke not wanting children was his impotence. He did not contest the divorce. Later, I heard, he remarried one of my hostel mates.

I became a lecturer in my old college—the J. J. School. Being a single woman I found the college atmosphere extremely stifling. It was not possible to speak to male colleagues. If a woman spoke to a man, it was assumed they had something going. One male colleague began pestering me. He first made a pass or two. I warned him. I said, "You are running after a shadow."

He was so persistent, he at once answered, "It is fun running after shadows." Then I confronted him and said, "will you leave your wife and children to marry me?"

"Where will my wife and child go?" he moaned.

"Where will I go?" I asked. He wanted me to be his girl friend, mistress or something like that. I could not work due to these harassments. I decided to remarry. The proposal came through a marriage bureau. I remarried a planter, divorcee with two grownup children. He said the children will not mind one way or another. I told him about my earlier marriage and the rough times. I was keen to have a child. We married in 1980. I am still married. But it is a cold relationship. My husband does not want children. He too forced me to have unnatural sex. It caused me such a serious infection that I nearly died. I had to operate one kidney. I live only on the second kidney. Today my husband's priorities are his children. He wants to live with his children, his mother. I cannot adjust to this idea. His children do not know me.

Their mother is alive. She is said to be insane. I do not know if that is true. But, financially, I enjoy a little freedom. My husband does not mind giving me a monthly allowance of Rs 2000. He encouraged me to travel. Thanks to him, I went abroad, met my friends. But I told him; I cannot live in a joint family. If my husband goes back to the garden, I will join him of course. I like that life. Otherwise, I am on my own.

From my own savings, I have bought a flat in a small town. One of my sisters, who are fond of me, lives there too. All my life, I felt like a dependent. I enjoy these feelings. I plan to retail small Indian items of handicrafts from the house. In case, my present husband wants a divorce, or to remarry, I have no objection. I shall not contest. Now I am on my own. I am only bitter about the exploitation by my first husband. He exploited me, my friends. These are sour memories difficult to forget.

Not that I remember them everyday but when I do, I feel very bitter indeed. My present husband on the other hand is generous—I enjoy the privileges of being his wife. Which is all I got from this man. To me, friends have meant more than family. One's family expects too much. I would rather die in a friend's home than in a relative's. This is what life has taught me.

ARUNA

I was actually married off.

I use the word *married off* at the very arbitrariness of the manner in which I was married to my husband. Brought up to believe that I could always go in for higher studies, this was a great emotional setback. I was a motivated child. We were eight sisters, but father made us feel that being a girl was not a problem. I was free to do so many things. If I wanted, I could go abroad for higher studies. The whole world seemed to be open to me. I was deeply involved in that little world of mine...music lessons, my dancing, my academic curriculum and of course, poetry. Out of the blue, father tells me I am going to be married in a month! I was just 15, going on 16....

To Whom? Why?

"It's a wealthy family. They will allow you to finish your education." This piece about education was offered as compensation by my family.

"I haven't seen the boy," I tried to protest but no one seemed to hear me.

"We KNOW best," was my family's attitude.

From then on it was a constant play on my sensitivity...

"You are so frail."

"We are so worried about you," and the inevitable finality, saying: "It's for YOUR own good."

I had such implicit faith in my family, although I was hurt and indignant inside, I could not protest, nor could I revolt. As if my father guessed my vulnerability, he said, "The boy is studying medicine. Both of you will go abroad." At that point, in the state of disbelief and confusion that I was plunged, the very fact I would be allowed to study was some sort of compensation for the unreasonableness of the whole thing, or even its suddenness.

During the traditional Bengali marriage—the moment of *subhodrishti* is literally the first glimpse a bride has of her husband.

My *subhodrishti* was shockingly disappointing. At that age you cannot conceal your emotions, and my husband never forgave me that. I was fond of music, dance, I had romantic notions what my husband ought to be or looks like. I remember it even now. Through that pomp and pageantry put up to impress the community ... the shrill sound of conch shells, *ululation*—seeing this person, my husband with disbelief. He was so much older, obese—unlike any vision of a man I would want to marry. I could hear my friends' voices whisper, "It is a shame, she is being married to an old man!"

The culture shock, which began with the announcement of my marriage, worsened when I reached my in-laws' ancestral home in Jhansi. The feudal atmosphere stifled me. I had not seen women in *purda*; never seen them segregated. No rules imposed on me, except as a child. Overnight, the child is told to confirm to certain rules—told she is a *woman*. Being reminded all the time, "Now you are the *bahu* of this wealthy house."

What is this wealth? I felt no joy. I was not impressed. And on the night of my marriage...I just cannot describe it...I was so shocked...the next morning...I thought to myself: Is this marriage? Is this all there is to it? My views were not taken into account.... It was as if this man had acquired a right over my body...somehow I came back home to give my exam. I was already expecting our first child. The first few years were just confusion, trying to cope with these sights and sounds. But, above it all was this very violent element in my husband.

He was forever "demanding." Not only from me, demanding from everyone. That was HIS world, HIS domain. He could get what he wished. I still carry this vision of a tyrant, a bully. In fact during one of his violent outbursts against me...when I was running down the steps in fright, I fell and lost the child in my womb. I was sent to my mother's place in Bombay. When I went back, recovered after the miscarriage, all I asked my husband Naren was, "Could I study?" In that state of confusion and fear, my books were all I could identify with.

He shouted, "What study? Why do you need to study? *Bahus* of our house do not study."

My father-in-law's adamant "NO" about studying made me resentful. Even though Naren was verbally abusive that was the first time he slapped me. For being resentful about his father's order. It was not just one slap but a series of slaps which left crimson marks on my cheek for days. I was so shaken, humiliated, and indignant that I decided to end my life. I remember having noticed a pistol in my father-in-law's closet. I took it out hoping to use it.

Again, ignorance. I did not know the pistol was without cartridges. Barely six months after this failed attempt, my mother-in-law committed suicide. Today, when I analyze her death, it is clear that she was frightened of what was happening to me. Naren's mother did not want me to endure the same tyranny she had. Whenever we were alone, she kept saying to me, "We made a big mistake bringing you as our *bahu*. We should have brought someone more dominating in this house. A tough girl from a rural background, not an educated girl like you."

The news about my mother in law's suicide was quickly supressed. This is just to tell you how powerful, how ruthless the Das family was. After her death, demands and restrictions on me increased. I was not supposed to have friends—friends would corrupt me. Not supposed to remember my past. I was expected to conform to that household's image of a dutiful *bahu*.

And what was that image?

Most of the time it was giving in to demands. I learned to cook, to entertain. I enjoyed being an excellent hostess. You want me to be in the house and cook all the time—then modernize the kitchen, I cannot use a wood stove, I appealed to my father in law. This fell on deaf ears.

My three children became the reason for my living. I found great peace and joy in bringing them up. Once again I was not allowed to raise them according to my ideas of morality, discipline.

A time came when I did not know what was going to please anyone anymore! If the *phulkas* were not ready, hot and fresh at any time lunch or dinner was demanded, there would be a diatribe. Lunch or dinner could be at any time. Male parties extended beyond 4.00 a.m. But the first cup of tea had to be served at 5.00 a.m.!!

In this situation, a friend of the family took me out one afternoon. I could go out only with friends the family approved. She took me home for tea and empathized with my circumstances.

Instead of coming back home at 4.00 p.m. as ordered, we returned home at 6.00. My heart beat in childish panic, God, I have to go back to that house! This was how I felt always, *that* house. It was never my home. And that awful terror of going back! My father-in-law and husband were impatiently pacing outside the gate when we returned. The friend literally deposited me in their hands as if to say, here, take her, I have brought her back safe. No sooner had she left, a tirade was launched:

"Why are you late? Why did you come at 6.00 and not 4.00?"

I replied, "...she took your permission and how does it matter if I am a few minutes late? I was with her all the time."

My reply was provocation enough to inflict burns. See these scars on my arm ... I was burnt with a cigarette butt. My father-in-law stood there instructing my husband:

"Naren, control her! Don't let her get out of hand." These were the words continuously used: "Control her or she will get out of hand."

If I reacted to these irrational acts of violence, I was told I deserved worse. My children were witness to my humiliation and degradation. It was worse when they were told, "Don't be like her...."

After my first miscarriage, I would have preferred to have no children. I loved children too much to want any in that stifling atmosphere. Besides, the very touch of my husband repulsed me. Even if I pretended to enjoy his demands, he sensed it and subjected me to a barrage of accusations night after night:

"You must be wanting someone else. City girls like you have had it too easy. Now you want someone else." Every night rape was committed!! My children are products of violence. Each one, imposed, against my will. It was my husband's philosophy:

"I will give you eight children to keep you in your place."

As I said before, for the sake of my three children I conformed more and more. Each time I came to my mother after incidents of brutality, I was to be told, "GO back. This is your *Karma*. We found such a good family for you. Learn to adapt, to sacrifice. What will be the fate of your unmarried sisters?" or "you have to live there for sake of the children."

It seems as if the children were an excuse to unleash even more unreasonable demands on me by my husband.

Then a time came—this was soon after my son's birth—when I simply lost the will to live. I had become depressed and suicidal. I was reminded again and again that THIS was my fate. How long was I to suffer? If that was my fate for the next 20 years, I had no strength or desire left to endure it. Behind it was this dread: I don't want this man to touch me ... perhaps if he had just left me to be a mother of his children, left that little part for me...I would have remained in the house as the mother. But it was as if to take advantage of the fact that I was a mother and utterly vulnerable, that all kinds of accusations were heaped against me.

Demands piled high...as I became increasingly more suicidal. After the last assault, I took an overdose of sleeping pills and sent to hospital. My husband called my mother long distance to complain that I was insane. My mother told him, "She is not insane. Send her back to me." I was sent back. But he kept the kids back. That is how I was forced to leave. Slowly, I recovered but I realized, even for the sake of the children I could not take the violence any more. But I had no options.

My mother's attitude was: Now that you have come back, we will endure you. But not the children.

As though the children were their property. "They have so much wealth, they can look after the children ..." was my family's attitude. I could not live in my mother's house as a "person." I had to exist as someone who had to forget her past, forget the children, rebuild her life, just continue to live. At this point, I asked for a legal separation.

I wanted the custody of my children. I wanted to file for a maintenance amount. But the lawyer engaged was incompetent in matrimonial matters. Again, ignorance—or was it the way we were raised? Kept out of touch with the real world! I did not know custody could be denied to a mother. Even the judge called me into his chamber to suggest:

"Let your husband look after the children. He has the means and money!"

There was no suggestion of alimony or provision for the children. To my family seeking legal redress was socially unacceptable, "Oh! What will people say!" Wanting to hush it up... Besides I had no money to afford a better lawyer. I was told, you have access to the children during school holidays!

All along I had survived in my in-law's house because of my children and now..., to be in this country without my children, it was end of the world for me. Overnight I was homeless, childless, and penniless. My family said:

"Look at so and so, how she has rebuilt her life...."

At that point I was too traumatized, too devastated to learn lessons from other women's examples. Unable to cope, I fled to another country.

My younger sister Gita was a hostess with an International Airlines. She helped me fly to the US. I didn't know what a visa was, nor had I learnt to fend for myself. I had no idea what awaited me in the US. I had no prior experience of the world outside our threshold. But I said nothing could be worse than the state I was reduced to. In that condition every step I took, each moment in a new country without moorings, was like crossing a torrential river in a small boat. I learned to use qualities of openness to people, my thirst for learning, and developed my inner resources of fortitude and spirituality. My first job was with a Consulate. Then I resumed college. Did all kinds of odd jobs, worked in a restaurant, gave lessons etc. to maintain myself. Education was a beacon of inspiration. It compensated for everything that had happened to me. Finally, it led to my Doctorate.

Of course, all this meant, I had to go without food and sleep for long hours. But it was a distraction from the gnawing pain for my children. I wanted to be a role model for them, for women. Positive letters poured in from my children, "Ma, we are so proud of you. Finish whatever you are doing, and don't worry about us."

My research was about women's issues. This helped me understand myself, understand others. My pain had become universal...it was no longer personal, nor exclusive to me. I understood I was not alone in my struggle. I came back to India after all these years hoping, I'll do something for the women in India. Before that I must pick up the threads of my own life.

Once again I sought legal redress as my son refused to stay without me. He ran away from home on several occasions. My girls were in their teens. Despite their attempt to understand my circumstances, they were scarred by it. I sought the custody of my son, the youngest of my kids. I was told, "It may take years.

Your husband's family will use every ruse to delay, accuse you of deserting them...."

And here I am, not able to get my own son ... he was sent back to Jhansi yesterday. He kept crying "... if you don't take me with you, I'll kill myself .... I will run away from home."

I know he means it. Last time when he was not allowed to see me, my son started for Bombay on his cycle! A truck driver rescued and took him back to his father.

What is this system? Is there no justice? Does it always reward the culprit...? Or those with money. Are women nothing? How am I going to live...or heal myself, when my son is in this desperate state...?

Postscript: Aruna's experiences were recorded in the winter of 1982. It was a cold and bitter winter in every sense. Aruna had tried hard but failed to get the legal custody of her 14-year-old son, Babloo. Dejected by the experience, she returned to the US. Applied for citizenship and a teaching job in a local high school. Even child custody and vacation access to which she had a legal right, was denied to her. This was a shattering blow for Aruna.

One day, to her great surprise a lawyer friend came up with a simple solution. She suggested Aruna should forget hopeless legal battle fly down to India and whisk her son away! Heartened by this bold suggestion, Aruna flew to Delhi in early February 1983. Her visit was a secret. Determined to take Babloo back, she already had a US visa for her son. Her phone call from the US, was merely that she was keeping poor health. The two daughters with Babloo reached Delhi to meet their mother. That very night, with the help of her air-hostess sister, Aruna took a midnight flight back to the US. This time, with her son. Back in the state of Virginia, Aruna settled down to work. She put her son in school. In the course of the next few years, both her daughters joined Aruna. Eventually they married and settled down in the US.

The most amazing climax of Aruna's life is how her former husband transformed. He came to terms with her struggle for self-determination. Age had mellowed Das. He bowed before Aruna. Das realized, that his power tools for emotional blackmail were useless. Aruna was compassionate to her former husband— the same man who once held her in terror. During one of her visits, Aruna even flew down to look after the ailing Das.

Let me quote from one of her letters to me. Aruna's words reflect her profound conviction in women's continuous struggle against violence:

...one can only build a home on a relationship that is meaningful, where two people achieve their objectives through dialogue and understanding... not by brute force. But women have to keep up the fight against oppression on a personal and social front. The social fight will be successful only if women have integrity and fight their personal battles simultaneously. We have to empower women and our children through education, about social issues heralding a country's progress. ...

Aruna hopes to come back and pick up threads of life again, devote her time in raising awareness and consciousness of the role of youth in helping oppressed women and the aged in a more constructive way. Developing focus through spirituality, she is firmly convinced that a spiritual basis (not mere religious dogma) will enhance every effort made towards alleviating oppression in all sections of society.

BINA

It was Ravi's eldest uncle who came with the marriage proposal. Someone from the family had seen and liked me. This uncle said, they wanted a girl just like me to be their *bahu*.

Ravi's family could not ask us for dowry. It is known as *tilak* in our community. They could not ask because this was my husband's second marriage. Before we got married, I had gone out a few times with Ravi. This was to know him better. He gave the picture of being the injured party. My in-laws claimed that Ravi's first wife was insane. They said she was not just mad, but also immoral! What else could they say? She had two kids already and expecting a third at the time of the divorce. They painted a nasty picture of Ravi's first wife. But I believed them. I was young and newly married. I chose to think Ravi was innocent.

After several visits from the uncle, I agreed to the marriage. As I said, I had gone out a few times with Ravi. It was like a love-cum-arranged marriage.

Pitaji was against the marriage from start. He told me:

"*Beta*, you have grown up and lived in an urban society, how will you adjust to life in Patna?"

Every one said there is a lot of dowry harassment in Bihar. *Pitaji* said the same thing. I did not want a dowry marriage. Ravi's family demanded nothing in the beginning. My husband used to tell *Pitaji*:

"Think of me as your son."

I wanted to continue my studies. I mentioned this to Ravi. I had studied only till graduation at the time of our marriage. He said, "Everyone is educated in our family. Everyone is an advocate or something—you won't have any problem."

Those days *Pitaji* was going through a bad time. He had lost a lot of money in the film business. I was in college. My brother was in school. For the wedding my parents gave dowry according to their capacity. There were clothes for the in-laws' family. They did not give a full suit for Ravi. But I think we bought good quality stuff. At the wedding ceremony my mother-in-law complained:

"*Dhoti diya hai, kurta nahi.*"

They had negotiated the marriage saying, "We have everything, what do we need?"

Soon they changed the tune. My in laws said:

"In our side we give the full bedroom furniture. Give at least a dressing table for the girl."

They wanted a silver leaf, a silver beetul nut, and a silver glass. We immediately gave these. Still they complained:

"Why give only one glass, why not a whole set? Surely your father could afford to give that much." I forgot that I was a newly married bride and had to play the part. I could not help answer them:

"You have everything in this house, for you, it is a drop of grain in the camel's mouth."

My mother-in-law did not like my saying this. She taunted me:

"See how she answers back. She is from the city after all, that too a writer's daughter. What else can she do but spout dialogues?"

That was the first time I was stepping into my in-laws' ancestral home in Patna. Everyone poked and touched me as if I was a shopping parcel from the big city shop. It was simply awful. At the entrance of our room the women stopped me:

"What has your father sent for us, let's see." My *nanad* asked for her *neg*. That is what they call it. My mother-in-law said:

"*Usko dena parega,*"; that it was customary to give my sister-in-law.

I felt very bad. I hadn't brought anything especially for her. I was put to shame over this. My mother-in-law kept repeating:

"*Kya lekar ayi hai baap ke ghar se?*"

I finally said to her, "*Main kuch bhi nahi layi hoon.*"

With great authority my *nanad* demanded a gold *kangan*, "*Mujhe sirf kangan hi chahiye.*"

Even when I went for the first night—*suhag raat* as we call it, everyone stopped my entry to the bed room demanding for something. I felt so very small and lonely. You know how it is when one has nothing to give. My mother-in-law is the only daughter at her home. She used to boast, "*Mujhe to sone main tolke diya hai.*"

Literally, she had brought a lot of dowry. From a pin to a car. Everything came from her *maika*. I believe my father-in-law was not doing well when he married her. The fact she brought so much dowry was her personal triumph. She ruled the house. She was so powerful, everyone bowed down to her.

It was said that my father-in-law had many love affairs. He had kept a mistress. Everyone knew about the other woman. In fact it was accepted. The mistress's house was called "the small home." When my husband had affairs, my mother-in-law naturally expected me to accept it. She had done it, so why not me?

Demand for goods continued from those first 6 months, up to now. At every step, I was reminded that Ravi could have married someone else and brought in a lot of money or consumer items.

My husband was totally under his mother's thumb. We could not stir out of the house without her permission. We had to take permission from one and all. Even to buy his cigarettes, or eat *pani puri*. Ravi had to ask his mother for money everytime. As a newly married woman, I craved to go out sometimes. My mother-in-law complained:

"Iska ek pao ghar main to ek bahar."

From the day we had first entered, my heart stopped beating—I felt suffocated. It was so different from the picture Ravi painted. I thought I was marrying into an educated family. When I saw that big house, the feudal atmosphere, so different in reality, my heart cried out:

"What have I done, what shall I do now?"

Before our marriage *Pitaji* once visited my in-laws. He saw their big house, met them. I remember he came back from Patna and said, "That place is not for you. Even now change your mind." I remembered his words. He was uneasy. *Pitaji* used to talk about one of his sisters who ended her life of slavery by committing suicide. He was afraid for me.

In those six months I was at Patna, my mother-in-law never left us alone. I saw a change in Ravi's attitude. He grew indifferent. Neglected me. One of his younger brothers—an unmarried *devar*, about my age—treated me with kindness. Once we were all to go out. The entire *khandan*. But something happened and we could not go. I came back to my room crying with disappointment. My *devar* followed me:

"Don't cry, *Bhabi*," he said to me, "we will go another day." That was all he said.

My husband charged into the room yelling at his brother:

"How dare you speak to her like that and do *natak* with my wife!" insinuating there was something between the two of us. I wanted to protest and say something, Ravi attacked me physically. That was the first time he hit me. I was in a state of shock. I did not expect Ravi to beat me. That's how it began.

The language spoken in my in-laws' home was vulgar. I cannot repeat it. It was crude and obscene. My mother-in-law would say awful things to Ravi if he took my side. He had to please her by abusing me. He literally, had to. He depended on his mother even for small cash. If anyone praised me or what I cooked, my mother—in-law retorted:

"You think she is good?—for you may be." *Devarji* felt bad about this.

The family had asked my elder sister-in-law, Ravi's elder brother's wife to get Rs 100,000 for the younger *devar's* college admission. She could not get it. She had brought in a lot as dowry. But they never stopped asking. Later I heard she tried committing suicide twice. I used to talk to her. Give her a little courage. She suffered from acute depression. Most of the time she was morose. I felt sorry for her.

When I was expecting my first child, the in-laws decided I should go to Patna, because it is cheaper that way. I was sent to an ordinary municipal hospital, though my in-laws are rich people. The excuse for not delivering in Bombay according to my mother-in-law was:

"Bombay expenses are too high. You have to pay for her return fare from Patna."

However, once we came back from Patna, she used to send Rs 500 as monthly allowance. What is that much money? She wrote to Ravi, "You have your father-in-law. Ask him." Every time we were short of money it was "ask your *pitaji*." My father was not in position to help us every month. Of course my family supported me. One sister sent money for a maid, others did what they could. But *pitaji* said:

"I have two other children to look after. How much can I do?"

On the other hand, my father tried to get Ravi work. He referred or recommended him to people. But Ravi had an attitude problem.

"Either I will be in the main lead, or not act. Either I will be a producer or nothing."

It was only natural no one would give him work. He actually refused work. I wanted to work. That was unacceptable to Ravi. He said his first wife had an affair, he was insecure about me. He was also very jealous. If I looked out of the window he'd ask:

"Why are you looking out? Is someone there?"

If I was late from the market or my mother's home he yelled, "Why are you late? Whom did you meet?"

Ravi didn't mind my borrowing money from anyone. He didn't feel bad if *pitaji* gave us money—but he was against my working. This is why our marriage broke down. His mother wrote to him often. I have kept those letters. She urged him:

"Keep her at your feet, not on your head. Let her beg for money, that is the only way to treat women."

Imagine Ravi kept the provision cupboard locked. He literally measured spoonfuls of rice and *daal* every day. He never gave money, but expected me to use it well. He thought I was lazy. This is how our life went on. One by one the two girls came. They had to be admitted to school. I was expected to run around for this and I did.

When they were old enough to attend kid's parties, Ravi refused money to buy gifts. He would either slip out exactly at the time the kids needed money or send them to me. I felt so bad for them. They were kids after all. Why make them suffer? I tried to make up for everything. My family stood by me. We had to keep our status in society. Ravi never bothered. And his mother kept instigating:

"Keep her down. Control her."

In Patna, a working woman is supposed to be bad. That's how narrow minded people there are. Whenever I visited they would compare me to my older *jethani*. She had brought a silver dinner set. My mother-in-law said to everyone aloud:

"Thank the almighty, she has got this. You have done nothing in comparison ... let us see what the third daughter-in-law gets!"

They never let me forget that I had failed their expectations. My younger *devar*, a man with physical deformity, received several rich proposals. That became a daily taunt. I used to feel suffocated— break into headaches, and cry every evening. Whenever I cried, my mother-in-law complained:

"See , how she is acting!"

Whether I cried or laughed my mother-in-law criticized me.

She was a superstitious woman and believed some ill-omen would befall the family because we are not supposed to even laugh. The kitchen was considered a holy place. In my mother's home too, we never enter the kitchen with shoes. But in Patna, they had two different cooking arrangements. One stove was for the *roti* another for rice. These were cooked on separate fires. One could not touch the other. If I touched anything my mother-in-law immediately cried:

"Look she has polluted my kitchen."

I could do little. Everyone liked my cooking as it tasted a little different. My mother-in-law felt threatened by this.

As I said, the conflict in my marriage was due to two reasons. One was Ravi's excessive jealousy, his obsession. Coupled with his negative attitude to my working. It became necessary for me to work with a growing family.

An incident I remembered now confirms my husband's intense jealousy. Once we were going to a party. A friend had come from abroad. Ravi who was busy at work told me, "You go ahead I will join later." I knew it was wiser to wait for Ravi. But his friend insisted we go ahead.

Against better judgement, we went to the party. Till 11 in the night Ravi did not come. I was uneasy and fearful. There was no phone in our home. I decided to leave. We reached home a little after eleven. We found Ravi at home. The kids were with mom. He behaved in a peculiar manner. That night he did not speak to me. But he could not do much in that night as the friend stayed over.

Next morning he became extremely abusive. He started calling me names. Dragged me by my hair, beat me, tore my clothes. I was bruised and hurt badly. I am grateful my daughters were not home to see this ugly scene.

My constant fear was about my daughters. When they saw me being beaten, Ravi gave them some excuse. He said I was going mad. Or that I was a bad woman. The girls were upset and scared. They cried, begged him not to beat me. Even his daughters appeal did not stop Ravi! His language and his behavior was obscene. In our Bombay flat or in Patna, the way Ravi dressed shocked me. He wore only a *lungi*, pulled it above his knee, and drink from the bottle. My sister-in-law used to dip her hand into the food vessel and said:

"Come on *bhabi*, eat like me."

I was disgusted by them. After the picture Ravi had painted, this lifestyle was shocking. My father-in-law was an advocate. Educated only on paper. Basically they are uncultured. I used to cry silently:

"What have I done? What shall I do?" No one asked me why I cried. They had no feelings. They would just say:

"Yeh sab natak hai, yeh dialogue bolti hai."

As for my mother-in-law no one dared say a word, nor contradict her. I have said before, she ruled the home. She was really powerful. My father-in-law has important political contacts. One of Ravi's brothers murdered a man. He was released on anticipatory bail. Everyone in Patna knows the family. They can do anything. They have mafia connections too.

When I filed for custody of my children, my husband accused me of adultery. What else could he say? They moved the court in Bihar so that I am harassed every time a hearing comes up. Last year I went out of town to work, my two daughters, 3 and 6 years old, were kidnapped from the school. My father was waiting to pick them up from the bus stop. The girls did not return. My parent's went to Ravi's flat. There was a lock outside. The watchman said he had left town.

It took us seven days to find out where the girls are. Unfortunately I cannot lodge a kidnapping charge—Ravi is the father, their natural guardian. My girls need us both. That is why I did not want to break up this marriage. They are intelligent kids. By taking away the children my in-laws want to destroy me. Break me down psychologically. This is the cruelest form of mental torture. In the beginning, I could not live here. I stopped eating, sleeping—every little thing in the flat reminded me of my daughters. I went to Bihar once with *pitaji*. They locked me up in the house. I could not talk to my girls. They are brainwashed. Told lies about me. I am not allowed to speak to them on the phone. I called on their birthday—but Ravi did not give them the line.

They are prisoners there. I had to escape in the night, scaling the wall. Otherwise I had no way to return. If I stayed longer, they would have made me sign papers, and get me thrown out from this flat, which stands in my in-laws name. My constant worry is—how will my girls grow up in that atmosphere of hatred, where women are worn like shoes!

My father-in-law managed to bring a stay on the case. There is no progress. The advocates only want to put the meter down and get their fat fees. I am frustrated by legal procedures, dodging games, delays. What can I do? My in-laws have the power and the money. They can get anything done.

I have not given up. Tell me, are not the laws of the Indian judiciary same for us all? It is not their personal property! I will fight till the end. I will get my daughters back. I live from day to day. Try to forget my sorrow with work—there is no other way.

Postscript: Bina's brave struggle to get her daughters back was unsuccessful. However she managed to retain Ravi's Bombay flat, which was transferred to her mother-in-law's name. At this point of time, both her daughters continue to live in Patna. It is apparent they have succumbed to pressures and forgotten their mother's existence.

DEEPA

Deepa, the fourth of her parent's seven children was a bright little girl born after three brothers. Deepa always topped her class. In college, she held a high rank. Good at debates, Deepa was also a keen athlete. Her family—known for its academic inclinations, is devoutly, Catholic. As a result, her parents worked for their local Parish. Deepa's mother is a rare example in their community—she is a champion for women's education.

Deepa fell in love with Krishna, one of her batch mates, and a Tamilian Christian by birth. Her family was fiercely opposed to Deepa's romance with Krishna. As her family's opposition grew intolerable, Deepa decided to elope with Krishna. The couple left Bombay city. Soon they were married.

The young lovers continued to work together—taking projects for rural development issues in Marathwada. Later Deepa pursued her interrupted academic career, completing a PhD thesis with Economics. In her crisply worded statement, Deepa explains why she chose to remain married to Krishna despite severe—often violent differences:

When I crossed over to the other side of age 25, my eyes were opened to many myths I had about marriage and men. I had married at the age of 22. I was a rebel. I ran away from home with the man I loved. Left Bombay for Pune. And married my husband against my parent's wishes. The first four years of marriage were not really unhappy. I was deeply engrossed in my own world trying to complete my studies, adapting to a new city, making friends, building a home. Also a great part of the time I was trying to earn. My husband was a student union activist. I never bothered what he did from dawn to dusk except what he volunteered to tell me about his work, or his latest achievements. When it happened to be one of our birthdays, a feast or our wedding anniversary, we celebrated.

In the year 1986, I became pregnant. This forced me to be away from home continuously for three months. I went to my parents in Bombay, as was the custom. After the delivery, I returned to our Pune home with a baby boy. Obviously a little nervous with so many new responsibilities but a proud mother all the same. It was at this stage when the real trouble began. I heard gossips about my husband having an affair with a woman working in the same union.

Then there were letters and phone calls from women he knew but I had never met, never been introduced to or bothered to find out about. I grew angry, resentful, and very suspicious. When I asked Krishna for explanations, I was told it was none of my business. So I nagged him about it. We two complained bitterly and he shouted. The baby boy fell ill very often so my husband was forced to look after him. He was also compelled to bring home more money as I was unemployed due to pregnancy and the burden of child rearing.

Soon the past began unfolding before my shocked eyes, as I discovered all the relationships he had maintained with numerous girl friends. He had taken them out to restaurants. Treated them to dinners and meals with the money I had earned for the home. As I recalled the many nights I sat awake waiting for him to come home thinking he was busy at work, I began to grow militant and adopt a "no nonsense" attitude. I started holding on to any money gifts that we received. I began to keep track of his activities. Every time I caught him lying, I had an argument and every argument ultimately ended with Krishna lifting his hand or leg on me to prove his male superiority!

For years I had deceived myself into believing that some degree of equality between men and women was possible in the home if there was love, compatibility, and both had a progressive outlook. But my own experiences with a comrade who is also my husband, left me disillusioned. I was a changed person, a matured women. No matter how progressive, sympathetic or ideologically motivated men were, I realized they never grant women full equality. This is true even today.

My husband and the other men who work alongside him in the union, profess equality for men and women at the workplace, organize women to demand their rights at the factory gates and are ever willing to run to the union office in distress. Yet none of these male activists show equality to women in their own homes. Their wives, mothers, sisters or daughters are treated with contempt!

Patriarchal domination still exists in the homes of these union leaders. Male egos have always to be appeased; if hurt by their women who may refuse to toe the line, the result may be beatings, walking out of the home, threatening affairs with other women or curtailing financial support for household expenses.

My own experiences of being a victim of marital violence and my husband's infidelity, has made me want to reach out to other women. I wanted to share my experiences with them and gather knowledge that will be of value to us in future.

I want to caution other women like myself of the dangers of being complacent, easy going, and idealistic. I wanted to warn them of existing reality and the need for all women to stay alert to their rights. I try to make them aware of the risk of being having their personalities abused or their spirits crushed. In order to express solidarity with women who suffered like me, I became a founder member of a small local women's group. Today the group is an outlet for my anger, my militancy. In an organized way it provides us a scope for creativity and innovation. The same group has helped me understand women's problems in depth. At the group meetings, I made many friends with women who have similar experiences like myself.

I decided to stay with the man I married. That does not mean all my marital troubles have ended or been resolved.

There are times when I want to walk out on Krishna and start life anew like many courageous women have done before me. But our son just adores his father. The other, more serious reason being, I have seen divorced women reduced below the poverty level, having an awfully tough life fending on their own. There are always enough men prowling to exploit their insecurity, seduce and ill-treat divorced women.

Even today I feel most vulnerable. For these reasons I chose to remain in the marriage struggling to assert myself, my rights and hoping that my struggle will help me grow in conviction and strength. I pray daily that I will find the energy to work with and for women.

GANGUBAI

I have six children, they are all girls. Two are from my first husband, four more by the second. The youngest girl was breast-feeding when I began to work from one house to next. I lived very far, in the eastern suburb of Chunabhatti. From there I went all the way to Mahim. Sometimes I had to go beyond Mahim, to look for work. My parents were both dead by then. Father was the first to die. Mother died only four years ago. My father and mother, worked in the Swastik cloth mills, in Parel. I did not go to school. How could I go? My leg got twisted into a crooked shape when I was a child. It happened when we were playing games. My sister, who is a little older than me—pulled my leg in fun. The joint was dislocated. Since then it is crooked and looks bent. There is no pain—but I cannot walk straight.

My parents got me married. At what age I cannot say for sure. I had begun to have my periods. For my wedding *ai–vadil* gave the usual stuff which was not much. I got a pair of ear rings and a nose ring—that is all. From my in-laws side , I got a *mangalsutra*, and silver anklets. They gave me three sarees with it—one was for the wedding, another for *tilak* and a third extra.

After the marriage I went to live with my husband. Went in the sense, it was close by—in the same compound we lived. My husband worked in the mills. He was a much older man but a good soul. My husband gave me no trouble. He looked after me well. He did not drink or beat me, why should I lie? But he was a sick man and died suddenly. I had two girls already. One was 5 years of age, another very young. I myself was young. I kept thinking what will happen now? Who will look after me and the girls? Where can I go? We lived in a rented room. I left it after my husband's death. My parents were so old they could die any day. They told me, "Don't look to us for help anymore."

I left the two girls with my husband's brother, and his wife. They looked after the two daughters. By then, I had met a man.

It was a matter of falling in love. I was a young woman and he seemed so nice. We began to stay together. My brother had warned me—do not go out with any man without being married—but it was too late for me.

I gave him four daughters. He looked after us and was good to me. As long we stayed together I did not have to worry. I did not have to look for the ration shop, the market. He provided us everything.

To be honest, I did not know where the shops or the market place was. He brought everything for us. He gave no money in my hand but he took care of our daily needs. We never got married. He used to tell me:

"Gangu, I will marry you some day."

But not once did I ask him to marry me! What difference would it make? Wasn't he the father of my four girls? We were living together for 10 years or more. And one day he just comes to me and says:

"I want to marry again."

I did not answer him at once. But could I say anything? He repeated again:

"I will marry. You have not given me a son. You have only girls. I will have to marry."

True, God had not blessed me with son. I said:

"Alright—go get married."

Was there anything left to say? His mother had found the girl already. They approved of her. Before the marriage, he brought a piece of paper to me which said:

"I will marry her but look after both of you."

"Sign here," he pointed.

I put my thumb mark where he pointed out on the paper. He got married soon after that. I went to the wedding. His mother-in-law had a room in Central Bombay chawl. He and the new wife went to live there.

Before the marriage he had talked sweetly and said:

"I will look after you".

Once he was married, he did not turn back. My youngest girl was still breast feeding. I took the four girls to my brother's place. Left them there, and got out of the house looking for work once again. Since that day I am working. Washing clothes, utensils, cleaning. I used to beg of all my *memsaabs*:

"*Bai*, advance me a thousand, I have to live with my four girls somewhere."

Like this I borrowed from my madams. I continued to beg till I got money for a room. We changed places, when the rent period ended. The girls began to grow up fast. I took them with me to work. They helped me. And we managed to live. Not once in all these years did this man come to look for us. No asking how we are, what we eat, how do we live? Yes, he did visit me sometimes.

He came, we spoke. I cooked him food. Not once by mistake did he bring me a glass bangle or *choli* piece. I heard his mother-in-law died leaving them the *chawl* room. He sold it, for over a lakh of rupees. This money was divided between the two—him, and his wife. Now they have returned to the village. I hear he comes sometimes. He does not ask about me or the girls.

If I say anything, he will quarrel, fight, beat me—why barter my dignity like vegetables? I say nothing to him. At the time of the eldest girl's wedding he gave us some money. But my girls had earned well too. After that he gave us nothing.

Once when he came to visit, he said on his own: "You won't get along with my wife. She won't like you."

"May be not," I said. What else to say? It was in my destiny not give birth to a son. God denied me a male child. But my daughters are good to me. All the girls are married now. The last one, married four years ago when my mother died.

The girls look after me. I live with one of them. There is no one in this world except my brother. I don't see him that often. He drinks too much after his young son died.

I depend on no one. I eat with my daughters. My son-in-law is good to me. They live near the subway. I have a room there. Once a man says he will look after you, but does not—we have to go our own way. I have no savings. When I am ill—I cannot afford to go to the doctor. I go only if there is money. My daughter scolds me, "Go and see the doctor." She takes me if she can. I have unpaid loans on my head after all these marriages. But I don't want his money. If I asked, he is sure to say:

"Where is money? I have nothing to give you."

He will argue, quarrel, or beat me. Why loose my respect? I work everyday. If I feel like a holiday—I stay home. The *memsaabs* grumble a lot. But I am back the next day working. Expenses have gone up. It costs three rupees now to travel by bus. I have to pay one hundred and fifty for my room. There is no electricity. We burn an oil lamp. All these are extra expense. It adds to quite a lot. But when someone doesn't want to give money—why ask him?

I am telling you all this as it happened. This is the truth.

Postscript: Gangubai heard about the book project from a neighbor where she works as part-time maid. She was very keen to be featured. Our neighbor's family had known Gangubai for long. They know about her ordeals with her so called "husband." They supported her whenever the need arose. Several times, the police had to be called.

Gangubai complained often about her husband's beatings to the family. When she spoke to me, Gangubai never talked of her frequent physical abuse—except to make passing references. I think it is important to share this observation with readers. It highlights Indian women's compassionate nature, their capacity to forgive, or graciously accept those men who abused and exploited them. Gangubai says she cooked food for the man after he heartlessly abandoned her. See Aruna's postscript on this.

From Gangubai's oral history it was abundantly clear her pride was wounded. To be rejected after 10 years by the man she loved as a young widow! If she felt betrayed by him, she felt equally betrayed by God for not blessing her a male child. She could absolve the man for punishing her on this account, or denying her the social legitimacy of marriage. That her former lover shrewdly chose to marry a younger woman, also owner of a room for selfish gratification, did not strike her as odd. She continued to believe, had she produced a son, the same man would never stray.

HANSA

My Father was a staunch follower of Mahatma Gandhi. In 1947, the same year Gandhiji went on *Satyagraha*, I was born. I remember the *Khadi* clothes my father wore until the last day of his life. By profession, father was one of the leading advocates of the Bombay High Court. Our family had a reputation in the legal profession. Since the past few generations, the Desai's (my maiden surname) had produced several leading advocates. Perhaps I was expected to follow the family profession. But there was no pressure from anyone on that count. I have an extremely understanding family. Being the youngest in my family, I was given a great deal of freedom. Needless to say, I was also pampered. In retrospect I think, it is I who abused that freedom. I was keen on fashion and films, and a little glamor struck as well. All the same, I completed my graduation with economics reasonably well.

The first time I fell in love was during my student days. My dream man was none other than the boy next door. We were classmates. Everyone knew about Kirit. He was from the same community. We often went out together. Our marriage was taken for granted—a matter of time. One day Kirit told me he had fallen in love with someone else. I was only 18 years old and madly in love with him... you know how it is after years of youthful romance, declaring our undying love like in Hindi movies. I was shattered by Kirit's admission. My world fell apart. No sooner had he told me, Kirit was engaged. And before I realized, he was married. I suffered like hell.

One day after Kirit's marriage, I decided to see theatre with friends. At the theatre I met a businessman by the name of Ketan Shah. He paid me rich compliments and a great deal of attention from that first meeting. Perhaps on the rebound, I was quick to respond. I knew nothing about this man. Except what he volunteered to tell. We went out often—either for a drive, or tea, or even dinner. Ketan began dropping me back home. Sometimes it was pretty late at night. At home no questions were asked. We had grown up with brothers and their male friends. It was not considered wrong in my family to go out with a male friend.

In only a month's time, Ketan was chasing me in real earnest. Our family always spent the summer holiday at the Matheran hill station. Ketan turned up at Matheran! My family's first concern was for my future. They were naturally protective since the time Kirit jilted me. We are a caring close-knit family. When Ketan was busy chasing me all over the place, an uncle decided to find out more about his family background.

I forgot to mention something important that happened before our Matheran trip. Ketan and I had gone to a seaside restaurant for coffee. Out of the blue he said:

"As you belong to a legal family—I think you can help solve a riddle!"

I encouraged him to continue. "I have a married friend" he confided, "who has fallen in love with another woman. If you were in the other girl's place what would you do?"

"Are you talking about yourself?" was my frank reaction.

Ketan flatly denied he was the "friend." I believed him.

I remember saying to him, "Well, if the man truly loved me—I would like to marry him. But first he will have to divorce his wife."

To this day, I recall that evening's conversation in all its detail. I do not hold it against Ketan for pretending he was talking about a "friend." But I was certain he had a hidden message for me.

My uncle came back with the shocking news that Ketan was a married man, had a son, and his wife was pregnant. He also gave us the bad news that, Ketan is a wealthy business man's son who lived off his father. Emotionally, I was far too involved with Ketan to care about these unfavorable reports. My family was ready to support me in any decision I made. Their concern was my happiness. First Kirit ditched me, then this awful news about Ketan being a married man. I know exactly how they must have felt.

We could not marry under Hindu law—so the easy way was, convert to Islam. My name was changed to Ayesha and Ketan's something else. I cannot remember his Muslim name. We had a secret marriage ceremony under the Islamic law. A Mullah was called, we even got a *nikanama*. At home, we carried on performing the daily *pujapath*. Our conversion to Islam was purely for the sake of convenience. I was not prepared to live with Ketan without solemnizing our marriage. I thought it would be wrong. Looking back I think it was wrong to convert just like that. Besides, we cannot change our souls, our tradition or culture over-night can we? At that point of time I felt extremely helpless and chose to take the short cut.

We broke the news of our marriage to my family. Even if they were upset, they did not show it. On the contrary, my family was full of understanding. They arranged a small ceremony for my sake. My family wanted me to have the satisfaction that they had done everything according to our tradition. I was given all the items of ornaments they had preserved for my wedding—and much more.

I got their blessings, their love. If this thrilled me, it thrilled Ketan much more.

For a few months everything looked fine. Ketan did not mention his wife to me. He showed no signs of regret. But the problem was, being extremely lazy, he hated to work. Luckily for us, he had access to his family's finance. His father was working in Hong Kong. We decided to go there for a few months. For me the trip provided a great opportunity to take a beautician's course. After the Hong Kong beauty course, I could earn. Meanwhile I was delighted to discover myself pregnant. This added to my physical discomfort but I was overjoyed. Imagine my horror when Ketan got furious hearing I was expecting. His temper tantrums upset me. I always wanted children—I loved children. But Ketan was adamant not to let me have a child. He kept saying, "Not now—later. Wait!"

I did not want to make an issue of this though I was deeply unhappy. I had no choice but to obey my husband. I did not want to argue or quarrel with him. Anyway, Ketan forced me to abort the first child. It was at this stage, I realized Ketan could get violent. Earlier he had verbally abused me. Ketan used foul language but I ignored his language, thinking it was no big deal.

One day Ketan told me, "I heard your uncle is seriously ill. You better go back to India."

We were married for hardly a year. I found it odd going back alone. Ketan did not intend to return with me. He said, he would follow soon.

Again, I did not argue, or question him. I flew back to India alone. It is true my uncle was ill but it was not serious cause for me to return. My family was happy to see me. I did not talk about the abortion. I never told my family Ketan used foul language—this would indeed be a jolt in a Gandhian home. Why hurt them with my problems?

Ketan came back to India after a few months. I did not want to live with my family with Ketan—though no one asked us to leave. Ketan had no home. He agreed to the idea of buying a flat. We found a small, pretty flat in the western suburbs. Happy to be back in India, I got busy turning the flat into our home. Ketan used to return home late. After this happened too often, I asked him about it. Ketan was so angry, so offended that I had to stop asking. And our life went on as usual. Until I discovered I was pregnant again. I had to tell Ketan about it. The second time, I desperately wanted the child. The minute he heard I was pregnant, Ketan went wild. He declined to give our child his name:

"Go on you …! You can have a bastard baby," Ketan raged.

He abused me so much that I got terribly depressed. Finally, Ketan had his way. There was no way I could have the child without his support—or his permission. I went for a second abortion with a faint heart. As though that was not enough of a torture, a friend called me to say, Ketan was seen with other women. I caught him lying to me several times about small things. He was drinking far too much. After my abortion Ketan said he had official work in Delhi that would keep him away for a few days.

I was weak after the last abortion. I wanted Ketan to stay with me. Despite my requests, he left me. He was to be in Delhi for a week. In Ketan's absence, Jaya, a common friend, dropped in to see me. When she asked where Ketan was, I said, in Delhi.

"Are you sure?" she quizzed me.

"Of course, he is in Delhi for work. But why are you asking?"

"He is cheating on you Hansa!" said she with a tone of finality. Before Jaya left, she confirmed seeing Ketan with another woman in a Jaipur hotel. I heard buzzing sounds in my ears and felt I will pass out. I kept asking Jaya:

"Are you sure it was Ketan, no one else?"

"Hundred percent sure. Ketan saw me. He made me promise I would not tell you. Whatever he is doing is very wrong."

Many things began to fall into place. His frequent disappearing acts. Late night outings, those mysterious blank phone calls. I prepared to face him when he returned. You can imagine how awful I felt. My face showed it. That day, my younger *bhabi* asked me:

"What's the matter Hansa, is everything alright?"

I burst out crying. I told my family what I had been through. Talking to her lifted my spirits a little. Worst thing was I was pregnant again. And I was determined to have this baby.

When Ketan came back home, I confronted him. He denied it at first. When I did not give up he became hostile and arrogant:

"So what if I was seen with a woman? There is nothing."

I hid the fact I was expecting until it began to show. By then I was in the fifth month of pregnancy. Ketan was the first to notice. He ordered me:

"Go for abortion. I refuse to give the bastard my name."

I was equally adamant, to have the child. Our row lead to a terrible incident. Ketan pushed me down on the floor. He sat on my stomach, beating me with a hanger all the while. I screamed, calling loudly for help, and then lost consciousness. I was very serious. My head, banged continuously was bleeding. Due to severe beatings, the fetus was damaged. I had to be rushed to the hospital in that condition. The doctors said it was a matter of life and death. My family was present in full strength at the hospital. They helped me to pull through and took me back home. For many weeks after this shameful incident, I was unable to speak, or sleep .... so shattered was I by what had happened.

I realized it was hopeless hanging to hopes where none existed. My bigamous marriage to Ketan was over. The family advised me to recover my stamina before making any decision. In my mind I decided I did not want to lead this double life. That it was time, I left him.

Once I recovered, I asked Ketan to leave the flat and give me a *talaq*. He did not contest. I also told him to put the flat in my name. Surprisingly, he agreed. I got my divorce without any difficulty. My family's care helped me heal. Their support was an effective pressure on Ketan. My brothers took charge of the matter and got it sorted out.

Obviously, I have a number of regrets. I know I wronged Ketan's wife. The poor woman must have gone through a rough time when we married secretly. Several years later I plucked up the courage to admit this to her and personally apologized.

We talked openly, how both of us were treated by Ketan. He had gone back to his wife. Unlike me, she is a traditional Gujrati woman. It made a big difference to her life when Ketan returned. Of course, she had forgiven him completely. Their children have grown up, got married. Ketan's first family live together.

I live alone. My only wish is—to have a child. I wanted to adopt a baby. But the adoption agencies have a stiff rule, not to give children to women above forty. Again, I lost out. I keep myself busy working. I have many friends, I go out, party, watch films—spend the weekends with mother. My life is neatly organized. The strongest support has been my own family. If they did not stand by me—I would have ended my life long back. My brothers wanted me to not remarry. They are right, I am enjoying the fruits of freedom at last.

I have decided never to surrender my freedom to any man.

JAMUNA

Jamuna, was the only daughter of her parents. She had a kid brother named Kartik. The two siblings were deeply attached to each other.

The small family lived in a large house at the foot-hills of flourishing coffee and pepper plantations. Jamuna's family were *Kshatriya* by caste. In the rigid hierarchal order of the Hindu caste system, the kshatriyas are warriors by profession. The Kshatriya community has sent hundreds of young men to the Indian armed forces. Apparently the Kshatriyas observes an indigenous form of equality between the sexes. The women, for instance, are said to enjoy a few social privileges. They are highly educated, articulate and many women hold property titles, run estates. Although funeral rites are performed exclusively by male family members, women are not denied entry into crematoriums. Apart from these so called social privileges, women marry husbands chosen for them, sit separately from boys in classrooms—and generally adhere to traditional norms passed down from one generation to next. A first person account follows:

By the time I was in my teens, I knew my mother's constant warning by heart, "you are a big girl now" she warned "don't mix with boys." But otherwise, quite unlike the women of her own generation, my mother was determined to give me education.

I was 17, studying in high school when marriage proposals began literally, to pour in. I remember quarrels in the home over my marriage. Mother was often reduced to tears. She argued with father about the importance of me continuing education. Mother firmly believed women had to be educated and prepared to stand on their own feet. Thanks to her staunch support I Mastered in Philosophy and Politics. I was 22 years when I finally, got married.

Between me and Kartik we had an amusing time turning down marriage proposals! We fussed about each prospective groom. Argued about some one's dark complexion, or that one man was too short, another too fat. Most matches were successfully rejected by us. Finally there came an offer from a man named Gopal Rao, working abroad. Father asked me the inevitable question:

"Have you any man in mind?"

"Do what you think best," I had replied my father. This put down the lid once and for all on the tedious ritual of groom hunting and rejection games!! The match was settled through formal exchange of letters between our two fathers. After which I was allowed to write to Gopal in Bahrain. He answered back with great speed. Reading his very first letter I felt something was not right. I cannot explain that nagging feeling of unease. Nor can I pinpoint what it was. But the truth is, I did not like the tone of Gopal's first letter. I liked his photograph even less. I accused my poor mother angrily: Do you want to get rid of me, marrying me off to this uncouth man?

By then the wedding was fixed, cards printed. Relatives began to arrive in droves. Gopal sailed down for the marriage. It was obvious from everyone's shocked expression, that no one liked him. I confided these misgivings to my brother. He was of the opinion I should break it off. But our wedding date approached fast. Our's is a prestige—conscious community. Had I broken off, my father's name in our society would have been sullied for life. I could not bring myself to heap insults on my father.

I consoled myself thinking, may be the guy is nice after all. Our marriages were elaborate three-day affairs at the time. The modern version is reduced to a one day event. But the most distinct feature of the wedding is retained. Two separate marriage ceremonies are held.

The boy marries in his own home, the girl, in her home. They do not sit together. After these ceremonies, the groom comes *to claim* his wife. This tradition is based on medieval legends when men carried women off as acts of heroic bravery. I went to my in-laws residence after the ceremony. Next day it was the customary home coming of the bridal couple to the girl's place. That day again I moaned to mother:

"You are *not* celebrating my marriage, but my funereal" I said.

What else could I say? My husband showed no interest in me. I am a warm, fun loving person. He was the opposite. We realized he had lied to us about his educational qualifications, his financial status. He held only a SSC certificate. His finances were zero. He asked me to bring money from my father. This was an insult. But I had to obey. He fought all day long. During our honeymoon, he vanished all night, leaving me behind. When I asked him, he shouted, "Shut up."

From the honeymoon we flew directly to Bahrain. My in-laws had no home of their own. It was a joint-family arrangement. Gopal's parents, an unmarried brother, all lived together. It was a culture shock for me. Abroad I had no friends—nor family. At times, my husband stayed out all night.

I made the mistake of asking him where he spent the night after one of his frequent disappearing acts. He slapped me very hard and dictated: This is the first and last time you ask me that question. I never dared repeat the question. One day my father-in-law informed me, Gopal was deep in debt. He gambled every day. He said I should work to repay my husband's debts. I began to work. I forgot to mention before, that soon after the marriage, I had miscarried.

I was depressed, and terribly unhappy. In no time, I lost weight rapidly. I never thought of writing about these things to my parents. More than anything my silence consumed me from within.

Gopal held me in constant terror by brutal mistreatment. No sooner had I begun to earn, my husband extorted money for gambling. If I dared refuse, he used physical force.

For instance he used to twist my arms behind me. He hit me with spiked cricket boots. First on my feet, then on my stomach, and other parts—this was his way of demanding money. I was beaten practically every other day. I began to carry marks and bruises all over my body. No one came to my rescue. At times, he beat me right next to my father-in-law's study. The old man never came to my help. My brother-in-law was nice—but he did not oppose or stop Gopal. I had no support. As if these brutalities were not enough, one day my father-in-law openly made sexual advances. I was shocked. I told him he was like my father. But the mental trauma of this incident left a nasty aftermath.

I realized, my mother-in-law had been a victim. She used to have temper tantrums, throw fits. But when she was calm, she addressed me as her daughter and showered care. That was my only solace in the morbid house. For a long time I did not want to face the truth of what was happening to me.

My isolation in that foreign land, absence of support, poor health, depression and constant abuse diminished my sense of well being. It never occurred to me that I was actually in danger living with an excessively violent husband. All through my pregnancy, I was mentally and physically abused. Four days before the child was born, Gopal assaulted me brutally with spiked boots.

When I was expecting my son, the father-in-law complained bitterly about the expense childbirth involved. He taunted that my parent's had not fulfilled their duty. According to him they had to take me home for delivery. He insisted they pay hospital bills. I did not utter a word. I had saved a little money for the delivery. I had hidden it until required.

I worked till the very last minute. My labor pains began at the work place.

I remember that day so clearly—Gopal had again disappeared. He was nowhere to be found. My colleagues set up a search party to find him. He was found after hours and then I was taken to the hospital.

I carried my savings with me to hospital. As they wheeled me into the OT, I handed the money pouch to Gopal. I told him it contained money for my delivery and hospital bills. I begged him not to gamble it away. By the time the baby was delivered Gopal had vanished from the scene. He came back the next day. My husband had happily blown the money in a gambling den. It was a very awkward situation. Besides those were politically turbulent times in Bahrain.

The country was riddled with internal strife. Riots broke out between the two sects *Shia* and *Sunni* Muslims. Bullets whizzed past our home. Soon after my son was born, a bazooka hit the hospital building. The newborn baby screamed. I thought he would go deaf. Fortunately nothing happened.

The birth of a son made things more difficult for me. I had a child, as well as a 9 to 5 job to handle. The violence at home continued uninterrupted. After exactly three years, I plucked up enough courage to face my parents. From my modest savings, I bought a return passage to India.

When my mother set eyes on me, her instant reaction was, "You are not the same daughter."

I had been reduced to a bag of bones. My eyes had changed color, I cried so much. My skin was an unhealthy pallor. Altogether, I looked miserable. Despite these tell tale signs, I did not breathe a word to my parents. My father was an old fashioned conservative man. According to him, marriage was one's destiny. Good or bad, we have to bear its consequences. Knowing my father's ideas only too well, I did not open up. I had only two weeks holiday. I returned before it expired. My job was dear to me—it was a symbol of my economic independence.

On my return, I was assailed by unpleasant political changes. In the job market non-Bahrainis were being made redundant. My work permit was cancelled. No questions could be asked—I packed my bags to return home to my parents. Gopal, however, continued for some time. This time, I was determined to tell my family about the misery and ill-treatment I suffered.

I was finally ready to break the terrible silence which was slowly devouring me. I told my family about the tortures I had suffered. I appealed to them, if my life had any value, they should allow me to divorce Gopal.

My brother was a solid support. But Father would not hear of it. He enjoyed a distinct social standing. His position mattered to him more than anything. He merely relented that I could stay in our parental home.

Living in the security of my natal home for one year was a welcome though temporary respite from Gopal's ill-treatment. My peace was short lived. The day Gopal returned from Bahrain my oppression began all over again. The only difference being, my brother Kartik could intervene and subdue Gopal.

Every time I was intimidated or Gopal created ugly scenes, Kartik came to my rescue. He threatened Gopal with dire consequences. Gopal would retreat for a while, only to return. It was apparent as long as I was his legally wedded wife, Gopal would not leave me in peace.

When a new job offer from Bombay presented itself, I moved there. Gradually I rebuilt life in that unknown city with my child.

Gopal stayed behind with his parents. My peace was shattered once again, when Gopal's father threw him out. He lost no time and moved to his sister's Bombay flat. It was easy for him to trace me.

At this stage, a few elderly relatives from our community prevailed on me to reconcile with my husband. Similar pressure came from father. Out of respect for elders I agreed to give our marriage another try.

By this time I owned a flat. My job was fulfilling. I was feeling secure for the first time. Gopal's reentry turned my life and everything upside down. I was being humiliated, beaten. It was awful and then I conceived after nine years.

Life had become unbearable. One incident I remember vividly from this long nightmare phase—was the day I was beaten black and blue with a bamboo. I had to rush to our doctor.

The docter was aghast. She sent me directly to the local police station. The duty officer told me: "How can an educated woman like you tolerate this?"

From the year 1969 to 1983 my torture continued unabated. Witness to scenes of assault for years, my elder son revolted one day. He gave me a stern ultimatum: Either you leave father, or I will have to murder him. The tension for us was unbearable. My sons used to get verbally abusive towards their father. Gopal was always provoking these scenes. One day my son picked up a hockey stick to kill his father. I realized things could not go on like this. I filed for divorce. I must point out here, I had great difficulty in getting a divorce lawyer. One or two lawyers turned down my petition on the pretext they were reluctant to help me break our family.

While the divorce petition was being heard, the worst thing was having Gopal under the same roof. Once he broke my arm. Another day I returned from Court to find hired goons sitting at home. I was fortunate in having a good Judge. He called us to his Chamber and chastened Gopal:

"Why do you want to harass your wife and children? You do not care for them. Let them go."

I am fortunate my legal battle did not last more than two years. Gopal had applied for immigration to the UK. It came through just in time. He left without making any provisions for us. His behavior did not bother me. I had already risen to rank of Assistant Manager in our printing company.

In the past, I tried to commit suicide, but I never gave up fighting for justice. I have regained peace of mind at last. Both the sons live with me. I view my future with positive energy.

I always say my divorce was the best thing to happen in our lives!

KARUNA

I am exactly 69 years old. My father was a Mathematics professor in Allahabad—the city of my birth. I never cared much for school but loved to dance. Of course, dancing lessons for girls in the 1930s was unheard of. I consoled myself by participating in school programs and choreographing when I myself did not perform. But these diversions hardly made up for the intense passion I had for dancing. Studies suffered, naturally, till I opted out of school altogether. I did what seemed to be the ideal way out on not being permitted to learn dancing: I got married. A handsome man, my husband came from a reputed family and above everything else, he was extremely erudite. He was a Marxist and a Tagore scholar, never mind the contradictions which form a part of the arrogance of any Bengali intellectual. By profession, he was a dealer of imported books and earned reasonably well. But his business collapsed just before our wedding forcing him to take up a government job.

We shifted to Delhi, his first posting. For that first one year of our marriage, life was sheer bliss. It was paradise on earth. The difference in our ages simply melted away. Very soon I went back to my parents because I was pregnant. Sadly, we lost our first child. By this time my husband was transferred to Bombay. Over the years, we had three children, two girls and a boy and our family seemed quite complete.

I tried to make up for my lack of intellectualism by reading a lot, at times guided by him, sometimes, on my own. But three lively children and household chores soon turned life into a busy schedule for me to have time for any kind of serious reading except fiction.

Life went on. It had its usual ups and its downs. If there were arguments, it was nothing more serious than money matters or the children's upbringing. This gave me no cause to worry.

One by one, we got both our daughters settled. My life had more leisure after that for a change. I went back to my childhood love: poetry. And took up reading English and Bengali poets. At this stage, my husband achieved something great. He had become a famous homeopathic practitioner with a roaring practice but his aim was to treat the poor for free. So, though money flowed in generously, it was always much less than what might have been required, had he made money a priority. An idealist at heart, my husband treated money with contempt.

I, for one, did not get much of glimpse of that money he earned because he had very expensive habits: collecting for example rare books of Maratha History and art books, collecting coins and antiques. It never occurred to him to take us all into a more spacious home, or even to buy a flat. I did not nag him because we lived in a very nice neighborhood and did not care to move into the suburbs.

When he saw me venturing into poetry, my husband was thrilled. He encouraged me in fact to read. But his thrill lasted till *my* own poetry got published in a reputed Bengali literary magazine called *Desh*. That is when I think my life and our marriage began to fall apart. By this time our son too had got married. The new daughter-in-law appeared to be the catalyst who toppled the matrimonial boat. She was a highly educated girl from a rather poor family. Understandably, we had not demanded any dowry at all. Soon after her arrival, I could tangibly feel the reins of my family slip away from my fingers. Did I say slip away? Seized would be more appropriate: the reins of my family were seized by my husband, indirectly, even by my son.

I might have called this a mother-in-law versus daughter-in-law syndrome in reverse. But that would be unfair to the daughter-in-law because I was not dependant either on her or my son for my well-being. I was economically dependant on my husband who still earned handsomely from his homeopathic practice not to speak of his good government pension.

Over a period of time, I discovered, with shock, that I was slowly being reduced to an unpaid maidservant in my own house. My husband now began to ridicule me and my poetry but that made me all the more determined to go on. My husband, that nice, cultured man with decent manners, began to lead a double life: polite to everyone else and indecently abusive, both physically and verbally to his wife. He began to subtly hint that I must leave the house! The subtlety was lost on me so he became brazen: he was actually commanding me to leave the very house we had built together for 40 long years!

After 42 years of marriage, a day before my son's birthday, on 21 July 1983, I walked out, with the clothes on my back! I expected, in my heart of hearts, shamelessly, I confess, to be called back. After all, I was his wife of 42 years! I went to stay, not live, with my elder daughter and her family. We had thought this would be a temporary arrangement.

We were wrong. It appeared as if they were expecting that I would leave. I had simply walked into a trap without imagining there was one, cleverly and diabolically laid by the very people I had cared for and had grown to love dearly. I went back again and yet again, like any shameless woman who is foolishly in love with the husband she married 42 years ago. But he wanted nothing to do with me.

All attempts by my daughter and her husband to bring about the desired rapprochement, directly or through a marriage counselor, failed. I began to persuade him to give me a monthly allowance, a small one, so that I wouldn't be too much of a burden on my daughter and son-in-law, when my husband was alive and affluent.

He refused. If his refusal hurt me, the grounds on which he refused finally made me very, very angry. I had never been so shocked in my life. He actually said that since we were married many years ago, and that too in Allahabad, with both my parents having passed away long ago, where was the proof that we were married at all?

If his response to my final cry of help broke me, it also made me strong. If it made me wish myself dead, it inspired me to live. It thrust the decision of my life in my own hands for the first time in so many years, without the usual guilt feelings women are needlessly conditioned to nurture. I had no reason to feel guilty, I told myself, because he was the guilty one.

I gathered the courage and the moral strength to file a maintenance suit. Thanks to my very sympathetic lawyer, I won it within a couple of years with retrospective effect from one year after I left home. The triumph was not in the money it brought me which was a pittance. The triumph was in disproving what my husband had argued: that I was not his wife. The court decided that indeed, I was his legally wedded wife.

I continue to write poetry. I have two published collections of poetry to my credit and am planning to get another published, soon. I still live with my daughter's family. I draw my widow pension every month as my husband passed away in 1989 at the age of 79 refusing to speak to me or my elder daughter who sheltered me these years, though both of us went to see him, whenever he was ill, regardless of the altered nature of our relationship.

I refuse to wear widow's weeds because, to my mind, he had already died on the dawn of 21 July 1983, when I walked out and he sat there, calmly blowing rings of cigarette smoke into the air, not caring to stop me. They only cremated him six years later. He was not the man I had married so many summers ago. I still love my husband, the husband who inspired me to love, to read, to be generous to those who are in need. The man I had married never died. The man who died was not my husband.

Am I happy? Not always, because I still do not have a home of my own. The question is: Did I ever have one? My parents named me Karuna, meaning compassion. My husband renamed me Mita meaning the good friend. Today, as I traverse painfully, through the last phase of my life wasting away physically with my mental faculties more alert than they were before, I am a diffused blend of the two names: I am a good friend to all who care for my friendship and my sympathy lies with everyone, including all those who wronged me: my husband, and specially my son and my daughter-in-law whose lives are stalked by the tragedy of their beautiful nine-year-old daughter's death.

I cherish sweet memories of the times I had with my husband, days full of laughter and cheer and good spirit. Days of rehearsing amateur plays in the drawing room as I ran back to the kitchen to fetch hot cups of tea for everybody.

Days when we had little money to spare for a movie but we went all the same, tagging the children along, tucking in hot batata vadas or crisp chips during the interval.

And I am full of sadness because I still do not know why he deserted me at the fag end of our married life. He began to hate me for some mysterious and imaginary reasons. Was it because he realized, that despite his professed intellectual superiority, I was the more creative and the more talented of the two?

Postscript: Karuna would have been 80 years old when the book was completed. She passed away in early 2001.

KATY

We were not exactly wealthy. But from the time I remember, most, if not all, our worldly needs were taken care. The best part, of course, was we four sisters grew up in a family overflowing with love and affection. My father, Dara Vakil, was an old fashioned, sentimental kind of family man. Papa could get extremely difficult at times. He was short-tempered and lost his cool easily. Needless to add, at home his word was law. Papa passed away in early 1984.

Our mother, Sillo was very traditional in thought. Being a dutiful wife and mother was of supreme importance to her. Mama took it upon herself to preserve Parsee family traditions handed down by our female ancestors. Now whether these were right or wrong, did not matter to dear Mama.

Of course, I grew up not questioning my parents' their views about life. Suddenly one day I said to myself—wasn't it time I "educated" them a little? By educating them, I meant, make my parents aware that other kinds of views existed. For instance, I had my own view about life! While my parents were always bothered "what people would say?" I firmly believed "to hell with what others say." But I must say one thing—my parents were rebels in their own way. They fell in love. Had to elope and had a runaway marriage. Now this is something I am mighty proud of!

We girls were truly blessed growing up in a no-problem, happy family. My parents had their share of trouble—mostly about money matters. Papa managed to sort these out. During my childhood I made a secret pledge with myself. I swore, come what may, I would make my parents' old age comfortable. That is precisely what I did. What's more, I did so without surrendering my freedom, or my individuality. Not that my parents demanded this of me. I wanted both of them to know I cared about their welfare.

Talking about our lovely childhood days ... we sisters were a cheerful, fun-loving lot. We would laugh at the drop of a hat. Play silly girlish games and enjoyed life to the full. With parents as loving as ours, bless them, we had not a care in the world! We grew up with the hot sun's glow on our back, and sand grains caught in our hair. *Juhu*, the suburb where we lived, resembled Goa those days. I still live in Juhu—but it is not the same Juhu of our childhood. Carefree and content—that is me. It's quite possible I have remained young, due to my airy spirit. Never mind the chronological age. My sisters never tire of scolding me. They believe I should learn to behave and act my age! Nonsense!!

I can smell the salt air mixed with the tantalizing aroma of *bhel puri, ragda pattice, nariyal paani* ... the salty sea-breeze, and sand storms, if you can call strong gusts of wind, storms. Oh! those Sundays! How dearly I remember them! Sundays were special. Like in any Parsi home. From early morning we pestered Papa to take us swimming. When we returned home, pink cheeked, and terribly hungry—a special Sunday brunch Mama prepared was neatly laid out on the table. Freshly caught Bombay Ducks fried crisp, lots of eggs, jam, bread, cheese, butter, fruits and other goodies were the treat!

I often remember those cool summer nights spent in the courtyard. Our entire family assembled in the open air—Papa played the harmonica and all of us burst into songs. Yes, sometimes we slept in the open-air bed room. Stars twinkled over us. We slept soundly under the open sky.

Up to the seventh standard, I showed no spark whatsoever of progress in my school work. At one stage, Papa was even considering I become a pianist. He had noticed minor musical flair. Regular schoolwork did not interest me. I loved painting. Loved music. And of course writing was the greatest love of my life. Papa and mama encouraged me to pursue these. My sisters had total freedom of choice. They cannot complain anything was imposed. We have all done exactly what we wanted to. My three sisters married men of their own liking. Each one is happy with her individual family.

I remain to this day, a daydreamer. Dreams are my companions. I switch to my dream world regardless of where I am or what I am doing. That is why my attention span is no good. I am lost in my dreams. I enjoy being a loner. Lonely? Who says? I have no time to be lonely.

Another childhood companion was the radio. Remember the radio Ceylon station? Belting out popular Hindi film songs by dozens! And *Binaca Geet Mala* nights! That was my favorite station. I loved watching movies, Hindi, Bengali, English, all kinds of films. I almost lived for cinema. I loved cinema for cinema. Not for the glamor it projects. In any case, the glamor of cinema quickly vanishes and the reality beneath is far from beautiful ... but lets not get into that issue ... my childhood, quite simply, was super. I loved school, adored most of our teachers. I have fond memories of them ....

One thing I realized quite early in life was that one achieves one's true potentials only if independent. At a very young age, I took the decision to work first—earned and learned my way, you might say!

Immediately after school I completed a commercial course and was lucky to get work. College came later. Learning continued. I worked and did my Bachelor's with literature and psychology. Next I did a course in mass communications, with Cinema, Radio, TV, Journalism, and Public Relations. Believe me, I topped the class. Besides this, I learnt *Hindustani* and light classical music. Took a degree in *Bharatnatyam* from the Allahabad University. That is not all—there was more.

By the time I was 20, I moved out to live on my own. I chose a place near the family flat—to be within easy reach. Soon I purchased a car. These assets were possible with company loan. To repay loans, I worked over-time. It was a period of intense struggle. But I took pleasure in that struggle. Not once did I lose sight of my responsibilities, my duties towards my family. At times, there was tension at home because of me. My family wondered why I was doing what I was doing.

A dreamer and a chronic romantic! That's me. Naturally, I ended up having a few harmless crushes. I was determined about one thing however—that was, not to get married. I did not want to be controlled by anyone. The young guys I met wanted me to give up everything. Devote my entire life to their families. Imagine! I was expected to chuck my family for theirs! In any case I never wanted to marry a mama's namby–pamby boy.

Although I am born to Parsi parents, my outlook was cosmopolitan. I detest any kind of discrimination—communalism, caste system. Hindu philosophy fascinated me. I could not see myself as anything but an urban, cosmopolitan woman. My true cultural identity was cosmopolitan. Unlike the rest of our family.

I brought up the issue of being a Parsi, as I was raised to believe, I could marry only a Parsi man. Otherwise, I would be fried alive. To me a Parsi husband was unacceptable! On the other hand, if any man happened to display interest in me, I was watched by a hundred pair of eyes.

At the high school level I accidentally discovered—that I was attractive! I liked what I saw in the mirror. Friends paid compliments. Heaps of interesting young men just died to talk to me. This was a new experience! We had no brother at home. I studied in a strict girl's convent. Belonged to a generation where looking at the opposite sex was cardinal sin. So at home and in school I didn't dare express these new sensations about myself. It was a secret from all.

There was another strange fear that plagued me during adolescence. God knows why, I thought of myself as a cheap and fickle girl. Everyone seemed so terribly straight-laced, clean, good. No one owned up their true feelings. Most of my classmates were giggly girls—not be trusted. Parents, Nuns—even close friends—made you think something was wrong with you—that you were a rotten apple. I was an outgoing person—forced by circumstances to be an introvert. I honestly believed I was a bad person. It is only now I realize how utterly naïve I was. And this feeling of being "bad" persisted till I began working.

The glorious mid-60s made me glow! Many of the guys hanging about confessed their romantic interest. Fear and confusion, made me drop them. Frankly, I did not know how to cope with these eager flirts. To cut a long story short, positive I would never be allowed to date or marry a non-Parsi man—I turned these suitors away. But unwittingly, I had paved the way for my sisters to marry non-Parsis, even half Parsis!

While I was tossing in this kind of emotional roller-coaster, Dame Luck decided to smile! Out of the blue, I met the man of my dreams. We actually met at work. Within six months, he showered me with love. Of course, I was thrilled but tense at the same time. He 14 years older. And married with four children! His eldest daughter was just 10 years younger to me. He was a decent man—not the kind to carry on extra marital affairs. Why then, I wondered, did he "want" me? Boldly I decided to visit him in his family den.

The man, Vivek Shanbag, 34, was a *Gaud Saraswat* Brahmin, living with his wife and four kids in a suburban flat. He was not surprised to find me at his doorstep. He was, in fact, delighted. Vivek introduced me to his wife Ambi and their four kids. My unexpected visit turned into a pleasant meeting. Vivek's wife was a simple woman.

From the moment I set eyes on Vivek, I knew here was the man in my life. After meeting the family, I took a solemn oath—not to break his home, or hurt his wife. I wanted to be their friend. This may sound improbable but I was sincere. Vivek, a full-blooded man seemed physically unfulfilled. His wife Ambi had a complex about her looks. She refused to accompany her husband, avoided even office parties. At times they went to movies together. Vivek's elder daughter was growing up with a severe personality complex. She was jealous of everyone around—including her family. Anyway, this is not about the girl!

I confess being hopelessly attracted to Vivek. It was reassuring he loved me back with ardor. Not handsome in the usual way, Vivek had a pleasing personality. He was a charming man in a quiet sort of way. That made him sexually very attractive. Vivek was a highly qualified scientist. The only thought in my immature mind was, the man loved me and I loved him. I did not want any force in the world to break us apart ever. He was not seeing anyone else. I knew because I made it my business to find out. He spent most weekends researching in libraries.

I guessed, Vivek did not have a good sexual relationship with his wife. My parents would never let me marry Vivek or a non-Parsi for that matter. I decided, why wait? Why not go ahead? I am fortunate Vivek turned out to be a good man. Not the kind who abused a woman.

In no time, we were friends. And then it was inevitable for us to become lovers. Our two families got closer. That we loved one another as man and woman was a secret for a long time. Years later, when it was discovered, there was an unspoken "acceptance."

We had no choice but make love in hotel rooms. I was terribly uncomfortable about this, though Vivek understood my sensitivity, we were helpless. We were extremely passionate individuals. Vivek used to say:

"Katy, my personal life would have been dry without you. I am fortunate you came into my life at a time when I was learning to repress my needs."

He did not invent these lines. Nor was he bluffing me. We enjoyed a long-drawn love affair and companionship of 24 years. Being highly educated, Vivek encouraged me to educate myself. He began to groom me. But I took care to leave space to be myself. He gave me that freedom. His consideration made me respect him all the more.

I would like to mention, that never was I treated like a "kept." At the back of Vivek's mind was the nagging fear, one day we may not be together. If anything was "kept" by Vivek in our relationship, it was my higher education. He would get me the registration forms, pay the fees, buy my books, pick me from night classes and exult over my success. He wanted me to be independent in every sense.

Vivek used to take great joy in seeing me dressed in silk. He bought me heaps of sarees. He loved to fill both my wrists with bangles. Perhaps out of guilt, when he bought something for me, he bought the same for his wife. Sure we had our ups and downs, had major fights—especially after his children grew up to become questioning adults. We suffered in our own way. But we also stood by each other in thick and thin. Over the years I had become bold and no one—I really mean no one—could say anything to me against him.

Towards the end of our relation, I distanced myself. That solemn pledge, not to hurt his wife, had failed. If I had hurt Vivek's wife, I had hurt myself thousand times more. I realized with a start that it was convenient for his family to have me as their "friend."

When Vivek suffered his first heart attack, I was by his side. I told his wife to be present. But she expressed her confidence in my ability to handle the situation. Again, convenient for all concerned. I was with him day and night. This coincided with a major promotion to a managerial post in our office and my presence (in the office) was crucial. But what did I care?

It was the Parsi New Years Day, I remember. My parents rushed to the hospital. My sisters sat by Vivek's bed side when I was out. His family did visit him. During his illness our relationship gained silent acceptance. That was the twelfth year of our relationship. It would last 12 more years.

Vivek's brothers, their wives, children, were fond of me. They are in touch with me even today. They believed, Vivek would not have known true happiness had he not met me.

After his ailment, there were bitter rows between us. Vivek's two elder children got married. I was not even told. The issue simply was, why did he exclude me from the marriages? Make a secret of it? I was not going to show my face or sabotage the weddings. Once when I called Vivek's number, his new daughter-in-law acted smart. She answered my call, saying it was a wrong number. She stopped him from answering my phone. Had Vivek's wife had done this, I would have understood. But not a rank outsider? She did not know who she was dealing with. Within seconds I was at his doorstep and made a big scene. An indignant Vivek charged out! He isolated me from his family! Even now, I feel awful about that scene and a few others.

All of a sudden, Vivek began to hide things from me. At first, it was a few lies. When I got to know, I was naturally hurt. It was not because he was hiding from me, but the need to hide. Our relationship continued. But I was unhappy by his lies, his deceptions. We met only on Sundays. And this would have gone on, even now. Or may be I was expected to look after him, nurse him again when he fell ill.

What I am mighty proud of—rather pleased about—is how I encouraged and supported Vivek to start his business venture. Even from this I cut myself off when his sons grew up to take charge. They are still in business.

A year before Vivek died I met a man (I did not know then) who was virtually to be the last man in my life. Vivek died at the young age of 59. I was not by his side. No one informed me. Later, his elder daughter requested me not to attend Vivek's funeral. Her in-laws were present. This hurt me deeply. But in my heart of hearts I did not want to attend the funeral of the man I loved so deeply. He who shaped and pampered me, gave my life a new direction, taught me to communicate, to learn and enjoy financial independence. I could not bear to see him dead.

What Vivek did not realize, was he had carved a permanent place in my heart. For me, he is alive in so many memories. I wanted a lover, not a husband. He was that lover of my dream. Thank God I experienced the most fulfilling intimate relationship. I was to realize this forcefully when an uncouth idiot invaded my home, my life soon after this tragedy.

His name was Deepak Srivastav. This man, shockingly, controlled my life for eight-and-a-half years after Vivek's death. The result, I am out of love with love! Something I never thought I would admit. The story of a woman—beater started with my relationship with Deepak.

Deepak, was literally—tall, dark, and handsome. Endowed with a charming smile and seductive ways to woo women. "For goodness sake, what do you see in him?" is a question I did not stop hearing from my friends and well-wishers.

After Vivek's death (from which I have yet to recover), I was at my vulnerable worst. This man succeeded in paving roadways to my life and ultimately my heart. Like Vivek, I met him professionally. Don't ask me what profession! Till this day I do not know if the guy is a media man, an aspiring model, a garment exporter or anything else he glibly claimed!

Deepak was from an obscure place like Bulundshar—in UP (or is it MP?). Deepak said they owned ancestral lands, farm, etc. He insisted being a graduate—an impressive achievement those days. People even printed B.A after their names! Said he was a Police Inspector in Gwalior, before setting foot in Bombay. All this sounded grand. But I doubt he had seen the inside of a college. There are no ancestral farms or *havelis*. There never were. He wanted to impress me by laying it thick. Deepak pretended he was younger than he was. He was 38 years to my 44. Six years younger. He tried hard to give me a complex by our age difference.

Deepak was attracted to me to the extent he stalked me. He staged accidental meetings and phone calls. This is not to flatter my ego. He was attracted to a woman he believed was wealthy, independent, owned a flat, was cultured, and charming. A single woman he could control. I was to learn these facts too late.

Shamelessly I admit, I lost my heart once again to this ruthless man. I was foolish and obsessed. For eight-and-a half years he lived with me. We had a lovely time together and were happy, because I chose to make it so. For me, he was a soul mate. A man to whom I gave and gave and gave and gave—everything I possessed ....

When we first met, Deepak was a paying guest. He complained of having a bad time with his landlady. He said, she troubled him, gave him no peace of mind. What he concealed from me, and I learnt by accident, was that his landlady Mrs Das, was also sharing his bed. She was separated from her husband and had three grown up children.

One evening Deepak complained, "Mrs Das keeps pestering me to marry her daughter."

The truth was, he fancied her young daughter. And the daughter hated the very sight of Deepak.

By then Deepak meant the world to me. Hearing about his trouble, naturally I asked him to move in. I had already taken a car loan on his behalf. Ghostwritten TV scripts for him. We dined out practically every night—and guess who picked up the tabs? I had done a great deal in an awfully short time.

After Deepak moved in, menacing telephone calls started to come. The callers were all female. When I asked who these women were, his answered by bashing me. He had bashed me before. If I said anything witty which he suspected was critical of him, he got physical. Deepak first raised his hand in the very month of our meeting. Scared to loose me, he apologized profusely. His temper bouts, too, I had begun to see earlier. But I took no notice of these—nor considered them warning signs of what followed. I was stupidly obsessed. I never knew what made him violent. After his apology I was forever willing to forgive and forget, erase the nasty memory. Pretend it never happened. Life went on like this.

Every once in a while something odd began to happen.

One evening two strange women turned up. We were not home. They rang our neighbor's bell. Questioned her about Deepak. Next day, my neighbor told me about the visit. She said it looked like pretty fishy business. I was grateful to her. But I was also terrified. I did not tell Deepak about the women. Again someone came. I did not recognize the person and never opened the door. But this time, I told Deepak. He brushed it off as my imagination!

Another time, I taped a long conversation. Even though I did not speak the woman at the other end went on teasing. Deepak seized those tape. What he did with it I have no idea. There were many incidents like these.

I introduced Deepak to the entire family, my friends. We went for meals to their homes. I recommended him to several people for work. My entire life revolved around him. The one thing that took priority over Deepak was my work. Professionally, I was at my peak. This suited him only too well.

One particular incident, bizarre as it is, stands out in my memory. This is a graphic picture of Deepak's vicious temper. One evening, he said let us go out to eat. I agreed but warned him, I was short of money. He ignored the second part. He drove my car. We ended up at the expensive Sea Rock Hotel. Drinks and food was ordered. I was careful to order. He went ordering "get me one more *roti*," etc. Silently, I watched. I had no credit cards, for fear of misuse. I had not even dared buy a new car—which I badly needed. I knew it would soon become HIS car. The conversation at dinner, as expected, was only about him, his problems, his work and so on. I was a patient listener. However, I managed to pay the bill.

We got into my car, he took the wheel. Suddenly Deepak was raging mad. His left arm flew to strike my face. He pulled my hair, my sari or anything that got in his way. He drove on, bashing me all the time. He snatched my beaded gold chain, which broke. I did not know what was happening. I was protesting, naturally. The moment the car stopped at a traffic signal, I opened the door and fled. He drove away. There was alcohol on my breath. I was awfully upset when from a rickshaw I hailed a couple I knew came out. I had to greet them. Seeing my battered condition they asked if I was alright. Before I could answer, Deepak returned and pulled me into the car. Till this day I don't know why it all happened. I was living a life without a shred of dignity. Whenever he felt threatened that I would throw him out, he cried, asked to be forgiven. Again, we kissed and made up!

Those years we lived together, Deepak did not introduce me to anyone. No one in his family met me. Not even his friends. No one knew where Deepak lived. I was not supposed to tell. He had a post box address. Mobile phones had not come to the market. But I bought him a pager. If my friends asked him:

"How is Katy?"

He exclaimed, "I don't know! I've not met her for long." And he was standing right outside my gate. They told me about it later. If I questioned him, I was sure to be bashed up.

Deepak's bashings included, grabbing me by hair, banging my head against the wall; deafening slaps on my face; toppling the breakfast table; hitting anywhere, picking anything, a knife, a hanger—to hit me. Once he was going to pour kerosene on me. After he had cooled, I said to him that my friends know he abuses me. Should anything happen to me, he would be the first suspect.

Sometimes he got so violent, I had to summon my neighbors and whisper, "Please come soon." I was scared enough to confide to a police inspector friend, to keep him posted.

Distasteful and demeaning as it was, I put up for 8 years of degradation. Known to be a strong, independent woman—what had happened to me?

Things had grew from bad to worse. Everyday he demanded money for petrol. The excuse was, going for a long drive. He made me fill gas. Next minute, he picked a fight, drove me home and took off with the car tank full. I never knew where he went or for how long.

At one stage Deepak came late every single evening. After a hearty breakfast, he left home. Returned for lunch. Enjoyed a cool siesta with the AC in full blast. Refreshed, he went out again by evening. Where? You can't ask. How long will you be? You can't ask.

I often begged him, please tell me if you are late, I get worried. Begging him, was an excuse for a round of bashing. For the first time in my life I learnt to think before I speak.

I know people laughed behind my back. But the little good in Deepak erased memories of his abusive behavior. He was a house-proud kind of guy. Liked a tidy home. He liked to shop for the home—loved good meals. Of course, always, with my money. We cooked together. Watched films. Played scrabble. I would do some work for him. And invariably I found myself in the kitchen—breakfast, lunch, and dinner if he was home.

Looking back, it seems he could probably make a good administrator. He held on to a stupid complex about English. He was good in correspondence, handled the staff well in my absence. My family loved him. No one speaks ill of him. That is because no one knows his abusive side. I was silent about his bashing.

I guess what frustrated him was being deprived of my assets. Deepak thought I was blindly in love with him—so much that I will put everything in joint name. He underestimated me. I would never dream of doing that. Not with anybody. He must have believed I would give him the right to my flat. But the strong woman within came to my rescue. I put him in his place.

If you think I had put up with Deepak for love or sex, you are mistaken. I doubt if we had good sex eight times in those eight years. He kept me craving and enjoyed it. He had terrible hangups about sex. It had to be done with windows shut, in the dark. Soon there was no sex. It makes me laugh to hear friends say I housed a gigolo.

When I found money slipping away from me faster than I made it, I thought of investing. A friend suggested I put the money in a small flat. I signed for one. When Deepak came to know about this, his face fell. I helped him book one on his name, taking loans from a friend. Today he owns that flat. Although he paid only one tenth its value.

I knew if he has a separate flat, he would have someone. He did a lot in that flat quietly. Deepak waited for me to fall asleep. Then he locked me in the bedroom and made calls from the hall. One night I banged the door. He took a long time to open it, and then pretended that it was open all the time!

Deepak Srivastava was an extremely cruel man, a manipulator. He cared only for himself. He was full of typical North Indian double standards. The kind of man who lets his woman go out to work for him. Otherwise the woman has to be at home. He did not care for his family, or his old parents. He always boasted:

"I live life on my terms. No one tells me what to do."

I busied myself with my work. I knew in my heart, he was spreading tales about me. Just as he had done about Mrs Das, his former landlady. He told everyone, he was my paying guest. Paying? That made me laugh. Deepak paid for nothing. His clothes, food, laundry, stay everything was at my expense. I found happiness in giving. After he got the flat, I knew I had given him what he wanted.

By 1996 he was behaving very strangely. His birthday came in November. I treated him at the posh Library Bar of President Hotel. I was happy to be with him. Deepak was as quiet as a mouse, seemed sad, wanting to say something but unable to tell. I was surprised to find him subdued. He timidly explained there was some problem in his family and he would be going to settle it. I helped him again. I even packed a new white silk sari for his mother. I sensed trouble. I could feel it in my bones that he wanted to leave but could not let go of me. It made me uneasy. Deliberately, I did not question him.

I saw him off at the airport on 6 December 1996. It was a Delhi flight. He was to board a bus from Delhi for his village. I waited to hear from him. There was no news for a month. Meanwhile he got married on December 14. He simply phones me in mid-January 1997 to say:

"I got married *yaar* due to family pressures."

A 50 year old rebel bowing to his father's order? Sounded incredible.

I don't believe his bride is from Delhi. She was in Bombay all along. He must have carried on with her while living with me. Taking money from me to entertain her.

Deepak hoped I would get over the jolt of his marriage. And continue our relationship. He also thought, mistakenly, he could enjoy the comforts of my home. Lie to his wife. Be, with me during day and pass it off as being at work. Return to her by evening. He even thought he could beat us both—that we would silently bear it.

After those years with him, I wanted a clean break. What staggered Deepak is that I wanted nothing to do with him. I never questioned him after that day. I never asked about his wife or where he lived. He possesses a mobile phone. I even have the cell number—but I do not intend to use it. Never.

Deepak assumed I would take anything from him. He was not aware of my inner strength. My determination. I repeatedly ask myself what friends asked: how could a strong, independent, self-made woman who wrote her own destiny live with a man who bashes her? You forget, I was a woman in love! I failed to see the menacing, cruel man behind a charming facade. Failed to see the man had no feelings except greed for power.

I believe a daughter was born to him soon after their marriage. I wonder what if his daughter was to meet a woman-basher, two decades from now? Suppose I was to ask Deepak this question, he would jump up to hit me!

The only lover I have today is—work. I am insecure when not working. Completely wedded to my work, I value and zealously guard my professional reputation.

I think, the best thing about me is that I can be honest. Be like an open book. I feel no shame, no regret about what I have done, my relationships, the way I have lived.

You know, no one can blackmail me. I am willing to tell it all.

LAXMIBAI

No, I am not a *Lavni* singer by tradition.

We are *Kolatis* by birth. The *Kolatis* are carpenters. Most of the woodwork in our village was done by our family members. My father was a carpenter. His father did the same work. The male folk of our family were only carpenters. It was like that ….

My life turned a strange corner, when I was still in my mother's arms. Father died suddenly. Before him other relatives had died. That season our village was struck by diseases and death. Mother was a young woman at the time. Wisely, she did not want to suffer the cursed fate of young widows. So she chose to devote her life to Lord *Vithoba* whose most famous hometown is Pandharpur. Leaving me in God's lap, mother left for the pilgrim town of Pandharpur. Imagine the calamity! Elders of our village were thunder struck. No one knew how to deal with a six-month-old motherless orphan girl like me!

People of our village had a simple answer to solve the big problem. They married me off. My husband was about fifteen years old, now I have even forgotten his name. I was only six months at the time. But things like this are common in our village. I was raised by my *sasumai*. From the moment I could talk or walk, I had to do housework for my mother-in-law. Usual household chores! Washing, sweeping, look after cows, plough the fields, fetching water from wells. I don't remember doing anything else. But from my childhood I was mad about one thing—music. I loved to sing songs to myself. No one taught me. Anytime I heard a song or music, my hands and feet refused to work. I burst into songs and dreamed of being a singer. Every time I sang, I was beaten black and blue.

But beating did not cure my madness for music. I used to sing whenever my heart ached—and was beaten for this crime! I always said, let them do what they want, why silence the song in my heart? Luckily for me, our toilet was very far from the main hut. I sang in the toilet. I sang all the way to the toilet shed. If I was heard even humming, I was beaten. But you know, no one, not the worst beatings, could stop me singing. This is how I grew up. Sometimes, my mother-in-law punished me for singing or other imaginary crimes. I was locked up in a dark *kothi*, starved of food and water. My life rolled on like this. Villagers those days were more concerned about people than they are now. They knew I was illtreated. They talked about it when village elders met amongst themselves. But it was not until something drastic happened that my fate actually changed.

My entire family—except mother—had perished in the unknown epidemic that monsoon. I was the only survivor. Our family farmland belonged to me. My husband's family knew about this. Naturally they wanted to get rid of me, remove the only obstacle, or the thorn from their path to fortune. After that they could grab my land.

One night as I lay down to sleep, I heard soft footsteps approach me. It was very dark at that hour. The kerosene oil lamps had burnt down. I heard my mother-in-law, my husband talking and whispering in low tones. I was scared to death. I pretended to snore, and shut my eyes tight! Should they find me awake, God know what they would do! I heard the chopper blade being sharpened at the shed. My husband was busy setting up the chopper on a wooden plank for my head. Young as I was, I knew exactly what they were plotting.

I decided to scream at the top of my voice when they came to kill me. As luck would have it—a huge portion of the wall dividing our compound and the next neighbors had caved in the rains. I fearfully prayed to attract their attention by screaming aloud.

My mother in law bundled me towards the chopper. I wrestled with her and tried to break free. I saw a big sack beneath the chopping blade waiting to hide my body. I screamed loudly. Again and again. My lungs must have blown big like *phugas!* My piteous wails woke our neighbors and they rushed to save me in the nick of time. That is the story of how I failed my husband's murder plan.

After that night, our *Patil*—or the village chief—decided enough was enough. Word spread like fire in hay stack about how I was nearly killed. An urgent *Panchayat* meeting was called. Being an orphan I was the responsibility of the entire community.

The *Panchayat* decided to send me to my mother in Pandharpur. A kind villager offered to take me to my mother in the pilgrim town.

But the fact is, my mother had forgotten she had a daughter. I did not exist for her. She was not at all pleased to see me. But even mother could not ignore the village *Panchayat's* decision, I was left with her in Pandharpur.

I thought, at last I am free to sing as wild flights of fancy sieze me! Mother would beat me every time I opened my mouth to sing. She considered it bad for a woman to sing. I had an adopted brother. He would rush to save me from her beating. This brother was to become my first Guru.

He had a good ear for music to realize that God had gifted me with musical talent.

There used to be a famous singer in Poona by the name of *Godavari bai*. She was considered the best in the *Lavni gharana*. My brother said we should go to Poona. He wanted me to be trained by the best teacher available. Mother promptly agreed, she was only too glad to get rid of me.

In Poona, we met Godavaribai—the tough old *Lavni* queen in her home. She agreed to teach me. But many conditions were laid down. First of all, I had to do all her housework, I was to be her slave. Singing lessons were my wage for the work or call it my reward. What could we do—we agreed to Bai's tough terms. This is how my music lessons began. All day long I slaved for my mistress, my guru, Godhutai. She performed every evening without fail. How I longed for the hour dusk would fall and the curtain rise. At these performances, I accompanied Godavaribai, as an attendant maid.

I listened to her singing all night at the various concerts. I would hear roars of applause! Be lost in my imaginary world where it was I, not my Guru, seated in the spotlights, before thousands of adoring lusty fans!!

My Guru, Godavaribai was in no hurry to teach me. It was months before she would present me in Poona's music circle. Time dragged its feet … finally the day dawned. How I trembled, with hope, with fear. Would the audience like my singing? Would they hoot me out?

I need not have feared. My first performance in Poona was a roaring success. The audience cheered for me … clapped repeatedly, they wanted only me, they loved me … the other girls in

Godhutai's group were extremely jealous. But the worse blow of all was how Godavaribai was boiling with anger. In me, she saw a young rival.

After my first success, I was not given water to drink. I was given food only once a week but before the success I tasted, these were minor matters. I was giddy with my success. I continued to sing, food or no food. Continued to gain popularity ... my name spread far and wide ... once again it was time for me to leave the nest.

Godavaribai was a good teacher, but a cruel woman. After I left her, I hired my own musicians. We supported ourselves. Work flowed in. There were tours in villages, from villages to towns, from towns to big cities. We sang in tents, in homes of the rich, the powerful. We were the ruling *lavni* performers ....

Those were truly the days of Laxmibai! I was like a Queen .... you should have seen the crowd, heard them yell for me ... how they adored me! My music made me forget life's sorrow. I don't remember my husband, his name, or my past life—they are now like old faded pictures. I did not remarry. I am wedded to my art ... I have so many memories, happy ones and sad. I have become very old now ... but I have lived and enjoyed my life and my success ....

What else is there to say?

Postscript: I met Laxmibai at a performing arts workshop in 1987. Her struggle for recognition and social respectability inspired everyone who heard her speak with compassion, witty irony, touched by tragedy. When she tried to sing snatches from her popular *Lavni* songs, charged with erotic lyrics—her voice cracked. Laxmibai continued regardless as though intoxicated. She had distanced herself from her past, from bitter memories, forgiven those who abused her or her art. One of the most renowned singers of the *Baithaki* style of *Lavni*—Laxmibai faced society, life, death with rare calm.

In her remarkable piece there is clear evidence of societal violence. The *Panchyat* or the powerful local lobby had decided to marry off a six month old infant as a solution to her predicament. Then they decided she must be sent back to the mother who had cast her. Human concern for Laxmibai, as a helpless infant or, young wife, is absent in the *Panchayat* decisions. The *Panchayat* merely shrugged its responsibility and abandoned Laxmibai to her fate.

MAYA

Maya Chatterjee was born in Calcutta a couple of years before India's Independence. Her family shuttled between Calcutta and Bombay. Out of the blue one day her movie-star father was invited to play the male lead in a Bombay film production. At the time Maya had just turned one year. Since her father's work required him to be in Bombay for long periods, the Chatterjee family decided to move.

The family settled into a spacious suburban bungalow in the same neighborhood of a bustling studio. Famous for its movie industry, life in Bombay was more hectic for the Chatterjees. The only child of her parents, Maya had a stepbrother and sister from her father's first marriage. She enjoyed the security of a close—knit family and looks back fondly at her idyllic—almost charmed fairy tale childhood:

"I was treated like a little princess at home. Adored, greatly indulged and spoilt in the bargain. When my father took me to the studio, I spent an entire day on his film sets. Film studios in the early 40s were beautifully maintained. There was gold fish in clear ponds, dovecotes, fluffy rabbits, spotted deer and other studio pets that were required for shooting. Neatly cropped lawns and exotic flora and fauna made the studios like parks. Film studios had enough to keep a child entertained in our times.

My exposure to the glamorous tinsel world made me lose interest in school or study books. I became a reluctant student. Mother constantly worried about the fact. But by the time I was ten, I had settled down in school. A part of my childhood nostalgia is attending nightlong classical concerts. I invariably fell asleep in the warm comfort of father's lap. It was quite simply a wonderful childhood!

Our home was the hub of social activity. There were always guests at our dinner table. From that early age, I was encouraged to express myself freely. We were raised to mix with children of our age, boys and girls both. Somewhere discreetly, a vigilant adult kept watch. By and large, I had a liberal upbringing.

Loved, cared for, sheltered—perhaps too sheltered. I did not know what pain, or humiliation was. I was even less aware that pain could take so many shapes—as I understood later when life thrust misery in abundance."

By the time she was barely fourteen years old, Maya's academic performance was quite brilliant. The Chatterjee family had moved back to Calcutta. She was enrolled in the reputed and perhaps elite—Bethune College. Maya was the youngest student of her class.

Amit, her maternal aunt's younger son, had already appeared in Maya's life. A good ten years older to Maya, Amit was bowled over by his charming cousin. He took care to visit their home often. Unknown to her parents, Amit courted Maya with relentless zeal. He confessed being madly in love with Maya. The two were first cousins. They were in addition, a Hindu Brahmin family. Besides the fact that Maya's father was a celebrity made matters even more serious. Marriage between the two cousins was unacceptable. There was religious and social taboo against such a marriage. However, one particular incident at this point sealed Maya's fate forever.

One day Amit took Maya to visit a common friend. She was shocked to find the flat empty with no sign of their friends. Before she could protest, Amit seduced Maya in the empty flat. He continued to mount pressure on Maya to marry him. He backed up his marriage proposals with suicide threats. Maya recalls:

"Immediately after the incident of Amit forcing himself on me, I discovered myself pregnant. Abortion was illegal, dangerous and of course scandalous those days. I was afraid of the terrible outcome if anyone discovered I had conceived. It was under these stressful circumstances I married my cousin brother Amit.

I had no other choice open to me. Before the marriage, we rushed through a hasty conversion ceremony. It was only as Christians—or Muslims—we could solemnize our marriage. It was so strange having a Church marriage! Amit seemed to have a blue print ready for our future. He had secured a teaching job in a Christian Missionary school—this was in the wilderness of Bihar.

Within a week of our marriage we went away to that remote village in Bihar. We were allotted staff quarters. This was no more than a tin shed—with a cement roof. The place was extremely uncomfortable—hot in summer, freezing in winter.

I realized that I had deliberately been cut off from everyone I loved, and knew. Removed from the people who could support me. I was only eighteen years old, newly married, pregnant and completely defenseless. A small solace in my isolation was listening to music from a tiny transistor set.

If my husband walked in while I was listening to music, I had to switch off. Otherwise he would seize the transistor. Lock it up for days. Amit made it quite clear: look, you are not supposed to do this, or this, or this.

Take the food stuff he bought from the market. Mutton, fish, or even other goodies. These were just enough for one person. He had specific orders for me: this is fish for my lunch. Mutton for, dinner. You cook rice and *daal* for meals. Day after day I had to eat lentils that was actually cattle feed. I ate food hours after Amit finished eating. I was told to eat on his dirty plate, without washing it—as this was the traditional custom for being a obedient wife!

I had a special liking for sweets but my husband did not allow me to eat sweets. He didn't allow music in our house nor were visitors welcome. If anyone showed me warmth, he was suspicious.

Gradually I was so isolated, that I began to wonder what the human voice sounded like!"

In Bihar, Maya had no neighbors she could talk to. Their tinshed was located at the rear end of a wooded estate. At the center of the estate was a large bungalow where an elderly couple, Mr and Mrs Sen, lived. If she was depressed, Maya visited the old lady She took care to visit the Sen couple when Amit was away at work. If by chance her husband discovered she had been out visiting, Amit was sure to get suspicious.

The first time Amit hit Maya is imprinted forever in her memory:

"I remember the first time I was physically abused. My daughter was a three months old baby. We had a wonderful Nepali maid, *Parvati* to look after the baby. That wet morning, Parvati was going to the market. My husband insisted Parvati take the baby to the market with her. The maid had an umbrella in one hand and the shopping basket in the other. I objected to the baby being taken out in the rains. She was likely to get wet, and fall ill. Any mother would want the baby safely indoors when it was raining. No sooner had I said this he dragged me into the bedroom. And I was being bashed up from head to toe … I didn't know what was happening. Nothing like this had happened to me before. No one had raised their hand on me. I was never slapped by my parents, or anyone for that matter. My nose began to bleed profusely.

The maid rushed to my rescue. She threatened to call Mrs Sen, our only neighbor if Amit did not stop beating me. Her words had the effect of magic. He stopped. But I noticed, he was careful from then. He did not like the maid's intervention and her show of concern for me. In that God-forsaken place, our Nepali maid Parvati was a source of great solace. But I lost her. Amit hated anyone who supported me. He kicked Parvati out on some stupid excuse. I could not prevent her leaving.

Another incident I vividly remember involves a male office colleague of Amit. In a rare moment of hospitality, my husband once invited a male colleague to dinner. I had cooked the meal. After dinner, his colleague thanked us both. He made a special mention about my excellent cooking. Amit silently heard his colleague's praise. Summoning me to the bedroom, Amit accused me of flirting with his friend. He verbally abused me. So stunned was I by his wild allegations, that I could not utter a word of protest. My silence infuriated Amit. He smacked me on my face. Not once but several times. Deep red, finger marks showed up on my cheeks for days. Naturally, I could not come out in that condition.

After hitting me, Amit went out for a walk, as if nothing had happened. This shocked me more than his slaps. The little socializing we did stopped after this incident. Frankly, I was wary of having visitors. Amit's bouts of explosive violence, and vulgar language could occur in front of outsiders. What never ceased to surprise me is that both of us belong to the same cultural milieu.

Before the baby was a year old, I conceived again. By then, I was regularly in touch through letters with my parents. Though deeply hurt by our marriage, they responded to me.

Her parent's positive response lifted Maya's oppressed spirit. Mrs Chatterjee was keen to visit her daughter. If Maya was happy by her mother's concern, she was full of apprehension. Could she trust Amit's reaction to her mother? Maya need not have feared—Amit put up a charming façade. Maya's mother pretended to be pleased but her mature eyes had picked the telltale signs to indicate all was not well with Maya.

First of all, Maya's mother was appalled at the poor living conditions of their beloved daughter. There was very little Mrs Chatterjee could do at that stage. After a week with Maya, she returned, greatly disturbed by what she intuitively sensed. After the second baby was born, Amit lost interest in his job. He became moody and listless. Maya recalls:

"We had very little money at hand. I decided to visit my parents and give him some space to work things out. He allowed me to visit them—perhaps his consent was given in an unguarded moment."

When she was visiting her parents in Calcutta, Amit landed up without warning. He called her back to his parent's home. The moment she stepped into her in-laws' house, Amit accused Maya of having affairs with other men. Maya's feeble protests met with violence. When she was being battered in her in-laws house, Amit's mother, or Maya's aunt, did nothing to protect her. It was her father-in-law who stood by her. He threatened to take police action, if Amit abused Maya. Confident of his marital rights as a husband, Amit blatantly ignored his father's threats.

That visit to Calcutta ended abruptly. Maya returned to their tin shed home, broken in spirit, and sick with anxiety. She did not know how to mend her marriage. Very soon, she asked Amit to allow her a second home visit. To her great surprise, he relented.

Maya required her parent's support to make serious decisions about her life. She also wanted to resume her education:

"I decided to do my Masters in History. And that is when another phase of nightmare began. My husband was opposed to my doing anything. The very thought of my leaving home without my small kids, was intolerable to him. I had no financial support. I left home with exactly 36 paisa—the return fare for my college.

If my parents quietly gave me pocket money—it was taken from me by Amit. I had virtually lost all control over my existence. He used to follow me every time I went out. Each time I left home, he accused me of other intentions. That I was having extra marital affairs was his constant allegation. While all this was going on, one day something occurred that shook me up completely. That morning, my older daughter was severely battered by Amit. Blows rained on me trying to save her. I realized, that his violence was beginning to boil over. And that if I did not act, my daughters would also be his victims. I was not ready to take that enormous risk.

Without arousing suspicion, I asked father to send me the car. I did not remove any clothes nor did I change the girls'. As soon as the car arrived, I took the girls, and moved to my parents. On the way, I remember mentioning my decision to leave Amit to our old chauffeur, Alibhai. I told him I would never return to my in-laws house. He knew what was going on. And the loyal retainer that he was, Alibahi showed his warm sympathy to me. Back home with my parents, I told them about my decision to leave Amit. My father had not intervened so far. He told me:

'You are choosing a very lonely path my child. There will be many who will discourage you. Many fingers will point at you— with accusation. Do not allow these to deter you from the path. As long as you can answer your conscience—we are with you.'"

After Maya decided to leave Amit—she did not look back. With her parents' help she migrated to another city. Maya got a lecturer's job in a local college. Amit was unwilling to give up the golden goose so easily. He followed her. Intimidated Maya. Forcibly moved into her flat. Maya was constantly fearful he would take the girls away. As Christians, they would have to annul their marriage. Amit contested that. He contested Maya's right to keep the girls. Unable to get redress in court, Maya finally gave up the legal battle. For a long time, Amit tried to win her back with threats, or false promises to change his ways. Unmoved by his threats or promises Maya did not go back. Until his death, Amit had not given Maya a divorce. She did not remarry. For many years she had a meaning-ful relationship with a male colleague.

Maya is the Head of the History Department in the same college. She lives with her aged mother, and two daughters. The traumatic episodes of her past are mercifully behind her.

She does not wish to journey back into the past. Memories of her painful marriage haunt her still. At times the fragile mental equilibrium she has achieved is threatened. Today Maya says confidently:

One thing I am grateful for is the ugly violence in my life did not make me bitter. I have a marvelous relationship with my young students. Their affection, their respect for me has not suffered due to my unconventional past.

No matter how grim the battle, what is important is to retain one's humanity at all levels. I do believe we are entitled to a life of dignity and self-respect. Two invaluable assets I nearly lost in my hopeless struggle against violence. I was blessed to receive my parents support—without their blessing, I would not have survived this battle.

NEELA

I had heard about wife beating. But I was under the impression it did not occur in the educated class. Although my parents never got along, violence was never a part of their problem. Certainly there was a lot of bullying from both ways. A great deal of verbal abuse, but not actual beatings. My parents argued nonstop. No one knew what triggered their rows—the smallest and the silliest things could start it. If my father lost his kerchief—it was enough for us to be tense the whole day.

I remember being always nervous. I never knew what was going to happen in the next five minutes. We never stepped out of our room; my brother and me. Father had a phobia about dirt. I remember when the ironing board did not fit into our parents' room it was moved into ours. Father would iron everything—his belt, kerchief, socks, even currency notes were ironed. He believed ironing killed germs! And he kept washing his hands after touching anything ... for us kids it was the most tense part of childhood; the year the ironing table was shifted into our room. Father would explode over anything at us and at mother. So we always stayed in our room. We pretended to be fast asleep by eight in the evening and avoided coming out of the room.

As a child, I was beaten severely by both my parents. They did not dare hit each other but vented their frustration on me. My mother used to buy canes from local fairs for dogs and beat me with them. My father belted me. Between them I had my skin peeling off. Since I was five or six years old I was beaten every day by one or the other, whoever was in worse mood. I never protested. My parents had come to the conclusion since their marriage wasn't working and they were perfect human beings, the cause of the problem lay outside. They blamed me for their bad marriage.

Even now when I pass that Byculla neighborhood where we once lived in a bungalow that is now demolished for a high rise,

I shiver with terrible memories of what I went through as a child. Very often, mother used to have these bad headaches. When she had one, mother asked me to leave the house and go down in the garden. We lived on the first floor. Our Parsee landlords lived downstairs. In the early hours of evening, only the grandmother and a mentally retarded boy were home in the landlord's house. One evening I was playing as usual in the garden. The half-wit boy called me into their house. I went in. He took me into a room at the back. He undressed and touched me. After this incident, the boy repeated it several times.

I did not know how to avoid this nasty thing happening to me. Mother was lying upstairs with a headache. Once I tried to tell her about what the boy was doing to me. She shooed me off. After that, I never tried to tell her. The Parsee boy molested me for over a year. It stopped only after we moved to Poona. Once we shifted to Poona, I was put in a boarding school, or what my parents thought was a boarding. It was really an orphanage for girls who had no parents. At the orphanage, I got scabies. The nuns notified my father. He refused to take me home, as scabies was contagious.

As luck would have it, I was treated with heavy dosage of antibiotics for typhoid. The treatment cured my scabies. Only after I was well, did my parents take me home. At home, things got only worse. I was always made a scapegoat. My parents were convinced their marriages did not work because of me.

My younger brother Sunil suffered from serious psychological problems. His temperament is quite different. He made no contribution to the home. He had become passive and kept a distance from all of us. Perhaps that was Sunil's way to deal with the problem. He was also beaten but less often than me.

I always thought trying to please my parents will stop them beating me. So, I was forever willing to help. Always ready to run errands, shop, help mom in the kitchen. My parents used this as blackmail. When I was in college, I had to miss classes, because mom kept no servants. I was there to help her. Despite these pressures at home, I stood first. I lived with them till I was 19 years old. After my graduation I went to live with a maternal uncle in Bombay. He was separated from his wife. The original idea was I would live with my uncle till I got a job.

Uncle John's new girl friend was Peter's elder sister. I met Peter first at my uncle's home. The only person I liked in Peter's family was he. It was a pity I could not date him. Uncle John's girl friend Lily felt if I went out with Peter and did not marry him, it would spoil her relationship with uncle. Peter's family was always hanging around. We could not go out on our own. In those two years before marriage, Peter and I never had a conversation. We did not once talk!

I had no clue about Peter as a person. Even if we went out dancing together, strict conditions were laid down. His sisters had to dance with him too. It was more like a family outing!

The Gomes sisters made funny comments about slow dance numbers. Even the five minute conversation I could have with Peter on the dance floor was impossible. I did not feel like dancing with stupid comments all around. Those two years I thought he was a gentle, shy man—not a violent or abusive person. I seemed aggressive, in contrast to him! He is still soft and gentle with his family. They overwhelm him—he dare not utter a word against them.

By this time I had secured a work permit in Saudi Arabia. I was flying with an International Airlines. When I came down for a holiday, I met Peter again at Uncle's flat. I thought he was too shy to ever ask me out. I came to know from him later, about the conditions imposed by his possessive sisters. Once when we met alone for a brief second, Peter proposed marriage. He told me, he had already decided about us. He was older, and seemed mature. He also said I need not rush into a decision. But I was happy to marry him. Perhaps I was too naïve and did not know what marriage meant. I had only seen my parent's bad marriage. Greatly overwhelmed by Peter's proposal, I promptly accepted and said "yes."

I was blindly in love with my husband after our marriage. That blind adoration lasted one month. Then we began to have problems. This was mainly about what my mother told his mother or sisters.

These arguments went on for all the eight and a half years of our marriage lasted. That is how the abuse started. The only arguments were his blaming my family, abusing them for any little thing or vice versa. Later there was so much bitterness; we began to dislike each other intensely. Frankly, we had no other dispute, except about our family. It used to make him unbearably violent. Sometimes he beat me up to such an extent that I could not go to work for days.

One of the first beatings I remember was over a birthday card his sister Lily sent—or some silly thing like that. I did not realize

Peter was so touchy. He flew into a rage because I questioned about the way this card was sent. He beat me till I nearly fainted. I was expecting our son. Weak with my first pregnancy, I collapsed after the beating. The other time was soon after we married. I was standing in the kitchen. Peter instructed me how to cook, how to arrange the food on his plate. Where I had to put the curry, over his rice, in a clockwise direction, where to place the pickle. He screamed loudly at me that it was all wrongly placed and the plate of food I was serving fell down, with spoon. I couldn't imagine anyone screaming so much because the rice was not in exact position.

It began with small things like that. First came his shouts followed by massive blows. Initially it was only a few slaps. He would hit me with his bare hands or pull my hair. Because I did not resist, he got bolder. He used to pick up anything he found and throw it at me. Once he threw a heavy crystal animal. It broke into splinters on my feet. He broke used bottle, hit me with the edge, anything at all.

I never stopped him. I never protested. He grew bolder and bolder. Then a time came when he attacked me daily. I was in a shock in the beginning. But within five or ten minutes of the explosion, Peter became contrite and wanted to make love. I loved him so much that I was ready to sort out anything.

I remember screaming a lot at times. I screamed not to attract attention, but out of terror and shock. We were living in Riyad at the time. I soon realized if this is the way he is going to behave, I better stop reacting. Block my mind. He resorted to other kinds of cruelty. For instance, when we went shopping, everything we bought for me was selected by him. Apart for the fact he had good taste—this was how he controlled me.

The shopping *had* to be his choice of brands—in frozen food, the clothes we wore, even the lipstick shade I used! Everything was what Peter wanted. I did not resist, knowing it would result in beating. I am saying all this as I had no voice, no freedom to choose what I wore, or ate, or how we lived. It had to be *according* to Peter's decision. The only way I could deal with it, to retain my sanity was to block the mind. Not react. I said to myself let him make all decisions and avoid being beaten. But it did not protect me. By the time we left Saudi Arabia, I did not know whether I wanted to wear red or blue. In the beginning I used to scream, as I said before, not for help—my screams were involuntary, out of sheer shock. Later I decided not to scream. My husband is 13 inches taller than me. He is well built like an athlete. Physically, I was no match.

I never thought of retaliating. He used to call me names. Sadly our son picked these up. When I got the custody of my son after 18 months of separation … the first thing my son did was call me names. The first time he called me *"Mamam,"* I turned round to see if it was really me my son calling "mother"! I had got used to his calling me bitch, and whore. Even in court hearings the child called me these names.

The first six years in Riyadh, the beatings were not that frequent. It happened every time a letter arrived from Bombay. We had no telephone connection. All communication was through letters. I was beaten once a month to start with. I learnt not to express what I felt to avoid confrontations. Our conversations were one sided.

As a Catholic you are brought up with a strange notion that however bad your husband, you have to make the best of the situation. I followed that faithfully. When my husband was at work, for long ten hour shifts, I had time at hand. I would meet my girl friends, all of whom Peter disapproved of. I listened to music, went out for coffee—it made life a little bearable. I doubt many husbands disapprove of their wife's girl friends! After our return to India, I wasn't allowed to meet my girl friends. According to Peter every one of my friends was a bad influence on me. No one was good enough for his sophisticated family.

My poor mother-in-law had even a worse situation than me. She was constantly bullied by her husband and in-laws. I don't know if she was beaten or not. She used to be a French tutor. Her solution to this was to leave home by 7 a.m—go from tuition to tuition—and stay out long hours. There was no separation or divorce in her times for a Catholic woman. This was how she coped. In Peter's family people are gloomy by nature. They never laugh. Peter vented his frustrations by beating me. This was his way of dealing. Peter did not want to change or confront the situation.

For a long time, I told no one about Peter beating me. What was the point, I thought? I was sure to be ridiculed. Recently, a former colleague of mine confessed to me that her idea of a perfect couple was me and my husband. I had kept up the image successfully.

When I married Peter, I was working and economically independent. Peter agreed I could work two more years. But in ten days, he asked me to resign. I begged and pleaded to continue. He agreed to allow me a half day job. I looked at options. There were a few perks but for a half day job, I could get only half the salary I earned before. Still, I took it up. When we came back to India, I had to quit. I had a child of three, expecting another. My Provident fund money, gratuity etc. was with Peter. I was therefore totally dependent on him.

If you are told all the time you are useless, no good, that you cannot support yourself, it is bound to affect your self-image. I felt I was unable to live on my own. Though now I enjoy a better lifestyle than I ever did even as a married woman, I thought I was doomed.

I never thought a husband has a right to beat his wife. No, I was not brainwashed to that extent. My attitude was, when you have accepted life, keep quiet. As I said, it was cleverly dinned into my head, that I could not be self-sufficient. I felt the children needed a family, and they need their father, that is why I did not want a divorce.

I did not want to opt of marriage even though I was locked out during my pregnancy just before meals. Big rats were thrown on me in the dark while they took off the fuse! I was terrified of rats, and used to jump on tables and chairs. I was in an advanced stage of pregnancy, but Peter locked the bathroom and I could not use it, The two brothers, Peter and Charles locked the kitchen—I was left without drinking water.

I still lived with the hope he would patch up once I delivered the baby. I only accepted the fact that he had no intention of patching up when I went to hospital. Peter refused to take me to hospital at three in the morning. I was told the baby would be put in the incubator. Peter's sister said:

"Oh that would be the best thing—then the baby and she both would die."

I delivered the baby prematurely. That day they had put a live bloodsucker at the door entrance—I used to be terrified of rats, lizards, bloodsuckers. I took a long stick and tried to shoo the bloodsucker into the garden. Peter got very angry. He tried to hit me, and get the bloodsucker back into the house.

Fear induced my labor pain. In that state I walked all the way to the police station, without money. The police took my complaint, gave me two constables. We returned to the house, in order to identify the respondents. First I had to walk to a neighbor's flat and phone my mother. Then take a bus to my lawyers. I was afraid once I left for delivery, Peter and his family would stop my entry. My lawyer prepared an injunction motion. By then, it was nearly midnight. My pains had grown stronger. I went back to collect my hospital bag. Peter was in bed. I switched on the light to pack my the bag. Peter jumped up, ready to hit me. He said I was disturbing him.

Before I knew he kicked me in the stomach for taking his towel. This was exactly three hours before my baby was born. At first I requested him to unlock the front door. Still composed, I requested him to take me to the hospital. He refused to come with me and woke up his brother Charles.

Both of them screamed at me. They ordered me to open the front door, the downstairs gate, come back return the keys and take a taxi. All of a sudden the sheer horrible cruelty of my situation hit me!

When I redialed the police station, Peter snatched the phone receiver, and opened the door for me. I called for my Uncle John, who was married to Peter's sister Lily. But she had locked him from inside and uncle could not come to my help.

By this time the police were informed and a lot of people in the area knew what was going on. I guess the fear things were out in the open, scared Peter. They thought should anything happen to me, they will be implicated. Finally, I was allowed to leave, I took a police van at that late hour—picked up my mother, some money, and rushed to hospital. My baby was born premature.

After the delivery, when I returned, as suspected, they did not let me enter the house. I went with the newborn baby to the Crime Branch. I entered home with police help. The next six months were hell. Peter had disconnected the phone. Cut off water supply. Saddled with an infant baby—I was without water, without phone. My in-laws went round with pillows, ready to suffocate me. My mother was not allowed to come and my maid was threatened. They spread nasty rumors about my character, saying the baby was not Peter's child. Due to these rumours all our neighbors shut their doors on me. Only one lady let me use her phone. I moved the court within six month's of my new born son's birth. The cruelty was so inhuman, that I could get arrest warrants for the entire Gomes family. Their powerful Church connections proved futile.

I was able to get the family out of their homes. Afraid of arrest, Peter and his brother were on the run for ten months. During this time, I could stay in my matrimonial home and recover my few belongings. The jewels were recovered through the court.

I was able to negotiate for my belongings, my fixed deposits, provident fund etc. only because I was physically in that house. Possession is nine-tenths of the law I realized. If by chance they had managed to throw me out before I moved Court, all was lost.

Without money, I could not have asked for my older son's custody, or start any business venture. These ten months gave me time to sort out most of these things. Peter had not bargained for a long-drawn Court battle. He must have thought, I would give up.

Ironically, in that neighborhood, most houses have a similar history. Either daughters or wives have been thrown out. It is a predominantly Catholic area. For 65 years there was a law that no house could be demolished. As a result, estate builders did not operate in that posh locality. It was only in 1990 that law was struck down. Today builders swarm all over the area ... the violence in my life, or in the lives of other wives of that neighborhood have links with this new reality of real estate market value. We are seen as outsiders. All those old land holding families owning vast properties zealously guard their priceless estates against any individual they view as an outsider. Take my case, Peter divorced me. One sister is unmarried.

The married sister, Lily died soon after I left. Her husband, Uncle John, was summarily thrown out. Peter's brother Charles is a bachelor. The Gomes are a strange family. All those beautiful houses in that area have similar tragedies ... it is a question of inheritance of property ... they want to keep it in the immediate family.

I have no regrets any more. Though I loved Peter, adored him, I could not have survived in the Gomes family. My one fear is their hold over my young son—the only male heir to that vast property. I know someday Peter is going to fight back for his custody ... I live with this one fear. I cannot remarry or go out of Bombay—automatically I lose my son. That's why, I have to work at home, here, in this city, I wish I could have left this city and made a fresh start somewhere—I feel trapped ....

Postscript: The son whose court custody was such a contentious issue-began to abuse his mother from the age of 9. He terrorized his mother, maid, grand mother, breaking crockery and other things beating them up. His bouts of mindless violence occurred specially after Alan returned from weekend with the father. Unable to bear renewed incidents of violence from her own son, Neela approached a social worker, and her Parish priest. In a meeting with all parties, the custody of her son, was reversed. Alan was handed over to the father. Neela had week end custody.

It was after this Neela found a suitable job in the Gulf. She is still abroad. Her two children, in their late teens, visit their mother. But her ex-husband never acknowledged his daughter as his. Neela feels very bitter about his. She has transferred all her assets to her daughter.

SARLA

The greater part of my childhood was spent with a maternal uncle and his family in a North Bombay suburb. My father worked abroad. He was appointed the Technical Adviser to the Government of Oman for many years. Mother had to stay back in India to look after us. During the school vacation our family always reunited. Some times, father came down to Bombay. Alternately, we visited him in Muscat. From Muscat our family traveled all over the world.

In our homes, we were taught to speak politely. If ever we raised our voices, mother or one of the aunts was sure to tick us off:

"Is this how you will talk in your in-laws' home after marriage?"

In our home daughters are dearly cherished. We are showered with care, affection. At the same time we were taught frugal middle-class values; respect for elders, how to live a simple but meaningful life. Father earned enough to maintain a car. But he chose not to buy one. He believed it was not in good taste to show off wealth.

The two sisters, Vimla and I, were given freedom within limits. This was unusual for the extremely conservative *Marwari* community. We girls could go to see movies—but not to the market. I had boys as friends—but they were neighborhood boys from decent homes. Out-door work, like going to shops, or bazaar, was left for our brothers and male family members. Our childhood was quiet and peaceful.

We had never heard about any kind of violence. I always thought it happened in a certain class of people. One of our maids complained of being beaten by her husband. She committed suicide later. But I thought this kind of violence was not possible in our middle-class homes.

At 22, I graduated with an Economics Major. I was the oldest of my parent's four children. My attitude has always been total surrender to the wishes of our parents. They have given us everything—education, a sound upbringing, love, care—we owe them respect. I am what I am because of them. Shortly after my graduation, a relative of my mother's proposed marriage to a Professor in a college.

Our family was against dowry marriages. A few proposals were turned down when the groom's side asked for too much cash and dowry. My aunt was impressed with this match since the groom's side assured no dowry was involved. I got cold feet when I saw my future husband, Anil Tiwari. My first reaction was to say "no."

Family elders prevailed on me to give this match a second thought. They were impressed by the boy's background. He had a small family. They said this was another point in his favor. The most important point in Anil's favor was his avowed disinterest in dowry. I could not go against my parent's wishes. I had no convincing argument why I did not want to marry the man. In the end, I agreed.

Father gave gold ornaments worth 15 *tolas*, plus 21 pairs of clothes, bedroom furniture, vessels for the kitchen. My in-laws went on saying, "We don't want anything."

After our wedding, I went away to live my in-laws' ancestral home in Satara. My husband, Anil lived with his parents. The house was a funny building with two floors. All the bedrooms were upstairs.

When we reached his home my husband's first instruction was to pay obeisance to his divorced sister. She lived with my in-laws. Anil said to me:

"If you care for me, care for my sister. Do not ever hurt her."

My sister-in-law Brinda, practically ruled the house.

Within few weeks of our marriage, Anil's mother complained loudly:

"Is this all your father has given you? We thought he would give much more. He has worked abroad and acquired a lot of wealth."

At Diwali season, she grumbled, " You father could give a gold chain at least to my son." Conditioned from childhood not to talk back to elders, I did not answer her back. My mother-in-law grumbled daily. Those were very difficult days for me. I was trying so hard to adjust in Anil's household. What seemed strange was

Anil's family did not want to leave the home. They never went out—nor did they have visitors. I found to be such a contradiction to a provincial small town lifestyle where neighbors freely mix and keep open house. Another instruction to me was not to speak to anyone. If a visitor by chance dropped in, I was asked to open the front door but vanish out of sight.

But when it came to post-office, or the bank work I was expected to do these outdoor chores.

Anil's first violent outburst was during our first trip to Bombay. We had gone to visit my parents. One day my brother Ravi was watching a television program. Anil wanted the TV set switched off. There was no argument, nor did my brother do anything to provoke. Anil just got up and slapped my brother. Mother was so upset, she told Anil never to come home again. Anil's resentment knew no bounds after this incident. He stopped visiting our home.

Anil retaliated by slapping me without any reason once we returned to Satara. I was by now pregnant. During my pregnancy I was abused more frequently. My father-in-law tried to intervene and protested to Anil. He was or seemed, kind to me. It was much later I got to know Anil's father used to sedate me. This was to keep me subdued. They had to make sure I did not cry or raise alarm. Because of the heavy dosage of sedation, my son got obstructive jaundice. When he was only four-and-a-half months old, the baby's health took a very serious turn.

A family friend was asked to take the baby and me in that precarious condition on the ordinary state transport bus to Bombay. Anil packed us off saying:

"Get *your* son treated in Bombay" He did not give me any money—nor did he accompany us.

At the time of my delivery the in-laws had sent me to Bombay. They said this was an Indian custom—daughters delivered their first born, in the natal home. On both occasions my parents bore the entire expense of delivery and treatment. Anil made a quick visit to see our new born son after a delivery. When the baby was ill, my husband did not come once.

My mother was naturally anxious about my future. Although no one at home knew about my ill-treatment, I think Mom was intuitive to sense that something was wrong. She took the initiative to send a family friend to counsel Anil.

As the child was recovering in Bombay, my mother-in-law passed away. She was frail in health and quite aged. Anil reacted to his mother's death in the most unexpected manner. I clearly remember my welcome treat after seven weeks of absence. Hardly had I stepped in with our weak baby son when Anil pounced on me.

He started beating me brutally the moment he laid his eyes on me. I was wearing a yellow sari that day. My chin split open in the beating. Blood streamed down, streaking the yellow sari red.

He burnt me all over with a cigarette butt. He put the butt on the bleeding chin. After this incident Anil locked me upstairs— the food was sent there. I was kept upstairs perhaps to hide the fact of brutality from maids who worked for them.

At first, I was indifferent to my ill-treatment. My concern was the pain my parents would suffer. Immediately after the first baby, I became pregnant. Anil ordered me to abort. He screamed at me:

"Your first son devoured my mother. The next child will eat up father. Get it out!"

I was pressured to abort against my wishes. What could I do alone in my in-law's house? If I did not obey, cruel punishments lay in wait.

In spite of the battery and other awesome pressures, I did not allow Anil to stop me seeking an outlet for economic freedom. He was shrewd enough to realize that he would benefit from my income. I was trained in cosmetics and beauty treatment. It was easy to open a small parlor. A beauty parlor was quite a novelty in Satara those days. Business was brisk. I made two hundred rupees daily. Every evening when I reached home, the cash was snatched from me by Brinda, Anil's sister. I could do nothing nor protest. My earnings were spent to get Anil's daily quota of liquor, cigarettes, *paan*. I had no control over my earnings. By 1985 Anil was drinking heavily. He lost interest in his teaching job. I suspect he was jealous of my parlor's success. The fact I made a good income may have given him a complex.

Anil's unfulfilled ambition of becoming rich and famous by writing films made matters worse. There was a brief respite from my every day ordeals when Anil was asked to write script for a small-time Bombay producer. I went with him for the meeting. Anil's

English was not as fluent as mine. That was the only reason for my being with him. Things did not turn out as planned. The film venture ended in a disaster. Anil got bitter and very frustrated.

Anil's frustration drove him to the bottle. He aspired to a lavish lifestyle—like Bombay film stars. A lifestyle his meager Professor's salary could not maintain. He wanted an imported car, air conditioner. He used to taunt me, "Why doesn't your father give me a foreign car, or an AC? Doesn't he think I am talented?"

The last three years of our marriage were a nightmare. Anil was rarely sober. He was demanding too much sex, unnatural sex. I was going out of my mind. The fact I was doing well at the parlor went against me.

The worse was yet to come. I discovered Anil had sold most of my gold ornaments during our absence with the ailing child. This fact was concealed from me for a long time. Even when I became aware of the loss, I could not confront Anil. A shudder still runs down my back speaking about the gruesome, degrading sexual torture Anil put me through.

Father had gifted us a VCR soon after the marriage. Anil kept the VCR in our bedroom. Every night he watched blue films. Some of the films were disgusting. He insisted I watch blue films with him. In one film a man has sex with a dog. He subjected me to these tortures. In the beginning, he would make our son sleep next to us while he made love. Today I realize it was to keep me silent.

Sarla mentioned one particularly difficult period when their son Sumit volunteered to sleep between his parents. She believes her son sensed something was wrong. This was Sumit's way of offering his mother support—by his physical presence. For Sarla—her son's physical proximity while Anil made love, at times unnatural sex, was the ultimate form of mental torture. She recalls one particularly cruel incident:

That night I was running a high temperature. Suddenly I was freezing cold and requested Anil to give me a blanket. No sooner had I said this, he ordered me to undress. There was such a threatening menace in his tone I had to obey him. Shivering with cold, I was forced to undress. Then he climbed over me, and made love. I remember him gloating triumphantly, 'Unless I make love to you when you are burning with 103 degrees temperature, I will not know how it feels to have sex with a woman in this condition!'

Very often he ordered me to walk naked into the kitchen and make tea. I was paralyzed by the shock of what he said or did—but I was afraid to disobey.

The last three years of my marriage were agonizingly painful. I realized if I lived with this fanatical man, my sanity was threatened. Desperate to escape I used to pray Anil would die some how. I prayed that his scooter should meet with a fatal accident. The very next moment I repented.

The final upshot came when Sumit was eleven years old. He had a serious streptococci infection. Treatment was delayed until he was critical. We rushed him to Bombay. My parents spent over Rs 15,000 for Sumit's treatment. Anil was absent all the while when our son lay suffering in a Bombay Hospital.

I nursed my son back to health with day and night care. For over seven weeks I was in Bombay. My parents stood by me. They were a source of tremendous support. I decided to own up to them about Anil's brutality. After listening to me, they said: Don't go back. Stay with us, after all this is your home. Foolishly I wanted to give my marriage another chance. I thought, my son needed his father. I went back for the Ganapati festival. My parents were scared something terrible would happen to me. When I returned, my husband accused me of being unfaithful. He cursed me for sleeping around with doctors when Sumit lay ill! His wild suspicion spared no one—he even said I was having relations with an uncle! Anil pestered me about this. He quizzed Sumit if I had met this uncle. We both said yes, we met him. Then he said: "Now you are coming out with the truth!" For half an hour after that, Anil spat on the floor. He asked me to get a mop, and clean his spit. He ran his fingers over the furniture, and ordered me to wipe it fifty times. I had to obey him.

I stayed for only five weeks more in my in-laws house. A sudden change in Sumit alarmed me. He was being pampered too much by Anil. Sumit was being treated to goodies, taken to wine shops and video parlors. Sumit was answering me back. He was behaving aggressive, demanding. My son began to resemble his father. One day my son asked me to buy him the He-man toy series. It was an expensive kit. I told him I couldn't afford to buy such an expensive toy. Immediately Sumit retorted: "when papa beats you, you give him hundred rupees. I am asking you nicely, you won't give me Heman!" I realized the awful harm abusive home environment was doing to a child. I was convinced what the child needed more was a healthy home and not an abusive father. He would grown up decently even fatherless. It was not easy for me to walk out from my husband's house. I made a call to Bombay. My family sensed trouble. A false telegram was sent to Satara saying: Mother ill come at once.

Anil did not stop me as he did not suspect I was leaving for good. I took a small bag—packed four or five clothes and caught the first train to Bombay. Everything father gave me—TV, VCR, Furniture—was left behind. I did not want to arouse Anil's suspicion. Once I came back—he has not bothered to come. I was told he is accusing me of many things, of cheating him.

Father-in-law came to negotiate my return. He tried to convince my parents that if I went back, he was ready to guarantee not a hair would be touched. Father gave a fitting reply: "Why didn't you stop your son earlier? My daughter will never go back. We do not want her to die."

Mother sounds cheerful about my future. She said, "How can we allow our daughter to suffer? We care for her. She is part of us."

Father gave me a one room flat. I live with Sumit there. My son has recurring nightmares about our life in Satara. Sometimes Sumit comes out with disturbing solutions. Once he said: 'Mummy why don't you hire goondas to murder papa?'

I know he is disturbed. Knowing my son's aversion, when access for the vacation was given to Anil, I appealed against the Family Court order. My son has been through untold mental torture. Why does the Court give his father an opportunity to manipulate my son? Anil is a bad model as a father for the boy. I don't want him to go back to that awful house. Sumit does not want to go with his father. That is why I have denied access—but the case is far from over. I know my husband will move against my appeal.

Postscript: Sarla's healing process and recovery from the trauma of a bizarre marriage was entirely due to her family's exceptional support. A support that is rare as it is exemplary. Her father, Mr Agarwal encouraged his younger daughter Vimla to make her own choice in marriage. Both the Agarwal sons have settled in the US Sarla and Sumit live with them.

Sarla's divorce proceedings had not concluded when we spoke. This frail, soft spoken woman displayed true grit. In her quiet but firm manner, Sarla challenged two powerful social structures—the family and the Judiciary. Her splendid stand against violence, in its countless ugly forms has transformed Sarla with new self-confidence.

SITA

SITA grew up in a small coastal village in the district of Ratnagiri (Maharashtra state). Lashed on one side by the raging ocean, the region is isolated from its neighboring towns during the fierce monsoon months. Sita's parents were farmers. Like thousands of Indian peasants they are victims of what economists call a cycle-of-poverty, the tragic process of descending lower in the social ladder by which farmers become sharecroppers, and are finally forced into exile as migrant labor in any of our urban metropolis.

At the crack of dawn Sita's parents leave to work in the rice field. When they leave, Sita takes charge of the household. One of her first chores is to sweep the court-yard in front of their home. After that she gives fresh fodder to the livestock before going with the clothes to the common well. Sita does not return home until the mid-day sun is up in the sky. The earth road seems to be on fire. She returns in time to roll out mid-day *bhakris* for her parents. At all times she keeps a watchful eye on her young brothers. One brother goes to school. Although education is made free, girls are inevitably pulled out. They are allowed to study for a year or two. Female children stay home in the rural community—supporting parents out at work. In this uninterrupted pattern of rural society it is considered a matter of great concern, in fact, a dishonor, should a girl remain unmarried on coming of age.

Sita had reached that tender age. Like girls in her community she did not decide her own fate or who to marry. Questions about her fate were decided by elder male members from the community. The elders ask a professional matchmaker to find a groom for Sita. This was how marriages have always been arranged.

A man who is reasonably sound of mind, able bodied, owns a hut, a piece of farmland, and some livestock is considered an excellent match. Tukaram was found exceedingly suitable for

Sita. That he was a widower, with a grown up daughter and three times Sita's age, was not a matter of concern in the negotiations.

Once the marriage was negotiated, the village priest announced an auspicious date for the marriage. Traditional wedding items such as bride's nine-yard wedding saree, two extra pairs of clothing, copper utensils, a mattress, a gold ring for the groom, if possible a cycle and suit-length, are soon purchased from the local market. Without these, no wedding is solemnized. On the wedding day, Tukaram came with members of his family. During the ceremony, he puts the black-beaded *mangalsutra* around Sita's slim neck. She was now accepted by the community as his lawful wife.

Sita's final departure from her family home is tinged with sorrow—like that of all Indian daughters. Women of the village weep aloud. Men stand silently on one side. Sita's brother Bhikhu, the family official, accompanies her to the new home. From that moment until her death, Sita has no other home in heaven or earth, but that of her husband's. The doors to her childhood home are shut to her forever.

It is not long before Sita realized her husband Tukaram—whose name she is forbidden to utter—does not work. If he went out of the hut, it was only for a drink. Sita's wifely duty was to wait, serve her husband hot food, tend to his needs, eat and sleep after him. Tukaram always came back violently abusive after his drinking bouts. He called Sita names like "prostitute" and "whore". He was extremely possessive about his pretty, young wife.

Sita said she remembered Tukaram used to fly into a violent rage if she dressed in clean clothes. She says:

My husband was suspicious by nature. If I wore clean clothes, he accused me. From my childhood I applied Kohl to line my eyes. I put flowers in my hair. But he shouted at me saying: are you going to the pictures? Are you going to visit a man? Why are you wearing that nice blouse, the new saree? I was upset when he called me the bad names—I am not a woman like that. But what could I do? He is my husband after all—I could not answer him back. I could tolerate his beating me. But I used to cry when he called me those bad names and suspect my character.

Within a year of marriage, Tukaram migrated to the Bombay city with Sita and his daughter Vasanti. In the cloth bundle they brought a few essentials to start life in the city. At first the couple shared a hut with another family from their village. Quarrels broke out over small things daily. Sita, meanwhile, lost no time in locating a dry spot where they could build their own home. Resourceful as ever, Sita collected bamboo, canvas, old cement sheets. Soon their own hut was ready. It was close to one of Bombay's busy building sites. In fact, there was plenty of work around on the site. She recalls:

I began to work as a building laborer on the construction site. The money was quite good. I earned between 15 to 18 rupees per day. My husband was given the work of a watchman. He worked only for a week before the drinking devil took him. He was out of job in no time. After two months of work on the site I conceived my child. I continued to work. Vasanti—my step daughter, found work as a domestic in a lady's home nearby. Between us we managed to run the home. But every day, my heart beat loud—if I was seen talking to a man, or was late by even few seconds, my husband beat me. He was always suspicious that I was going out with other man.

Sita did not express anger or bitterness against her husband. Tukaram beat her almost daily, at times, brutally. She said this was her fate as a woman. That it is written in her hand. For her the security of marriage, and the fact there was a husband living, was more than the security of house or bank balance. The thought of living alone, husbandless, frightened Sita.

"For a woman it is a big thing to be married and have a husband", Sita emphasized. The morning her labor pains started, Tukaram was no where in sight. It was not the first time he was missing. Neighbors admitted Sita to the hospital. She delivered a girl that noon. Sita was hurt her husband did not come to see her at the hospital. She says:

My husband did not visit me at the hospital. I paid for medicine and all other costs. In three days I went back home. Vasanti helped me with the baby—she went to work regularly. At that time, she was the only one earning because I was home. I saw very little of my husband. If he came, it was to beat me or forcibly take away any money. We tried to hide the money—he broke things in anger, and said he would burn the hut, or burn me. So we had to give him the money.

At that difficult time of their life, Sita and Vasanti went without meals—as there was not enough money. When kindly neighbors found out, they gave them leftover crumbs. Sita resumed work when the baby was only two months old. Add to the burden of a new born infant—was Sita's growing anxiety for her step daughter, Vasanti, who was old enough for marriage. She says:

When I joined work on the construction site, my husband began following me. He was an extremely jealous man. He hung out near the building. If I talked to any man, I would be beaten on the street. The harassment got so bad that I decided to quit this job. I thought if I worked in a home as a domestic servant, my husband might stop suspecting. I was lucky to get work in a lady's home who lived in the same area. My salary was much less—but she gave me lunch. This lady liked me to dress neatly.

If I wore a torn *saree*, the *memsaab* complained. At home, I used to hide a *saree* in my cloth bag, and change in my *memsaab's* house. If I got even ten minutes late, my heart beat fast.

I was scared he would come from any side and begin beating me.

Thinking it was about time to get Vasanti married, Sita began looking for a suitable groom. During this time there was one serious incident.

I was sitting in the hut one night, breastfeeding my baby. My husband came in, so drunk, he could not walk. He accused me of "getting too smart". He called me names, said that I was going out with men, sleeping around. I was quiet as a mouse. If I moved, or looked at him, he would start slapping me at once. He continued to abuse me, then he said: "I will burn you alive, just now".

I thought, he always says these things, what will he do? He is too drunk. But he took the kerosene tin. Poured it over me, when he was about to strike a match—neighbors rushed in. I did not try to save my life. I kept thinking, it is better to die, than live like this—I did not want to live.

After the attempted murder, neighbors advised Sita to lodge a police complain. She was reluctant:

How could I take such a big step against my husband? But my neighbors insisted. I took the baby and Vasanti to the Kurla police station. They took down my complains. My husband was taken to jail. They kept him in the lockup. He did not come home for weeks.

We lived in fear he would come back and kill us. We could hardly eat or sleep with fear. The same neighbors who asked us to lodge police complaints said, "Look at them, they are nicely eating as if nothing happened! When the poor husband is in jail."

These neighborly taunts hurt Sita—she felt guilty going to the police against her husband. However, when Tukaram returned—things were quiet for a few days. Then the beatings began—he broke Sita's left wrist in one incident. His attacks were now directed against Vasanti. Afraid Tukaram would seriously molest Vasanti—break her arm or limb—Sita hastened Vasanti's marriage.

After the wedding, Sita was alone. She said:

I thought my husband's beatings would stop some day, but they grew worse. I was too depressed to eat. At times I went to work after days of starvation. When the *memsaab* found me weak, she forced me to eat food.

I used to get depressed at work. One day the *memsaab* asked me the reason. I told her everything about my husband, how he ill treated me, and one day he nearly killed me. She was concerned for me. *Memsaab* knew people who help women like me. She sent me with a lady to the Special Cell for women. I was scared thinking what if my husband found out. He would kill me there and then. Every time I went to the Cell, and met the social worker, somebody had to come with me as I do not know the city roads.

Repeated visits to the Social worker resulted in raising Sita's confidence. For a long time she was optimistic, her husband Tukaram would reform. But during the counselling period, there were several incidents to prove her wrong. It was obvious Tukaram would not stop beating Sita—that sooner or later, he would assault his little daughter. It was this fear that drove Sita out of her mind.

Finally she decided to make a clean break. With the help of the Special Cell social workers, Sita found a new job. She was offered a 24-hour job as a domestic maid with a young doctor couple living far away from her old home. With the job, Sita walked out quietly. Her troubles were far from over. Tukaram forcibly kept their 3 year old daughter Sushila. He thought this will force Sita to return to him.

Sita was determined nothing would lead her back to a life of abuse and humiliation. She displayed great courage at this stage. Intervention from the special cell social workers, brought Tukaram to the negotiation table. He felt intimidated and tried to manipulate his way. Finally Sushila was taken aside and asked who she wished to live with. The girl simply said: "My mother."

Her daughter's statement was a moment of joy and triumph for Sita. It was an answer to Sita's prayers. She wanted her daughter to live a good life. Sita did not want a divorce nor legal separation. She knew that would give Tukaram another chance to fight for Sushila's custody.

She is happy at her new home, with her new job:

I may not earn as much as I did before. My employers are very good to me. They allow me to keep my child—send her to play school. I am no longer afraid—I can eat in peace, sleep without fear. I am a stupid village woman. I cannot read and write. That is why I suffered so much. Educated woman do not suffer like me. I want my daughter to be educated. She will study as much as she wants. She may be a doctor or a teacher—who knows. I don't want her to marry young, like me. She must not suffer my fate. If by misfortune she has a bad marriage, my daughter can at least stand on her own feet. She will be educated.

Sita's dreams to educate her daughter Sushila is supported by her determination to move away from Tukaram's tyranny.

Sita is not unique in her struggle against violence—there are many like her, coming from similar circumstances. They can survive—if they receive support like Sita got from her employers and the Special Cell. More importantly, it is Sita's grit and determination to live with dignity. Today the kohl—lined eyes of this illiterate village woman from Ratnagiri shine with a quiet pride.

TINA

Vivid childhood memories persistently haunt Tina. It is as though the nightmares happened yesterday. Tina was 6 years old when her parents separated she recalls:

"I remember so many things from our childhood ... some of those images have become sharper with age. There was one particularly dreadful incident immediately after we moved in with our maternal grandmother in Lucknow. This incident was going to change the entire course of our lives. My parents were by then separated. Father would come to visit us frequently. Dashing and handsome, father was an extremely charming person. None of us realized he had a violent temper, until that day.

We four kids looked forward to father's visits with great anticipation! He always brought us lovely gift—toys, sweets, cakes, jujubes, ice cream. That evening too he brought us loads of things. Suddenly his smiling visage became contorted with rage. Out of the blue, he began hitting mom viciously. Granny rushed to stop him. Father's heavy fists hit granny. The impact of his massive blows sent both mother and granny reeling on the polished mosaic floor. We children watched petrified. Afraid to move or even cry, we held our breath. I had seen nothing like this before...."

The following weekend, Tina and her brother Chris, the older two of the four Andrews children, went to visit their father, Mr Andrew in his large garden bungalow. Weekend visitation right had been granted to Mr Andrews. His two children played happily on the lush green lawns of their father's house. He sat with his lawyer in a wicker chair, close by. By sheer accident, Tina overheard snatches of her father's conversation. She says:

"Hearing the words, 'shoot her' I climbed on father's lap. I did not want to miss a single word. Being so tiny, just 6 years old, no one noticed my presence. Papa and the lawyer continued talking. I heard the lawyer say: 'shoot her.' He repeated this aloud: 'Take a gun and shoot her', urged the lawyer to my father. I knew by *her* they could only mean mother. Father had a firearm's license. He possessed an armory at home. He owned guns, revolvers, rifles of all sizes and shapes. I knew the threat to mother was real. After that weekend visit, I returned to Granny's with a sense of doom about what could happen next! Having witnessed Papa's rage the other evening I knew he was capable of doing terrible things!"

Quite soon after their weekend visit, Mr Andrews went to see his children. Tina has not forgotten that visit of her father:

"One glance at Dad and I fled screaming inside the house. I dragged Chris and our two little sisters under Granny's massive four poster bed. We hid under the bed, waiting for something awful to happen. Nothing happened, of course. But I was sure Dad intended to kill mom sooner or later. The suspense was unbearable. I believed quite sincerely that I could prevent mother's death by keeping a close vigil on father. I shadowed him all the while, stuck to him—not letting Dad out of sight as long as mother was in India. To my great relief, mom finally sailed for the US but at age 6, I had taken a conscious decision to stay back with father in India. If he harbored any murderous plans, I would make sure he failed to carry it out! This is the story of how 6 year old me was separated from my beloved mother!"

Mrs Jane Andrew's, in other words, Tina's mother, resettled permanently in America. She remarried after a gap of few years. The mother–daughter bond was sustained through regular exchange of letters. Meanwhile Tina's education continued uninterrupted. She studied in various convent schools. Influenced greatly by the serene spiritual atmosphere in convents, Tina's life took an unexpected, new direction. By the time she completed Senior Cambridge, Tina had converted into the Roman Catholic faith. She did not wish to continue higher education. Instead, after her Cambridge exam, Tina joined the nun's order—upsetting both her parents who followed the Protestant faith. She recalls:

"During an excursion with the Convent Nuns, I had gone out of town, and fractured an ankle. As a result of this I was laid up for many days in the convent nursing room. My general condition worsened. The Nuns, anxious about me, called Dad. As I feared, Dad bundled me back home with him. I left the Nunnery, gave up my habit, never to return."

The last thing Mr Andrews wanted was to see his daughter wear a Nun's colorless habit! Tina was the only family he had. They were extremely close to each other. More over, Andrews had retired from the services a reasonably wealthy man. He had a villa in the Country, surrounded by acres of grape orchards and farmland. In true Brown sahib country style, Tina's father enjoyed the luxury of his well-appointed hill-station home. The Andrews home was in the vicinity of a popular wildlife game sanctuary. Andrews, a veteran *shikari* himself, had the reputation of being a gracious host. Visitors from all over India enjoyed his expansive hospitality. Tina helped her father entertain his guests. This is how the D'Silvas, on a game hunting spree in the hills, met the Andrews. She says:

"Frankly, I remember little about Paul D'Silva who was destined to be my husband, from our first meeting. The local Parish Priest however made a point to mention that the D'Silvas were an influential family of Lucknow. At that time, I was too excited about my long pending US trip. Dad had promised me that I could visit mother! He even offered to pay for my return passage. Mom was keen that we meet, before I made plans for my future.

You can imagine tumultuous emotions rocking me! Reuniting with mother after so many years proved an intense emotional experience for me. I was both nervous, at the same time over-joyed. Both of us, mom and me felt extremely vulnerable at that point. Mom confessed to me later, that she too had suffered similar pangs of anxiety about meeting me. She was waiting to receive me at the airport. We hugged one another and burst into tears! The wall of painful separation melted away like magic."

Tina spent almost an entire year with her mother's new family in the US. Her stepfather, Robert Murphy and children from two previous marriages got on well with Tina. But Tina had to return home, sooner or later. She had not decided the next course her life—but India was where she belonged. Landing in India at Palam air port, Tina was a little taken aback. Waiting to receive her was her father, and Paul D'Silva. Tina and Paul exchanged formalities in the presence of her father. It was not the right moment to know Paul. The father and daughter left for their hill-station estate. Paul went back to Lucknow. She recalls:

"On my return from US, I turned 20. Being secure under father's protective wing I did not have to fend for myself. Born with a silver spoon in my mouth, every luxury and comfort in the world was at my disposal. I lived the life of a princess!

Dad was an old fashioned country gentleman. He hated the idea of women working. I knew, he would not agree to let me, his beloved daughter, go out of his sight. I might as well forget about working. But every passing day made me more restless. My trip to America had opened a new vista before me. After a great deal of coaxing father allowed me to take up a teaching assignment in the town's Missionary school. When the school shut for a week of Easter vacation, I traveled down to Lucknow city to shop. Someone casually mentioned there was a vacancy in a reputed Lucknow girl's school. The prospect sounded attractive. But I was assailed by doubts about father's reaction if I had to leave home and work. Once again, Dad gave in to my wishes, after several rounds of argument and persuasion. I was fortunate to get the job. The next move found me in Lucknow city. I took up a room in the same school hostel. The school was situated in the very neighborhood where granny once lived. My roommate was a girl called Mary. By a strange coincident she met Paul at a local function. It seems the two exchanged notes about me. Next day I received a phone call at work:

'Guess who is speaking?' Asked the man at the other end.

'I don't play guessing games,' was my rude reply!

That same evening, Paul came to meet me at the hostel. He behaved as though we were old friends. I was not uncomfortable by his show of familiarity. But when he proposed marriage in less than a week, I confronted him saying that I knew he was seeing a girl from his own community. And he should not come back to me on rebound."

Paul assured Tina he had broken up with his girl friend and the earlier relationship was behind him. Tina was uncertain about Paul's marriage proposal. Her father's letters in the meanwhile urged her to settle down, to marry. In one of these letters he even threatened: 'I have received several marriage proposals for your hand. They are from decent families. If you have no one in mind, I will accept one of those very soon. Do not blame me later!' Tina continues

"After Dad's last letter, I began to think more seriously about Paul's proposal. Rather than marry a complete stranger, I may as well accept Paul. At least he was not a stranger in that sense. Allow me to add, I was not in love with Paul."

Tina hoped the engagement period would give her space to think about her future with Paul. This was not to be. Paul's grandfather lay on his deathbed. The D'Silvas wanted Paul's wedding to take place before the old man passed away. She says:

"Father spared nothing for me. He gave us a lavish marriage. D'Silva family members were put up in the hill-station's most expensive hotel. Wine and spirits overflowed for days on end. And the wedding feasts were worth a king's ransom."

Mr Andrews gave a fabulous trousseau to Tina. Carved rose-wood antique furniture, household effects from fridge to kitchen appliances, priceless family heirlooms, ornaments, and clothes. Sadly for Tina, her mother could not fly down for the wedding. But she sent her daughter's exquisite designer wedding gown from New York. Tina says:

"For the wedding, Paul's parents gave me exactly four hundred rupees to buy two sarees saying this was an old family custom."

If her in-laws' meager wedding gift was a rude surprise, more culture shocks awaited the newly weds on their arrival at the

D'Silva's Lucknow home. Paul lived in a joint family with his parents. Tina was shocked to find the bridal chamber in disarray. A state of chaos everywhere was evident all over. Paul's house was a far cry from the picture perfect image Tina had painted in her mind. Many unpleasant family skeletons began to pop out. It was apparent that Paul and his father did not see eye to eye. The other two D'Silva sons did not go to work. They lived off their ancestral property. One brother had become a drug addict, the second, an alcoholic. What struck Tina as truly appalling was the ill-treatment meted out to her elderly mother-in-law. She remembers:

"Every time my poor mom-in-law was abused, I would protest. The fact I took her side resulted in alienating me from the rest of the family. I began to be harassed over food, over every day things. I asked Paul to intervene, but he gave me a lame excuse, that he would not speak against his family."

For several months after her marriage Tina continued to teach in the school. Early pregnancy put a full stop to her job. As long as she worked, her pay packet went into Paul's pocket. Tina gave the salary to Paul without thinking about it twice. She believed it to be her wifely duty. It was during Paul's serious appendix attack that Tina woke up to the fact that her in-laws' family were not concerned about Paul's welfare:

"Paul suddenly collapsed on the road when his appendix burst. I rushed him to the hospital and called my in-laws. No one seemed to bother about the matter. Seven months pregnant with my first baby, I nursed Paul alone without support from his family.

My in-laws showed up only during visiting hours at the hospital. They would leave immediately it was time to leave. I understood they did not care about Paul—how could they care for me, when their own son was badly neglected?"

The couple stayed with Paul's family for a couple of years. A second child followed the first. Tied down with two infants, Tina had no choice but quit her job. The couple was so hard up at the time that Tina often diluted baby milk with water:

"Paul never gave me a fixed household amount to run the home. If I asked for funds, he said he would give it later, or simply admit he could not afford it. Father bailed me out financially several times. I sold pickles, jams, to tide over our crises. While the children's milk had to be watered down—the D'Silvas kept up false social façade by throwing lavish parties to gain political mileage. They had to prove they were rich and influential."

Trying to cope with physical and financial discomforts, Tina remained optimistic her marriage could survive. However, there was one condition, that Paul take a separate flat. But Paul was reluctant to leave the family nest and get his own place. He put it off with one pretexts or another:

"One day, my husband asked me to pack our travel bags for father's home. Paul assured me, he will send for us soon. I stayed with Dad for 11 months! In the 12th month, a cousin of Paul's showed up to fetch us back. My son had missed a whole year of school. Living with my in-laws the children's life was badly disturbed. They never ate or slept on time."

In Tina's absence Paul had moved in with a bachelor uncle. Paul's bachelor uncle Joe was obviously a lonely man. He invited Paul and his family to take up residence in his large cottage. Uncle Joe lived down the road, few blocks away from the D'Silva's ancestral home. In the same compound lived the childless Uncle Tom and Aunt Maria. The latter had serious differences with Paul's father over their joint property.

Apart from a change of residence, Tina found no significant change in Paul's attitude to his own family. In fact, he had become more indifferent, even uncaring. A sense of acute loneliness cast a shadow over Tina's family life:

"I tolerated Paul coming home late. I spent those long hours waiting like a husband-worshipping Indian wife. I was playing the role of a good wife. What I could not put up with was Paul's blatant display of love. One day he met an ex-girlfriend. In front of everyone, Paul kissed her passionately on the mouth. This upset me very much. But Paul laughed on my face, he called me old fashioned. I began questioning myself, is this marriage? Is this family life? I was extremely unhappy at the way things had turned out. But I prayed daily for it to sort out."

During the same period Paul and Tina were in acute financial difficulty, the D'Silva brothers fell out with one another. Their quarrel was over property ownership. Tina's son, Robin was the only male and thus the sole legal heir. Robin was going to inherit the vast ancestral D'Silva property. Uncle Tom and his wife Maria, the childless couple, lived right behind Tina and Paul. They were insanely jealous about Paul's son enjoying this property. Had it been Paul, their nephew who inherited, they did not mind it. The fact, Robin, the son of an outsider—as they viewed Tina—who was the sole heir, to own the D'Silva estate, made the couple blind with rage. Driven out of his mind by frustration, Uncle Tom tried to knife Robin. The boy escaped by the skin of his teeth. This attempted murder of her son, so shattered Tina that she took to bed:

"It was well known that the D'Silva men were involved in violent and brutal property dealings. They murdered people for property. I knew they would attack Robin again. I could not eat or sleep out of fright. We lodged police complaints. Robin was escorted to school. My only prayer was to move away from that house. I wanted to send Robin to a boarding school. The tension played havoc with my health. I developed a heart ailment after the knifing incident and was bedridden for nearly a month.

By the time Dad arrived from the hill-station Paul lodged criminal charges against his uncle. There was tremendous pressure to hush up the whole thing. Paul told Dad, I was feigning illness. Making up stories!"

Mr Andrews took Tina back with him. She recovered after a few weeks rest in the bracing hill-station climate. Her father's tender care helped heal emotional wounds.

Fortunately for Tina, her father's influence was useful to admit Robin in a boarding school. His admission was a tremendous relief to Tina. She returned to Lucknow with new determination. Tina was now adamant about Paul finding a separate flat for his family. As was his old habit, Mr Andrews sent expensive gifts for Paul.

"Paul never stopped boasting to his family about my father's generous gifts. He used to say my pa-in-law gave me no dowry but he sends expensive gifts. That is why I send my wife to visit him! When he wanted to buy a car, I gave him money from my fixed deposit. Another time, he was short of cash, I pawned my gold chain."

Tina's firm determination to make Paul shift to a separate flat failed. Real estate price had doubled. Paul was content to live in Uncle Joe's small flat. The threat to his son's life from Uncle Tom next door was conveniently ignored.

By the end of 12 years, communication between Tina and Paul had completely broken down. Whatever Tina did, Paul dismissed as a fuss. Tina stopped eating beef for health reasons. The only meat Paul brought home was beef! At times Tina had no food. The couple stopped talking. As a last ditch effort Tina called a local parish priests for marriage counseling. This boomeranged. The mental torture was so intense that Tina moved into the children's room. She recalls:

"When I moved to my children's bed room, it was deemed an act of open defiance on my part. Paul spread rumors about me. He called me cold, frigid. He accused me of having affairs. This earned him instant sympathy from the family. I suspect every one believed Paul. When I went to church, icy glares greeted me. Not happy spreading rumors in Lucknow—Paul complained about me to Dad. I got angry letters from Dad—admonishing me to be a good wife. Paul taunted me all the time: "I will turn you on the street. I will close my doors to you." When I most needed my father's support—he turned bitterly against me. The only person who kept up my spirits was mother. She called me long distance from New York. When things deteriorated further, mom flew down. She advised me to find out the legal options."

One evening, Tina was surprised to find the D'Silva family assembled in Uncle Joe's parlor. Their Parish priest joined the group. The little group scene seemed rehearsed. Paul stood near his room. Daughter Polly, sat on her grandfather's lap. No one spoke to Tina. Anger, accusation and suspicion were writ large in their eyes. They gave Tina the cold and silent treatment for a long time. Tina was about to retire into the children's room, when the Priest stepped in front and addressed her in these words:

"I am the God's Shepard and I am saying, your place is next to your husband." The message to Tina was clear: Return to your husband's bed. She says:

"I was shocked by Father John's order. He was aware about my ill-treatment. I had consulted him several times to seek guidance. And there he was ordering, I sleep with Paul? That it was my duty to be in my husband's bed? I tried to argue with him. No one wanted to listen. It looked as though my marriage would work the moment I slept on Paul's bed. I was feeling exhausted and degraded. The only way I could save the situation was use Polly as a human shield. I insisted she sleep with me. Paul vehemently objected to this. His family urged him to control me. But I was stubborn. I passed the night in great fear. We could hardly sleep."

After the intervention, Tina lodged a complaint in their Parish against Father John. She was bold enough to openly question the powerful Church lobby and its authority to force a woman into a dangerous and violent situation.

Tina involved members of a women's NGO. Women activists supported her stand. They objected to the Priest's intervention saying the Church had no authority to oppress women or precipitate a violent situation. Tina's actions were like flying red flags before the angry D'Silva family. NGO members faced hostile opposition on their home visit to Tina. Paul's family believed themselves to be all powerful, and above the law.

When these agitations were being staged, Paul dragged Tina into his room one night. She tried hard to resist, getting hurt in the struggle. Polly was sent away for the night to Paul's parents' home. Tina bolted the door from inside. Paul begged Tina to open the door. But she was determined not to compromise to violence.

As Tina stepped out of her room next morning, Paul yanked her by the hair. Her head was banged on the wall several times. Tina was seriously injured. Her friends admitted Tina in the missionary hospital. The day she was to be discharged, Tina was visibly nervous. Two Social workers had to escort her home.

When Tina reached Uncle Joe's place, Paul was not present. The social workers placed a letter recording Tina's condition.

Uncle Joe signed it. The publicity Tina gave her case, was not only condemned by her own community, it made the D'Silvas desperate for revenge. Uncle Joe, who allowed Tina a free run of his house for years, turned hostile at this juncture:

"Uncle Joe dictated me what to do. He put down limits saying you can go here, not there, do this not that!! All the time he said it IS MY house. They cut off the telephone, which was my life line. But what Paul and his family did to the children was truly demonic. Polly was pampered by excessive attention, expensive gifts. She turned hostile to me. Robin was more mature. He refused to take sides. Due to this Paul targeted his son, Robin.

I filed for child maintenance—Paul contested it. He said he was unable to pay for his son's expensive boarding school education. I appealed against Paul's reply. The judge granted me a favorable order. Paul was asked to sell off his VCR, his television to pay for Robin's education. Paul contested this too. I had to take a job as a teacher in an orphanage. My earning was spent for Robin's tuition. But I was ready to do anything and keep Robin away from that evil house."

The last, most painful phase of her struggle was during the court case. She had prayed for an injunction. The court granted this. Paul and his family–including Uncle Joe in whose house they lived, were ousted from entering Tina's room.

Tina locked the room when she was out at work. Each time the court granted a favorable order to Tina, conditions at home grew more inhuman. She was intimidated on the smallest pretext. It was like crossing into enemy lines every day. Food stopped. Confused by these events, Polly failed her exams. Tina says:

"I was a helpless witness to my daughter's dramatic change. From a loving child, she had turned hostile. She abused me verbally. As a devout Christian, I constantly prayed to God. I knew he was my only answer. Meanwhile I was running around like mad for court work. Drafting applications, meeting lawyers, attending court hearings.

I was exhausted. Once Uncle Joe locked me up home. Neighbors called a friend. Just as the police were to be called, Joe opened the front door. Paul and his family had bribed the police.

They are a socially powerful family with political contacts. The church and police were prejudiced against me. However, one Parish Priest was sensitive to me. They maligned this Priest. Had him transferred to a remote Parish.

I realized I could not go on. Finally Paul left Uncle Joe's place. He went back to his parents. This was a calculated move on his part. I was left alone in his relative's home. But it was no longer my matrimonial home—since my husband did not reside there."

For over two years Tina survived in that volatile, inhuman atmosphere. By the end of which, she was reduced to a bag of bones. Her positive spirit never deserted Tina. She knew her sanity was bound to snap very soon. Taking the first opportunity, Tina left for the hill-station with Polly. She intended to seek her father's support. But Andrews had turned totally against Tina's separation. He remembered his own case and sympathized with Paul. Tina did not give up easily. She had a cottage from her father. This was her only hope. Although Mr Andrews rented it out, Tina appealed to him:

"I begged Dad to give me back the cottage he had kept in my name. But he was so angry with me that he said: first withdraw all your charges against Paul, after that I will consider it. I know this is not father's intention. I stuck to my point. Finally Dad agreed my children could spend their holidays with him. At least they had a home."

Tina took two important decisions at this stage. One was to admit Polly in the same boarding school as her brother Robin. Second, to secure a teaching job in a hill-station Convent. Her earthly belongings, clothes, furniture, jewelry, remained at Uncle Joe's home.

Tina's faith in the power of prayer grew from strength to strength. She offered God prayers in a number of ways. Tina did not forget the few friends who supported her in this lonely struggle against cruelty, oppression, and injustice. She says:

"My only prayer was to take the children away from that house of evil. The kids are innocent. Why punish them? I remain ever grateful to God, I could achieve this. That is all I had prayed for. The rest is God's mercy."

Postscript: When Tina was granted Judicial separation on grounds of physical and mental cruelty, her father gifted her a strange Christmas present. He shut his doors to her. Tina and the children had no home. Their only shelter was the school where she taught.

Unlike the other women's stories, Tina's story has a rather novel ending. Left without his wife, his children, Paul discovered Tina's true worth. He was full of remorse for his misbehavior. Paul asked Tina to forgive him. Tina and the children returned home. The best part of this happy ending was when Paul and Tina built a home for themselves in South Goa.

Tina devotes her time to Parish work. And even Paul has found a job.

ULKA

We lived in the slums near the railway tracks. Father worked in a plastic factory. Mother was an illiterate woman. She was black like a *jamun* berry. She was not at all pretty. Our relatives used to say of my mother:

"This plain girl is too dark. She will never get a groom in the whole wide world!"

When another relative was getting married, they decided to marry father to mother. They were only 5 and 10 years old. My parents are actually cousins. But in our community this is a common custom. Father's sister's son can be married off to brother's daughter.

I am the eldest in our large family of three girls and four boys. We sisters were sent to a free municipal school. Our brothers went to English medium school. This is the kind of culture we have. Father is good in front of outsiders. To mother, he is a big bully and the boss. He expects her to stay in the kitchen, and only bear children. Some how, I was different from the rest. May be, I was a rebel. When we were young, the *Seva Dal* came to our area. They wanted to construct a park for local children. Whenever I went to play in the park, I was beaten up. I still went out to play, and when I returned home, got beaten up! I studied and managed to pass the exam. If I got second or third rank, I cried. I was a smart kid. When I reached the seventh standard, my parents wanted me to get married. My teachers came home with my municipal school principal. They said to Dad, "Allow the girl to study till high school. She is smart at studies."

When the principle said this I felt confident, I could do something with my life. After the visit, Father sent me back to study. I started giving tuition to our neighbor's children. I charged only Rs five. Every month I earned Rs 20. I gave most of the money to mother—keeping a small change.

As I said, I began to earn from a young age. Whenever I visited other friends' home, saw their family life, I realized with shock, that my parents had given us very little, except feeding us. Take the husband–wife relation for instance—the way they behaved with their children—was so different. I used to compare our lives and become sad at the way we lived.

In the tenth standard I made a very good friend, called Lata. She was close to my heart. Whenever she visited me, she held her nose tight and jumped over the sewage to enter our house. Lata always said:

"Ulka, you can't live here!"

Lata went home and told her father about us:

"You are building many flats. You have got to give one to Ulka."

So one day Lata's father visited us. He saw our condition with his own eyes. After that he met Daddy and offered him a flat:

"You can have a flat in our block and repay the loan slowly."

That's how we got a flat in the housing board. Father put some money. Mother sold most of her ornaments. We were fed up with life in the slums living in only a single room with so many of us.

This flat was a big leap forward for us. It was too good to be true. We now had two bedrooms—a kitchen, a verandah. Again I felt, if we try hard, we can rise higher in society.

About this time, I began menstruating. My parents said:

"She *has* to be married now."

After my parents said this I threatened to leave home. And I really ran away to friends. After two days father came to take me back.

"O.K. we will not force you to *marry*," he promised.

Mother, father, at times even granny pressurized me. Granny was the least difficult one of my family. She understood me. Granny always took my side and told my father:

"Let her study. She is a smart one. So many girls study these days. She earns like a boy too."

If you ask my personal feelings it is granny who loved me most. She had suffered. She understood and supported me. After this incident, I began going out with groups like *Seva Dal*, *Chatra Andolan*—and others. In search of knowledge and to find out what I wanted with life. But I could see women were manipulated in these groups.

People used to join *Seva Dal* to find marriage partners. I did not like this idea. Soon, I stopped going. I began looking for a group where I could do projects. This work kept me out in the evenings. Father objected to my going out late.

I argued with him, "I go as I am, in my home clothes, I don't dress up,"—Daddy would not listen. Finally, I stopped. I felt economic independence was my strongest need. I started to give more tuitions. I earned Rs 250 and gave it to mother for food. Father's pay went to repay house loan. I took up three small jobs, at a typewriting institute, and in a telephone exchange. My income rose to Rs 800. This convinced me, I was capable of doing it.

Next I joined a local college. I studied only for a year. One day, a girl was abducted from our college. This incident scared us out of our wits. Finally one of daddy's friends convinced him to send me to a co-ed college in South Bombay.

"So many girls go to study in Bombay why not send Ulka?" Dad's friend argued. He won the argument. I was sent to a city college. Simultaneously I earned a tidy amount. All this before I was 18 years old! I had to fake a certificate, saying I was over 18 years to get jobs. I did it. My work was a great security for me. At home I created an impression that no one could pressure me for anything.

"Now you can't force me—if you do, I will leave home." This was my stand.

In 1982 my younger sister was going to get married. She was not like me—a born rebel. But I was happy for her sake and told her:

"Look Uma, my idea of a marriage is different. I refuse to marry for security or to produce children. I am not traditional in that sense. I will marry when I find a man I want to live with."

Granny was happy hearing me talk like that. She had suffered as a young woman. Though mother had suffered, she did not agree with my ideas of marriage. I think mom was also a little jealous. She had not enjoyed life with my father. Also, her fear was, whatever I did would backfire on father's reputation.

I had completed three years college by then. It was about this time that I met a man and fell in love with. We had met in the Club House. I had not gone out with him alone as we moved in groups. I grew to love this man intensely. It was platonic from my side at first. I thought if we gave more time to each other, he would change. He used to say:

"Don't get too involved with me—marriage is out of question." And my answer was, "One changes—it is possible you will change and think otherwise."

But he stuck to his argument, "Don't get involved with me."

And foolishly enough, I continued to hope, to believe in change. I had faith in the man and in myself. I kept a diary those days. I still remember writing one night: my friend refuses to marry. I am trying; trying hard to make him understand.

Emotionally I was deeply involved with my friend. I felt here was a man with whom I can grow. That we would both grow. The comfort you get in companionship, I gave him. He agreed I was good for him. He still maintains that.

He thought all girls in activist movement are out for fun and have no ethics, no moral scruples. This has been our constant quarrel for the last three years.

I argued with him: "Don't talk like that to me! In fact, you have no morals. You can have a relationship with a woman without making any commitments! That is not ethical."

All through our relationships, he was comfortable with me, but not interested in making a serious commitment. He made love, without wanting to commit. He was not ready to stake anything, as I was. I had put everything into our relationship.

When my father found out that my male friend was refusing to marry me, he said: "This is what the world is like Ulka! Marry for our sake. We will find a suitable match."

This was a stressful period for me with endless arguments without any answers. I began to think, love was a myth. Marriage for me was like a journey together. I was not ready to make emotional commitment into a relation without love. At least that would spare me the suffering, I thought. I said this to my father who was insistent. I had turned 24. With a final deposit paid for my room, I could move with a cooking stove and other things and be on my own. I continued to reject proposals my father got. Mother threatened to commit suicide if I did not marry that year—it was an effective emotional blackmail. Curiously, one man kept sending proposals again, and again. I did not understand his reasons for doing this. Finally, I succumbed to pressures. I was weary and wanted to end the mental anguish.

The day after our wedding, a friend of my husband congratulated him for winning the bet! It seems my husband had declared he would not rest till he married me. I can't express to you how small I felt that day. Add to the agony what my father-in-law said:

"My son is a cheat and a liar. We bribed a clerk to get his B.Com degrees. We have no responsibilities towards you two. As long as you are the wife, you can earn, cook, and feed us."

Imagine my feelings! I have no words to express my tormenting dejection. My husband was their only son. The in-laws confessed they had not disclosed anything about his background, for fear of breaking our marriage. They wanted a working wife for their useless son.

The other angle was, who would marry their son from the Brahmin community? He was already quite notorious. I said to myself, "I have nothing to do with anyone after this except with my husband. I will try to change him."

For three months life was smooth. Then the abuse began. By mistake, I told my husband about my previous lover. I had no guilty feelings. When we had problems communicating my husband blamed my emotional involvement with the other man. I had treated that as past. Yes, I did think of him, how could I not? There was a constant struggle within me. Nothing seemed to work. When he began abusing me over little things, I said:

"I refuse to stay with you. I will leave soon!"

I had conceived my first child in those three months. When I confessed everything to mother she only said, "Now that you are pregnant, how can you leave him?"

I said, "I got nothing from the marriage—no love, nor respect, not even one *sari* in these months. I obeyed you to marry this useless man—it has ruined life for me. I can support myself, even the child. I will earn. If you want, I will go to my own place. But you have no right to reject me at a difficult time like this."

Unknown to me, father had taken back the deposit I paid for my place. I was furious over this. Father explained in his own way, he said, he knows I have a restless nature. He had kept the money safely. But that day I realized one cannot trust anyone. I began meeting my former partner secretly. In his company I found emotional strength. But I had grown diffident. I could not say to him, I want to be with you or confess my husband was abusing me.

At home, my husband was abusing me more often. I told my mother in law one day, "Tell your son not to touch me."

After that, I began to sleep in her room. My mother in-law had a soft corner for me. She asked me not to leave and offered help. When she retired as the principal of a municipal school, she had Rs 95,000 in her name. But she never saw that money. My father-in-law took it away from her. He used to collect her salary. Those 36 years that she slaved, the poor lady did not get to see her salary. She had positive feelings for me. I realized my husband had picked up bad habits from his father. But the father and son did not see eye to eye. My husband mistreated his own mother. Even at that age, she was expected to cook, and wash. I knew I was wasting time trying to change this man who had no respect for women.

My mother-in-law realized we needed to get away. She gave me Rs 30,000 and with this I booked a place nearby. I thought we would try to live together. Once more I gave an ultimatum to my husband to stop drinking, stop abusing or I would leave him.

For him I was a physical necessity on bed. There was no love, nor attachment. He only wanted sex. Once our son was born, I felt no need to relate to him or even pretend to make our relation work. One day he beat me so much that I bled profusely. As was his habit, he left home after the assault. I was in a state of shock. A man beats you, your son cries in fear—as though some one had died, there was blood shed—and then he behaves as if nothing happened? That same day, he abused a school friend for taking my side.

After abusing us, he coolly sprayed cologne, and left for work. His doing that was even more shocking. I let him go but got a large lock from mother's home to replace the old one. My neighbors had seen me beaten, I told them, "Look, this is my lock. This is my home."

In the evening, my husband returned, with fruits, sweets, smiling in a jolly mood. My friends told him: "She won't go back to you."

I stayed in the bedroom; I had been treated at the hospital for my wounds. He screamed, "I'll break the lock."

I came when he screamed too much and confronted him, "You may do anything you want but our relationship is over."

When he heard me, he became verbally abusive. But I was surprisingly calm and clear in mind, as though the pain had left me after years. The struggle within had been too much. I used to worry all the time: What shall I do? Stay or leave him? But all that tension vanished. I felt calm. The marriage chapter was shut. Next day, my wounds, where the head was banged, were bleeding. I went back to the hospital for five days. His mother, father, my husband no one came to see me. On the sixth day he came to mother's place. I told her at once, shut the door. I have nothing to do with these people. He was demanding the child. The child was so terrified he hid in the bathroom. I refused point blank and said, "We can meet in court."

He used to beat the child saying, "You are just like your stupid mother! You lived in her womb, what do you have in common with me?"

His statements made me think he had a serious inferiority complex. He was unable to accept that I, a poor girl from the slums had matured spiritually. And he, a fair skinned, well built man, that too a Brahmin—had not. He has a kink about being a high caste. I, on the other hand, was content with my lot—my being from the slum background did not affect my self respect. All this puzzled him.

After I left he began getting drunk daily. He used to stand below mother's flat showering abuses. I asked my mother and sister to confront him with the truth. They need not hide the fact I left him because he was abusive, drank, and beat me. I told my family I need their emotional support in this struggle. I knew economically it may be difficult for them to support me and the boy. Unless they supported me in spirit—I was ready go away to a new place.

Many of my friends are from the women's movement. They support me. They are amazed how my husband could ill-treat an intelligent woman like me. They are confident I can survive on my own or find some one. My mother used to be shocked seeing some of the women smoke. I told her that I am not a child. If I wanted to smoke or drink, I will do it. All that talking has made her accept my friends.

My husband is in a great hurry to remarry. He has asked me for divorce by mutual consent. But he wants his mother's money back.

I refused on grounds that I will not claim child maintenance in the court. What is the guarantee that he will honor a court order? I will keep that money for our son. I have nothing more to give or take from him.

My former boy friend cannot make up his mind. He wanted our relationship to stay behind curtains. He claims, to dream of me. But also says, "I have no peace of mind."

I was quite blunt with him, "What peace do you mean? You think there is peace in another relationship? You say you love me, dream of me—but you used me like a disposable commodity. How can you even say, you have morals? You have no confidence in yourself or me."

His lack of commitment is a mental torture. I told him to end it. I am so depressed when I meet him that I cry. I can cry alone not when we are together. Last week he went back to his native place in Kerala to see a girl the family has approved for him.

At times a great sadness casts its shadow over me. I married and it did not work. I loved, but experienced no love in return. I have given so much into both. I am convinced what women give, not even 10 percent is returned back to us. We never receive an iota of what we give. Not even from the children we give birth. All this makes me very sad.

Postscript: Ulka was in a state of extreme agitation when we spoke. Her lover's indifference had hurt her more than the miserable marriage. She had turned bitter about life. After the interview, we lost touch. I hoped in vain, she will contact me one day—but I never saw Ulka again.

Zohra

Abba sold tickets in the village cinema hall. The hall was not far from our home. I do not remember our *ammi* at all. From what I remember, she used to cry in pain. She complained all the time of stomachache. I was this high (measures the bed height) when *ammi* died. Rukia, my other sister, was a little bigger than me. What a problem it was for Abba to be left with two little daughters. He got Rukia married that very summer. Next, he married me. I must have been six, or seven years old. My husband was 15 years old. He knew to drive cars already. Abdul was a kind and good husband. He did not scold me or beat me—nor did he expect me to fetch water from far away places. Why should I lie before *Allah?* We were married for five years when Yasmin was born.

One night both of us were asleep on the rope cot *Abba* gave at our marriage, when Abdul, my husband woke me up and said:

"Something has bitten me Zohra, take the lamp and look at my leg!"

I took the kerosene lamp, threw the light at the foot of the bed, just in time to see a long, black snake slide down the cot. I shouted for help. My husband was rolling in horrible pain. His brother rushed in with a bamboo stick. But even as he died, my husband begged his brother not to kill the snake. He was kind hearted even as death waited for him. In one hour my husband was dead. We could not even get the *ozha* to help. Yasmin was an infant in my arms. Next morning Abdul's family, my in-laws called me and said:

"How can we feed you and your daughter when our son is dead? You had better look after yourself from now."

Had I given them a grand son, they would not throw me out. After my in-laws said this, when Abdul was barely laid to rest under the shadow of the Mosque, I cried a lot. But I picked up Yasmin in my arms and went straight to *Abba's* home. My brothers had got married. Their wives did not want me to stay with *Abba*. What could I do? I went round doing housework from early morning to fill my stomach and produce milk for Yasmin.

There were quite a few men who offered to marry me. I was only 12 or 13 years, blooming like a wild flower. But I did not even want to look at them after such a kind and good husband. Few years passed like this. My sister Rukia had crossed over to India. She visited us from time to time. One summer she suddenly asked if I wanted to go away from the village with her. What did I have to hold me back? So I took Yasmin and crossed to India with my sister Rukia. Ever since that time I have been in your country. I used to live with my sister at first. Over little things Rukia quarreled with me. I did not mind her bad temper or her sharp tounge, she is after all my own sister, older, and the only family I have in another country. I never argued or answered her back.

Once she found me a house work with a *Sardarji*. This man had grown up children. His wife was nice to me. When the wife went out to shop, this man came to me, suggesting all kinds of things. He said he will marry and keep me like a queen. I knew what he was after. He always smelt of liquor. Everyday he pestered me. Sometimes he tried to touch my breast. I took my slippers and beat him nicely before leaving that job. Rukia was furious with me for leaving the old *Sardarji*. She and her husband even hit me because I left.

"Why couldn't you agree to do whatever the man said? He was going to pay you!!" Rukia shouted and called me names.

I was happy to be on my own with Yasmin. I only wished someone gave us, mother and daughter a place to rest our tired heads. We could make a living somehow. People were ready to keep me as a day and night maid but the moment they saw Yasmin I was rejected. Where could I keep a fatherless child?

My second husband was from Bihar. He worked as construction laborer. Until I agreed to marry, he pestered me. His friends and neighbors assured me: He has no other wife. We know him for many years etc.

These were lies as I found out later. He had another wife before he did *Nikah* with me. He had six children. He left his first wife to marry me. His first wife performed black magic to get him back. I have two daughters by the Bihari. When I was expecting my son, he left me suddenly for his first wife. He was a cruel man. He would beat me over anything and did not spare the two girls. There was no money—no food for us. He starved us and never gave me anything. All the time, he suspected me. The other day he died in an accident. Once the man left us, he never came back to me. I was only too glad—I was free from his cruelty and suspicion.

I said to myself, if one blanket does not protect you from the cold, can a second blanket keep you warm?

I am on my own again. My sister Rukia does not talk to me. If I go to meet her, she beats me, tears my clothes, calls me bad names. All this is due to the fact she wanted my daughter Yasmin for her son Babu. But I refused. I said: We don't marry sister's children to one another.

Since then she is mad at me. I got Yasmin engaged to a nice boy from Bangladesh. My son-in-law earns well as a polish wala. I hear he is from a good family. It was my good fortune to see them married.

But Rukia bribed my children. She called them over to her hut, treated them with fish curry rice and sweet words. She and her husband did Yasmin's *nikah*. I was not even told. No one called me to my own daughter's marriage—my tears have not stopped falling for the way my own blood sister treated me.

But I care for Rukia. She is my only family in this foreign soil. If I meet my daughter Yasmin when she goes to the market I ask: When will you visit me child?

She is scared of her aunt that she said to me: "*Khala* has asked me never to see you." I am grateful to Allah at least my daughter is safe and sound. She has a kind husband.

In Mumbai, we Bangladeshis live in constant fear. Anytime the C.I.D. officers can raid our area. They flush us out in the night with powerful lights. Someone is reporting about us to them. They come in big groups, in trucks and vans. We throw the covers, hide in corners, but there is no escape. Once the vigilance officers find us—they make no difference—woman, man, child—everyone is caned mercilessly, pulled by their hair, dragged and dumped into waiting vans. They pull down our huts. Thrown our cooking pots, trample and pee on beddings. We are driven away to the Arthur Road jail in Bombay Central. Children are pushed to one side, women and men made to stand in different lines. We are ordered to speak the truth.

"Where do you come from?" the officers ask. Show us your ration cards, they command. What is your name? How long are you here? If they catch us telling lies, they bang our heads on the wall and give us *lathi* blows. I have these wounds still on my back.

When we reached the Jail, my daughters were snatched away. They cried not finding me around. Only my boy was left with me as he was suckling my breast. Sometimes they release us after a month of jail term. Once the C.I.D. took us to the Bangladesh border with strict orders: Never come back.

These days the border has been sealed off. The police are ordered to shoot on sight. Our Bangladeshi people still smuggle themselves from villages to cross dangerously into India. They risk their lives. Some were caught only the other day and mercilessly beaten … I am frightened when I hear about all this.

But where can I go *Didi*? *Abba* died last year. As long as he was alive, I went home to pay my respect to him. Our two brothers work for rich *babus*. They drive the *babu's* shining new cars. They are comfortable, secure. They have homes, family, enough food, and clothes on their back. Neither of them look at us sisters, Rukia or me. Once Rukia tried to win them over with sugary words. She even licked their boots. But the brothers treated her like cowdung.

I have made many mistakes in life myself. A big mistake was to marry the *Bihari* man. Another mistake was entrusting my girls to a wealthy Sindhi lady. She promised to send them to school, look after them like her own girls. But she starved my girls, made them work like donkeys. When the younger one broke her arm they were sent back to my door hungry, dirty, lice crawling in their body and hair. I don't trust strangers who have a sweet tongue. I am not sending my girls back to work. They watch over their brother Shakeel who is learning to walk. I take the older one with me to do house work. I have found a job—washing and cleaning for Rs 300 per month. I am looking for other jobs.

When I returned from a visit to *Haji Malang*, my home was turned into a rubble heap again. Just a few vessels were lying scattered. There was nothing else left of my home. The Bangladeshi settlement people have decided not to allow the C.I.D. to harass us again. I have seen a dry patch near the Reclamation seafront … I will rebuild my hut—we will manage somehow, me and the three children—can you help me a little *didi*?

I have no one else in this world.

Postscript: My recorded conversation with Zohra was pieced during her unexpected visits to see me. She turned up any time she wanted to seek advice.

Rukia our Bangladeshi maid used to nag me to do something for her younger sister, Zohra. She told me how a Bihari man had dumped Zohra on the fifth month her pregnancy. Rukia seemed to have tremendous faith in my powers of persuasion. She wanted Zohra to give up her girls for adoption. Rukia herself was reluctant to take charge of her destitute sister. At the time Rukia's concern for Zohra seemed genuine....

But all this takes me back several years ... to the year 1986....

We had started HELP Center. One day, I asked Rukia to bring Zohra to HELP.

Remembering a young Zohra I am flooded by painterly mother images. Radiantly pregnant, her beauty, her youth gently gleamed through the worn out dirty sindoor—red hand woven saree. After hearing about the rough times she had been through, I talked to her for an hour. As we both spoke Bangla it helped us communicate. She spoke the rural East Bengal dialect—and I its urbanized diction. I explained to Zohra, naively I admit, that giving up her daughters for adoption was indeed a secure option. Provided she was ready for the pangs of parting. At the time neither of us knew about adoption procedures. We felt with her children taken care of, Zohra would be free to work as a maid. Unskilled, and illiterate that she was, the poor woman had few survival options but domestic slavery. Her sister had washed her hands off. The so-called husband had vanished ... and eventually died.

I talked about Zohra's case with a reputed adoption center. Many sessions later Zohra agreed, though with grave misgivings and reluctance, to give up her two girls, aged 3 and 4 years. During a counseling session Zohra was informed that once foster parents took her daughters, the mother became redundant. Even the right to visit them was denied to the biological mother. Outraged by what she thought was a cruel and unjust blow, Zohra rebelled. She refused to give her girls for adoption.

Zohra demanded to know, "How can my girls never see me, their own mother? I who gave them birth! My girls will die without me!"

If her outrage frustrated me, it also made me inordinately proud of Zohra. Without further ado, I informed the adoption center of the reversed decision, greatly relieved that I had not engineered separating a mother from her children!

During her tenure as my top maid, grim tragedy stalked this mother. One of her girls died. Zohra had no money to buy a piece of new cloth for the child's coffin cover. But what broke her heart was Yasmin's rejection. Zohra aged quickly. At 30, she looked 50. Then severe health problems wore her down. Despite these terrible calamities, Zohra managed to bring a smile on her pale countenance every time she visited. She remembered to make respectful inquiries about my health, my family's welfare.

For reasons best known to her, Zohra had chosen me her mentor. My home was her symbolic shelter against the ravages of an uncaring society. Zohra's quiet resistance against poverty and state violence won my admiration. Even more inspiring is her sensitivity, her humanity. It is years since I last saw Zohra—wherever she is, *Allah* be with this magnificent mother.

Chapter Four
Police Attitude and Women
Kalindi Muzumdar

Background

The Indian police system was established during the British rule. The British wanted to keep checks on criminals, and later on freedom fighters. The system had no provision to tackle human rights issues. This was proved immunerable times by the police brutality during the British rule in India. One case that comes instantly to mind is the infamous *Jallianwalla Baug*[1] incident in Punjab. The Indian police obeyed their British masters blindly without raising questions. After the independence, India inherited the legacy of British police system with its former prejudices and attitudes. Police personnel seem to forget they are public servants. As a result they behave more like dictators.

We have to bear in mind that our police force has emerged from the same society which has a culture of gender bias, deep-rooted prejudices and insensitivity to the female sex. The police have internalized similar cultural values from our society. A dominant trait in the police is their absence of respect, in fact, their undisguised contempt for women. Policemen, especially from the lower ranks, treat women as secondary citizens. Women's problems, according to the police, should be given the lowest priority. Women criminal are harshly punished even for minor crimes. There were cases of terrible brutality when the police branded the forehead of alleged women thieves with hot iron rods. Incidents of stripping women naked at police stations are common occurrence. The police nurture a *Sati Savitri*[2] images of Indian women in their minds. The slightest deviation from this culturally accepted womanly image provokes tremendous police hostility towards female clients.

Intervention in the Police System by the College of Social Work

The college of Social Work, Nirmala Niketan[3] (NN) has been responsible to a large extent for focusing attention on the marginalized, victimized, and exploited groups in our society. The curriculum and field practicum were planned to prepare students to work towards the empowerment of the above sections.

It has been observed by most social work educators and practitioners that there are three main systems which affect all vulnerable groups in our society, i.e. education, health, and the police (law and order). While the social work profession had involved itself in creating and maintaining effective interaction between the client system and the education and health systems, very little or nothing, was being done with regard to the police system. Despite articles in newspapers and magazines regarding police atrocities against people, especially against women and children that occurred in several police stations and lock-ups of India, scant attention was paid to tackle these issues with a view to initiate remedial and preventive measures. There was yet another incident that took place in 1982 in Mumbai[4] city which gave a momentum to the plan by NN to place students in the police residential colony as well as at various police stations. In 1982 there was a strike called by the police constabulary in order to motivate the higher authorities to improve the pitiable living and working conditions of the nation's police. The police system is considered an essential service by the Indian government and hence, has no legal right to adopt agitation measures for making or demanding any changes. The NN faculty took note of this and felt that social work intervention was a dire necessity to improve the functioning of the police. Consequently, permission for student placement was sought in the residential colony of the constabulary particularly at a suburb known as Worli including two other police stations in Mumbai city.

A Brief Description of Students'
Work in the Police System

Work in the Residential colony
concerned the following

- To identify needs and problems of the police community.
- Motivate youth and women to organize themselves to satisfy their needs and to solve their problems.
- Conduct training sessions on health, nutrition, sanitation, consumer awareness, and child care for women's groups.
- Conduct training sessions for youth on leaderships, teamwork, and conflict solving.

Work in the police stations

- Observe the functioning of the police in relation to the client system.
- Handle cases of non-cognizable offences[5] (NC) and demonstrate a humane manner of handling such cases.
- Conduct training programs for the police personnel on social issues and the responsibility of the police therein.
- Conduct awareness programs in the slum complex regarding rights and responsibilities of citizens vis-á-vis the police; handling familiar conflicts and organizing youth and women's groups to solve the problems of the slum complex.

Attitude of the Police Towards the
Students in the Police Stations

Primary Phase

1) At first, the police behaved hostile towards the students of social work. They(police) were threatened by the presence of students at the stations.
2) The police were also suspicious of students, thinking they were being spied upon to check alleged corruption.
3) Most policemen were indifferent to students.
4) Some were openly sarcastic.

Secondary Phase

1) Police began to adopt a condescending attitude towards students.
2) There was an "approach – avoidance" phase. Some policemen would try to cooperate and then suddenly withdraw.
3) The cooperation of the police was cautious and marginal.
4) There was a reduction of hostility, suspicion, and sarcasm in the behavior of the police.

Tertiary Phase

1) The police personnel were convinced about the sincerity and dedication of students towards their field work.
2) They began to rely on students to handle NC cases and to organize training sessions.
3) The police cooperated in the training programs.
4) Their behavior towards clients showed improvement.

Our Observations of the Attitude of the Police Towards Women

Any radical change of attitude in human beings is a gradual and long drawn process. The same would apply to police personnel, as the police are also "people." A brief description of the attitude and behavior of the Mumbai police towards women observed during the last two decades is noted below. From time to time, these attitudes of the police towards women have been challenged by social workers from various schools of social work such as NN to give one example. However, as mentioned change of attitude is a long drawn process. As explained before, our police force comes from the same society as ours and their behavior follows traditional patriarchal values. Some of these traditional values in the police system regarding women can be summed up as follows:

- Women have to obey the men in their families.
- Women have to tolerate domestic harassment, since this is part of our tradition and women's destiny.
- The attributes of good and bad women is firmly entrenched in the police psyche.

- A *good woman* is one who talks less and softly;
- is polite and obedient;
- suffers silently and never complains;
- serves her husband and family members;
- dresses in a traditional manner.
- A *bad women* is one who talks loudly;
- argues, asserts herself;
- values her own desires, individuality, and independence;
- dresses in a modern fashion.

Some policemen view girls or women merely as sex objects. This is demonstrated in the sexual abuse of women in police custody. Women who approach police stations for help have been unfortunate victims of sexual exploitation.

The Police treat women's problems as unimportant, or secondary compared to police operations in catching thieves, pick pockets, gang wars, protecting politicians, providing police *bandobast*[6] at political meetings etc.

On the whole, attitudes of tour police towards women ranges from intense to mild hostility, indifference, condescension, selective acceptance, cooperation and finally, collaboration. The goal of achieving unconditional acceptance and collaboration is still far from reality.

Sub-Inspectors are often heard to say, we can work with a hundred men but never with *one* woman! Women are stereotyped as talkative, jealous, quarrelsome, suspicious, and intolerant These generalizations about women's nature and behavior thrive within the police ranks. "A woman is her own worst enemy"—this belief was mentioned by police trainees at several training sessions. The police gave examples of dowry harassment and death where mothers-in-law were actively involved. While to an extent this was true, the root cause of atrocities by women was overlooked. The theory postulated by Pauolo Freire in Brazil i.e. the oppressed, once in power, become far worse oppressors, is reflected in the mother-in-law versus daughter-in-law phenomenon. None of us justify atrocities committed on women by women. However, the root cause lies in patriarchy—where women are subordinated.

In domestic violence cases, women are told by police *it must* be their fault for which they are beaten. Women are accused of provoking and angering their husbands or in-laws. In rape cases, the same is believed by the police. They (police) believe women are raped because of inappropriate dressing/behavior. They also believe that you cannot clap with one hand. This provocation factor in violence deters victims from pressing charges.

Women are strongly discouraged to lodge complaints of domestic violence in the name of protecting family honor. In crises situations, regardless of their intensity, police feel women should behave in the following manner:

- Sacrifice her self-interest for the sake and the welfare of her family.
- Protect the prestige of the family. As the police put it, *khandan ki izzat* (family honor) is at risk.

In cases of women dying of burns, the inspector present in the hospital ward, has been heard to say to the victim, "Why do you want to file a case against your husband? Who will look after your children if he is sent to jail? Why do you want to slander your family's reputation?" One seriously wonders whether the thought of the family's honor crossed the minds of the culprits while committing these crimes?

There have been frequent complains that the Section 498A7 of the Indian Penal Code, referred to as "the legal weapon in their hands," has been misused by women to punish husbands and in-laws, and get them arrested. In fact, this is a view surprisingly held by some lawyers. There are always a few people who break or misuse laws. This is a global phenomenon. Therefore, it cannot be denied that a few women may have misused Section 498A. If women have misused the section, they should face the legal consequences. However, professional social workers' experience in the field indicates that a woman suffers silently on an average 4–5 years prior to taking recourse to Section 498A. There are many reasons for this delay. It is primarily due to women's economic dependency on the husband, and their lack of social support systems.

I would like to end this chapter with two brief cases that adequately illustrates police attitude to women:

1) A battered woman went to complain against her husband. She had dark bruises all over and a few cuts in her arms. The constable at the police station tried to shoo her away saying cases like her case are not handled by police. At this point the woman began to cry loudly. She was allowed to enter the Duty room. The Sub-Inspector on Duty shouted at her to stop crying. He then told her that it is a tradition for the husband to beat his wife to discipline her. The woman was forced to return home without making any complain.

2) A man complained to the Duty Officer(DO)that his wife refused to do housework and spent most of her time on bed. The DO summoned the wife to the station. The wife could hardly walk or talk. She was running a temperature. She also said, she had a caesarian operation and her wounds were not healed. The DO said this was not a serious matter at all and asked her to resume her household duties.

Conclusion

The chapter on police attitudes will be incomplete if I conclude on a pessimistic note. The NN, TISS, other Women's' NGOs and the Police Department of Mumbai are working together to make the police personnel behave in a humane manner. Change, though slow, is discernible. We find women are treated with some degree of respect at most police stations in the City. The police are also learning communications and basic counseling skills. This is significant as the police from the lower rank such as constables are burdened with problems of housing, long working hours and stress.

The following instance is a positive example of change in the attitude of the police. At 9.00 p.m. one night a woman called to say her husband had thrown her out along with two grown up children. I went with her to meet the husband. He was quite adamant and declined to take his family back. He defied us to approach the police.

We approached the neighborhood police station. After listening to us, the Inspector phoned the husband, requesting him to come to the station. After a great deal of persuasion, the man agreed to come to the station. The Inspector and I spoke to the husband first. Later, we spoke to the couple. At a later point, the children joined the discussion. It was past mid-night when discussions got over. The Inspector's communication skills were successful in persuading the man and sending back the family home. In the task of improving the attitude and behavior of the police there are three parties involved, i.e. the state government, society, and the police force. The government has to seriously address the specific needs and problems of the police. They have to do away with political control and interference in police functioning and grant autonomy to the Police Department.

Society on its part has to actively encourage awareness building and sensitization of police regarding women's issues and the responsibilities of citizens therein. Recent incidents in Mumbai of a woman being burnt in broad daylight and a minor being raped in a local train in the presence of five passengers, should be an eye opener for us.

Simultaneously, I think women's vigilance groups such as the *Mahila Dakshata Samiti*[7] and other women's organizations should be supported and strengthened.

I would agree a great deal of work is yet to be accomplished, in Mumbai, and other metros but the ray of hope is already visible. Each State, each town and village has to put its own house in order so that we can proudly provide security for Indian women.

Notes

1. *Jallianwalla Baug*: on April 13, 1919 people organized a peaceful meeting at Jallianwala Baug in Amritsar (Punjab state) against the Proclamation issued by General Dyer on April 12, 1919 banning public meetings and demonstrations. The Police shut two of the three exits of the Baug. Hundreds of protestors died in Police firing or the stampede that ensued.

2. *Sati Savitri*: a truly devoted wife. *Sita* (heroine of the epic *Ramayana)* and *Savitri* (from epic *Mahabharat)* are considered amongst others as ideal women in the Indian mythology. They have been extolled as paradigms of feminine virtue. The prefix *Sati* is added to their names denoting selfless attachment to their consorts.

3. *Nirmala Niketan* (NN): School of Social Work for Women in Mumbai.

4. *Mumbai*: Bombay began with a population of 1,600 in AD 1715, by 1744 it had grown to 70,000; 235,000 in 1836; and 644,000 by 1872. However, Mumbai has experienced its greatest poplation growth since Independence in 1947. In 1947 the population of Mumbai was 4 million and today it is greater than 12 million. An increase of more than 8 million people, almost all from internal migration and more than half of that increase occurring between 1960–1970.
5. Section 498A of the IPC. (see also Introduction)
6. *Bandobast*: arrangement, to organize during events.
7. *Mahila Dakshata Samiti* (1978) activities: Campaigning, seminars, discussions, protest action in consumer rights and women's issues.

Chapter Five
Roadmap for Support
Rinki Bhattacharya

There is, of course, no simple answer to the question of wife abuse. As there is no conceivable remedy, no effective strategies have been developed to cope with violence in women's daily life. It is our experience that wife beating has social sanction. As observed in the Introduction, this is not the case merely in India, but domestic violence has universal social sanction. In England, there was a popular saying that a man can beat his wife with a rod no thicker than his thumb. The Napoleonic code of France advocated beating wives.

This concluding chapter puts forward suggestions based on the collective experiences of local activists, social workers, and victims for a road map to support abused women.

Given that wife abuse is not restricted to any particular age, or social group, we have to remember it may take the victim several years before she can perceive her mistreatment as acts of "domestic violence." Karlekar has pointed out:

In an interesting study of the impact of wife-beating on the women themselves as well as other members of the family, Vijendra Rao (1995) found that in three multi-caste villages in the southern state of Karnataka, only 22 percent women claimed to have been abused by their husbands. In fact during fieldwork, two women were hit by their husbands, in response to a question, the very same women did not say they had been abused. The researcher concluded that it was only if the beatings were very severe did women perceive themselves as being abused; the odd slap or blow was regarded as routine husband-like behavior (Karlekar, 1998: 1747).

Ghosh makes a pertinent reference to women who, having internalized patriarchal norms, do not perceive themselves as being abused (see Ghosh in this volume).

Karlekar and Ghosh's observations are based on empirical findings. Many victims, for instance Sita in this volume, regard physical abuse by their husbands as normal *husband*-like behavior. Therefore the great dilemma before women's activists and social workers has been *how* to render support to victims who are not aware of being abused. Friends, individuals, neighbors may report that a woman is being ill-treated either by her husband, or her in-laws. However, until the victims own up, social workers are at a great disadvantage, in fact they are unable to support the victims. Women remain in abusive relationships for decades without knowing how to cope. They know even less about how to escape. World over, victims of domestic violence continue to live with abusive men without realizing the grave risk this poses to their lives, their mental health and those of their children.

The situation of battered women is a grim one to say the least. In the Indian context victims are abysmally vulnerable. In Bumiller's essay about arranged marriages amongst the educated classes she candidly observed, "What I did not understand at the time was the powerful sense of fatalism that Indian woman have. Strict Hindus believe that their present lives have been predetermined by their *karma,* the accumulated sum of all good and bad actions from their previous lives" (Bumiller, 1990: 33). The author's assumption about women's belief that marriages are predestined affects most Indian women even today. Women are also plagued by ignorance; lack of education, and worst of all, economic dependency cripples them. Needless to add, very few women enjoy *real* bargaining power within their family. Powerlessness contributes abundantly to women's exploitation. Add to this the undeniable fact that there are virtually no support services, such as shelters for victims. The few services that exist are inadequate, conventional or old fashioned in their approach to victims. It is also more than likely, women are not aware about them. Unlike in the UK, women's refuges or crises hotline services do not splash posters at bus stops, shop windows or underground stations. During HELP we were fortunate to get adequate media coverage. The result was overwhelming. Our advertisement was flooded with inquiries—notwithstanding a few crank calls. Some victims preserved the hotline number and came to see HELP workers after several years. But women, in general, are ignorant about the existence of NGOs like *Nari Kendra* or *Dilaasa*. Neither have they any idea of their legal rights in the event of domestic violence. The inevitable questions before victims are, where/how do they escape, more importantly, how would they survive? It is this abysmal helplessness of victims, their isolation, which drove some to execute their tormentors (see Introduction). A battered woman, ready to leave her abusive partner—is therefore assailed by well-founded fears.

Providing humanitarian relief to a victim of abuse have several aspects to it. However, the key areas that deserve consideration broadly include:

- Safety of victims (including children)
- Re-building women's economic resources
- Healing and long-term counseling

From our experiences we understand that battered women fervently wish to return to their parents' homes. This is because the Indian family has been a cultural ideal. Wistfully, married women regard their own family as haven of goodwill and a place of natural nurturing.

There is a great clash of cultural values in this regard. On the one hand, women are anxious to return to their parents or the family abode. On the other, parents and the natal family offer stiff resistance—indeed view victims with the darkest of suspicion.

Working with Victim's Family

In their heart of hearts, married daughters in Indian society yearn to be welcomed home. They long to hear loving words from their family members. But "marriage" further dislocates or alters a woman's position, which to start with was an unequal one within her natal home. Once married, a daughter is regarded as *paraya dhan* (another's *property*). Married daughters are believed to belong to the kinship order of her husband's family. Marriage has robbed a daughter of her rights, whatever little she once enjoyed. Women find it extremely hard to accept this shift in their family's affection. It is even harder for them to accept their diminished position. Confronted by social disaster like widowhood or marital violence, victims have confessed their frank emotional expectations from the natal family. Struck by such misfortune, women have felt heartlessly betrayed by their family's indifference or rejection. Their family's indifference exposes them to exploitation. Roadblocks are deliberately created for women by their own brothers, or other family members in positions of authority. Women's return journey to the natal home is thus an uphill one. Few have the good fortune to receive unconditional parental support. There are some happy exceptions (see Hansa, Maya, and Sarla's stories) but generally the opposite is truer.

At HELP we handled the case of Leena, a young mother. Neighborhood police rescued Leena from her violently inebriated husband well past mid-night. She and her two children were taken to Leena's elderly parents. Next morning the parents insisted she send her children back to her husband. Leena was breast-feeding the infant son. Her parents made it very clear; they would *not allow* the children to live with them. They argued, the children's father might create ugly scenes or cause them harm. In this case the parents fears were indeed justified. Leena had no choice but to return to her husband.

Soon after this incident, the husband threw Leena out. She then moved back to her parent's home without the children. Leena was separated from the children when they were infants. The boys did not know their mother. Aruna used to be constantly reminded, "Go back. This is your *karma*. You have to live there for the sake of the children" (see Aruna in chapter three).

Even after women are savagely beaten, and their lives are in grave danger, the natal family ignores their piteous appeals by turning a blind eye. Women are ordered to "adjust," to "obey" the husband. Parents insist on "reconciliation." Reconciliation has been a commonly applied solution to women's marital problems.

No value is attached to women's lives nor do their personal safety merit relief (see Ghosh in this volume).

The aching love married women feel for their parental hearth, affectionately called *maika*[1], *babul* or *naihar* cannot be wished away. Women have acquired this sentiment from our specific cultural ethos. Poets and lyricists poignantly capture the moving sentiments in verse or songs. Women hope to return home in the best of times. In the event of misfortunes, women's first thoughts are to return home!

The tragedy of Indian daughters is that they are regarded as "unwanted," as outsiders in their parent's home from the moment of birth. Of the married girl it is said, that her bridal departure is a final exit point from the natal home. This Hindi proverb expresses that sentiment: *Yehase doli uthi hai ab uski arthi wapas ayegi* (the bride's *doli* has left, now only her hearse will come back).

A daughter's visit to her parent's home is legitimized during childbirth, specially for the first pregnancy. There are few and far traditional customs that give daughter's social sanction to visit the natal home. At other times, it is perceived as unnecessary, or even a luxury for a daughter to visit parents. In case a woman visits her parents other than the above occasions, relatives and neighbor's make it their business to pry. They loose their sleep over how long a daughter's visit would last, or the fear she is over-staying her welcome? These social pressure on a woman's parents force them to abandon their daughters. Women endure violence (see Ghosh) due to these unaltered circumstances.

Under the prevailing condition where daughter's are regarded as another's property or the moot fact that community support structures have not developed—sensitizing women's parents, as much as the city's police force (see Muzumdar in this volume) ought to be a priority on the agenda of Women's NGOs. But the task is a formidable one. According to Social workers at *Dilaasa*[2], natal support is not forthcoming. A few parents may occasionally accompany victims to the counseling center. Women have reported they have to adjust, and compromise in the natal home. Like Aruna, women who return after a failed marriage are made to feel they are being "tolerated."

A thin silver lining was visible on the horizon. *Dilaasa* workers reported that some parents agree their daughter deserved "to get her rights" from the husband. It was heartening to know many parents encourage a legal solution. There was general consensus however that the woman should not "break" her family.

Jamuna speaks about lawyers turning down her divorce case on the pretext they did not wish to be a party to "breaking up the family" (see Jamuna in chapter three). In a conversation with me during the shooting of the documentary *CHAR DIWARI* (1990/91), social worker Ashwini Yog, (TISS Cell for Women and Children) confided to me:

> The women's family is the last to offer support. Friends will stop listening. Victims can talk only to groups like the Special Cell for Women and Children. They feel legitimate in sharing extremely degrading intimate details. Women are ashamed and confused of being abused. At the Cell we can offer our support and give them a patient hearing. This boosts the victim's morale.

Rebuilding the Economic Base

Whenever there is has been any question about inheritance rights for women—the debate gets embroiled into the question of dowry. It is argued by many that women themselves are keen on taking dowry. In short the question about women receiving a fair share of their father's estate remains unresolved with women being blamed once again for dowry. It is perhaps true that young women cling to dowry at the time of their marriage as this is all a daughter gets from her parental estate.

Madhu Kishwar hit the nail on the head when she said,

> It is significant that historically, any attempt to ensure women's inheritance rights has been violently opposed by women's fathers and brothers (the supposed victims of the dowry system). For instance, a perusal of the parliamentary debates in the years preceding the passing of the Hindu Succession Act (1956), is very instructive in this regard. Men were united across party lines in opposing equal inheritance rights for women on the ground that it would create discord

between brothers and sisters. In other words, they virtually admitted that a key element in the asserted harmony between brothers and sisters in the disinheritance of the women. While some brothers accept their obligation to give dowry, few are willing to concede inheritance rights to women (Kishwar, 1989: 4).

The question about women's inheritance requires being contextualized within the Indian socioeconomic framework. Indian tradition upholds family values. There is emphatic faith in kinship ties. The silence on domestic violence is an extension of deep male reverence. It is believed that family disputes have to be resolved within the four walls. Serious apprehensions about litigation, and the expense involved have acted as effective deterrents. In the current scenario, many young wives may file for judicial separation or seek divorce. But it is rare to find daughters who actually challenge their father's wills to assert inheritance rights.

The following extract of a recent report from a study conducted in Kerala was published in *The Times of India* (2003: 5). Pradeep Kumar Panda (Centre for Development Studies) who conducted the report maintains, "Ownership of property by a woman reduces violence significantly. Even some access to an asset, land or house, dramatically reduces the risk of violence."

Emphasizing that the ownership of property by women has a strong negative effect on the violence suffered by them, the study points out that 49 percent of those who do not own property experienced physical violence and 84 percent experienced psychological abuse. In contrast, those who own both land and house reported substantially less physical violence (Katyal, 2003: 5).

It was pointed out in this report that women who own houses or property can exercise their options to get out of abusive marriages, and live independently. Most of the women interviewed by me admitted their regret not being able to do so.

In the same report, Anuradha Rajan of International Centre for Research on Women (ICRW) talks about another domestic violence survey done in West Bengal. Rajan reports, when women were asked to identify one area that would have helped them escape violence, all agreed it was ownership of property that would have helped them.

Although Panda's study was conducted in Kerala, his study, in general, forges a vital link to women's ownership of property and the decreased incidents of violence. His study argues that "right to housing and inheritance" are vital to prevent domestic violence.

Dr Julia Leslie offered the same argument in prevention of dowry murders:

Dowry is no real inheritance. However large the sum it may be, it is always pitifully small when compared to the brother's share. Furthermore, most of it may go not to the bride but to the groom's family. Thus it may never provide for a woman's security in the way that her brother's share, large or small, can. By associating the daughter's 'inheritance' with marriage and by handing most of it to her husband's family, Indian society treats her as a perpetual minor, deprived of what little she is given. In contrast, her brother will receive his inheritance as an adult and will, by and large, control what he gains (Leslie, 1998: 35).

In the same chapter, Leslie urged that:

we focus the legal aspects of our campaign on demanding inheritance rights for women. We need to separate property rights from marriage both in our minds and in reality. This will cut at the pernicious root of the dowry system. Once that root is cut, dowry itself will wither away (Leslie, 1998: 35).

Leslie observes that Indian society's attitude toward daughters, namely, treating them as "minors" is one of the main roots of women's oppression. A significant reform is required to change this antiquated attitude to girls, and daughters, married or otherwise. Without a wider social acceptance of women making their own life choice, be in charge of their lives—and develop as individuals—real social progress would remain a pipe dream.

Support Structures

Those of us working with victims of domestic violence must bear some important points in our mind. First, we have to understand that women who have been routinely battered by men they loved, who also happen to be the fathers of their children, are in extremely fragile emotional states.

> We have to quickly realize that a shelter is not just four walls or a roof over her head for a woman who wants to escape an abusive relationship. By the time a woman has taken this extremely difficult step to leave her husband and home, she has already been subjected to relentless 'victim blaming' from everyone. Empathy for her is primary support (Bhattacharya and Karkhanis, 1998: 250).

Noteworthy amongst newer NGOs, *Dilaasa* has been running effectively from March 20, 2000. The need to provide counseling, emotional support, and short term shelter has been made. It is significant to note *Dilaasa* operates from the premise at Bhaba (a public hospital in Bandra). Till March 27, 2003 *Dilaasa* had counselled 135 women. *Dilaasa's* Annual Report (2003) lists out its agenda.

Expected Outcomes of *Dilaasa*

- The hospital staff at all levels is sensitized to the issue of domestic violence.
- Doctors and nurses identify women facing domestic violence and refer them to *Dilaasa*
- No episode of violence faced by a woman goes unrecorded at the hospital.
- Other BMC hospitals start crisis centres (*Dilaasa* Annual Report, 2000: 1).

Women who come to *Dilaasa* after incidents of battery are first medically examined. Once the examination is done, if their injuries require more than first aid, the women are detained in the hospital. Victims enjoy a sense of security in the hospital ambience/premise. They utilize the safe space to contemplate about their position. Trained social workers help her understand the situation.

The following is an extract from the *Dilaasa* Annual Report:

- Women coming to the center are largely in the age group 21 to 30 years, followed by the age group 31–40 years.
- Most of them have expressed need for emotional support. A medico legal statement has been made for all women coming to *Dilaasa* after the immediate episode of violence.
- 33 of the 135 women expressed need for legal help.
- 50 percent of the women have followed up for counseling.
- Only two women expressed need for temporary shelter, which was provided through admission in the hospital.
- Hospital staff has referred 70 percent of these women. (Annual Report of *Dilaasa*, August 2000 to March 2001)

Shelters

Our experience of running the hotline HELP in Bombay, gave us insights into the specific needs of battered women. It is not necessary that victims would automatically move into Shelter or Short stay homes after incidents of assault. Spread across Mumbai we had identified about 20 shelter options. However, these places were rarely utilized. During the HELP chapter, out of several hundred cases, we referred two women to shelter homes, and only one to the emergency ward of a public hospital. *Dilaasa* workers explained that women are reluctant to use the option of moving to short stay homes. *Dilaasa* referred just two or three cases to short stay shelters out of a recorded 200 cases from their center.

The primary reason women do not move to short stay homes is that very few homes allow women with children. There are rules about male/female children as there are strict age limits. Women are tormented by fear of loosing their children and of course, their marital homes. But the worst fear is of the social stigma of staying in any institution. The fact a woman stayed in a "home" could backfire on them. It may result in a woman's character assassination: this deters them further from leaving their home. Victims hope that domestic upheavals will settle down or improve. Every woman clings to that slim hope. Leaving home under these circumstances would be jeopardy. In cases when battered women have left, they prefer informal shelters to any state run homes. This could mean staying with friends, or relatives. The fear of stigma is not an issue if women stay temporarily with a cousin or friend. In reality this is not the case. Friends sheltering victims have been accused of complicity or having immoral intentions. Revictimization of women has been a major stumbling block for social workers in this area.

The contrast between our society and US, or UK in this regard is dramatic. At the start of the second phase women's movement (late 60s, early 70s), autonomous women's groups in the US and UK demanded and acquired shelter homes as emergency refuge for abused women. Every provision was made for women with children at these excellently managed refuges. Once shelter homes sprang up, it did not take long to have them filled. Sometimes they were full beyond capacity.

A popular method used by women's groups in the UK was squatting inside unoccupied local Council homes. Women simply went and sat in vacant homes that were identified as suitable "refuges." These homes were converted with modern fittings, a community hall, TV sets, modern kitchen and other amenities. A close circuit TV monitored exits to the center. Cultural dietary needs of victims are kept in mind. Victims use special cabbies, trusted by social workers. In the UK the threat from Bounty Hunters was an additional risk for workers. In less than a decade, from the early 1970s to the 1980s, in Great Britain alone there were more than 200 shelter homes housing battered women and their children. In the US, the figure could be considerably higher.

In a conversation with me, Jalna Hanmer, the renowned feminist writer from Leeds, related the thrilling story how England's first shelter came into existence. At a women's group meeting, a women admitted she was being battered. The woman was shaken and terrified of returning home after the meeting. Someone suggested:

"If it is that bad, why not stay here?"

The woman agreed at once to this suggestion. At night she stayed at the office with her children. The shelter concept was an extension of this spontaneous support to a victim of violence said Hanmer. Soon after this incident more women from battering situations wanted to stay away from their violent partners.

Women's groups in the UK began to lobby for shelters successfully. It was not easy in the beginning. Fortunately, the need to provide alternative housing to victims of violence was recognized by local County Council authorities. The British media, both press and television, contributed in raising awareness. One TV coverage was taken to a refuge. The coverage showed a refuge meant only for 20 occupants packed with 100 victims who had nowhere to go. The appalling conditions shown in this program hastened funds and County council support.

Ashwini Jog from the Special Cell pointed out to me:

"We have no shelter homes, nor money to offer women who come for help in extremely dangerous situations. But we realized one important thing, that we can offer our friendship. Women come to us for moral and emotional support. After speaking to us a woman recovers her self confidence. This is very important for her when she has to face the reality at home. We send back the woman with the assurance that she was welcome to visit us any time."

Her experience at the special cell for women in distress (TISS) gave Jog a rare insight into specific needs for victims of violence. She confirmed that real support was "not four walls" but the capacity to reach out to victims. It was vital to assure women they were not to be blamed, nor was it a matter of shame. Least of all was it a matter of her "fate."

Recommendations

The following recommendations were drafted by Achala Daga after her pilot project on domestic violence was finished resulting in the structuring of *Dilaasa* (see appendix B):

Special Cells for women should have medical assistants who can conduct prompt physical examination and treatment in life-threatening conditions. The police investigation should follow only after the victims have gained adequate confidence. Female police officers should be posted in women's cells or hospitals dealing with investigation of domestic violence cases. To make quick references, it is required to have specially trained staff for emergency services to deal with the medico legal problems. All women cells should have alternative arrangements when women are discharged from hospital. Emergency shelters or temporary homes women should be available for them to come to terms with their situations. Counseling is recommended to reduce emotional trauma.

Women may require help to make FIR's at police stations. All those who work within the support structure such as medical officers, social workers, health care staff, nursing staff, should meet at regular intervals to review each domestic violence case. Home visits to survivors' homes should be made essential follow up. The police department should press criminal charges in cases where serious injuries have occurred. It is also recommended that legal advice should be made free for victims from poorer background.

State women's commissions should take appropriate steps to reduce crime against women. This present study led to drafting of women's law on prevention of domestic violence. The Women's Protection Bill 2001 recently introduced in Maharastra state is competent to deal with all gender issues. Education on health, legislation and the issue of domestic violence has to start at the grass-root level.

I believe both the electronic and print media can play decisive roles in spreading awareness, more importantly, breaking long held myths about domestic violence. Recently, one particular episode in the *Law and Order, Special Victim's Unit* (telecast October 14, 2003), showcased the case of a little boy who was the only eyewitness to his step-mother's murder by his father. His biological mother had fled when the child was an infant. The little boy grew up with lies his father fed him about his own mother. That she had run away with another man. He became deeply attached to his step-mother. When she was brutally murdered in his presence the boy lost his speech. What the episode forces viewers to acknowledge is the fact that men with charismatic personalities—socially successful—and from the affluent class—are wife batterers (see Afterwords). They are not above the law.

At times bordering on melodrama—these popular TV programs nonetheless bring up the issue of domestic violence forcefully—and confront viewers complacency. I believe, exposed to programs like the above, perceptions of viewers may slowly change to understand what actually happens in these cases, which always occur BEHIND CLOSED DOORS.

Despite the ubiquity of violence against women, the pervasive problem has not been considered a social or humanitarian disaster. The human tragedy scripted in each individual case resembles the aftermath of natural calamities like famine, flood, epidemic, or war. I would like to conclude with Del Martin's eloquent appeal for a more caring society and a just world, for countless women and children who are attacked in their own homes by those who are meant to love and protect them:

> Marital violence is a social disaster of similar proportions and its victims have the same desperate need for relief and support. Thousands of women and children need protection from injury, food, shelter, advice, and encouragement. The American government spends millions of dollars in aid to displaced persons all over the world, but the victims of violence at home are practically ignored. The problem of wife battery has been defined, the evidence has been presented, and the one immediate solution in the form of feminist run shelters, has been identified. What is your response, America? [India!] (Martin, 1976: 254).

Notes

1. *maika, naihar, babul*—are affectionate colloquial words for natal home.
2. *Dilaasa*, a joint initiative of *CEHAT* and the public Health Dept. of the BMC is a three year project to sensitize health care system.

References

Bhattacharya, Rinki and Karkhanis, Sudha. 1998. "Women and Shelter" in Shirin Kudchedkar and Sabiha Al-Issa (eds) *Violence Against Women Pencraft International*, New Delhi, p. 250.

Bumiller, Elisabeth. 1990. *May You Be the mother of A Hundred Sons*. Delhi: Penguin, p. 33.

Katyal, Anita. 2003. "Women Owning Property are Less Prone to Violence," *The Times of India*, 27 June, p. 5.

Karlekar, Malavika. 1998. "Domestic Violence," *Economic and Political Weekly*, Vol. XXXIII, no. 27, July 4–10, p. 1747.

Kishwar, Madhu. 1989. "Towards more just norms of marriage," *Manushi* no. 53, (July–August 1989), pp. 2–9.

Leslie, Julia. 1998. *South Asians And The Dowry Problems*, Gems No. 6. London: Trentham books, The School of Oriental & African Studies, p. 35.

Martin, Del. 1976. *Battered Wives*. US: Pocket Books.

Appendix A

Addressing Domestic Violence

1. Do not blame yourself if your husband is abusive.
2. When he is violent never argue, contradict or confront him.
3. Do not act like his therapist although he may push you into that position.
4. Beware of feeling sorry for your husband or even yourself.
5. Firstly, you have to understand that the violence is not within your control. Prayers may help calm you but will not yield miracles. Your husband needs therapy and counseling. So do you, not necessarily jointly, unless you want to keep trying for reconciliation.
6. Keep an emergency kit ready.
7. Make sure you have your own spare key to the flat AT ALL TIMES.
8. Keep important documents—bank passbooks, passports, flat deed, marriage certificate, ration card, children's birth and school papers with you.
9. If you hold a joint account, give written instructions to the bank not to negotiate anything without your consent or knowledge.
10. Keep bare essentials ready to leave without warning or at short notice.
11. Inquire about the nearest Women's group. Contact social workers, seek their advice.

12. Keep telephone number of local police handy. Incase you are abused, ring the police at once. At least make a complain, and get a copy of the FIR. This will give you back a sense of purpose and help you confront the problem.

13. Meet a lawyer to know your legal rights. Prepare for legal separation if things get too violent.

14. In case you have decided to end the relationship and need help, do not waste time. Turn to the list of numbers in the Yellow pages and call them NOW.

15. Look for local women's groups who will support and guide you during this extremely difficult phase of life.

Appendix B

Study of Domestic Violence in Public Hospital

Table 1
Types of Injuries Reported in Age Group 15 yrs Onwards

Classification	Number	Percentage
Assaults	1,097	48.19
Accidental injury	409	17.97
Poison	240	14.01
Burns	319	10.54
Falls	211	9.27
Total	2,276	100

Table 2
Types of Violence

Definite Cases	Number	Percentage
Assault by Husband & Family Members	537	26.49
Set on Fire by Family Members	17	0.84

(continued)

Table 2
Continued

Definite Cases	Number	Percentage
Possible Cases		
Assault by Family Members	528	26.05
Attempted Suicides	292	14.41
Assaulted Herself (set fire herself)	7	0.35
Unlikely Domestic Violence		
Accidental falls	211	10.41
Definitely not Domestic Violence		
Vehicle and other accidents	370	18.25
Assault by outsiders	65	3.21
Total	2,027	100

Table 3
Age-wise Distribution of Cases

Age Group	Number	Percentage
15–24 years	625	26.87
24–44 years	1,308	56.23
45 years & above	374	16.08
Age not known	19	0.82
Total	2,326	100

Table 4
Religion-wise Distribution

Religion	Number	Percentage
Hindu	1,105	49.35
Muslim	1,025	45.78
Christian & Ors.	109	4.87
Total	2,239	100

Table 5
Time of Admission at Hospital

Time	Number	Percentage
2100 hrs–0559 hrs	687	30.09
0600 hrs–1159 hrs	626	27.42
1200 hrs–2059 hrs	970	42.49
Total	2,283	100

Table 6
Description of Injuries

Parts of Body Injured	Number	Percentage
Head, Neck, Face, Nose	1,368	47.43
Chest, Back, Abdomen	628	21.78
Arms and Legs	888	30.79
Total	2,884	100

Table 7
Cause of Injury

Objects/Instruments	Number	Percentage
stick, iron rod, belt	564	24.12
Sharp instruments (knife, blade)	477	20.04
Slap/kicks/strangled/choked/bit	510	21.83
burns by fire or acid	82	3.51
Stove/burnt gas cylinder	481	20.57
Poisoned:sleeping pills, pesticides, other chemicals	224	9.58
Total	2,338	100

Table 8
Type of Injury

Injury	Number	Percentage
Abrasion	654	27.98
Contusion	717	30.68
Laceration	227	9.71
Profuse bleeding	228	9.76
Fractures	27	1.16
Burns	484	20.71
Total	2,237	100

Source: Data collected at J.J. Hospital, Mumbai, by Dr Achala
        Daga during 1996–98.

Afterword

A sensitive and socially challenging topic like domestic violence cannot be discussed in a couple of pages.

As a survivor of domestic violence I am aware of the enormity as well as the complexity of the problem, hence I will focus on only one aspect of domestic violence, "Battered Women." The issue is further confused when the broad term "domestic" referring to the household or the family is used. In addition, the prevalence and promotion of misleading myths surround the issue such as "it only occurs among the poor," "it only occurs among the uneducated," "it only occurs in a momentary loss of temper," "educated men do not batter women" or even worse, "we all know him personally. He is the most charming and kind person who would not even think of doing such a thing." Other common myths focus on the presumption that the women themselves must have provoked the assault.

Through my academic pursuit of the subject and years of research, I learned the problem exists in all cultures, races, occupations, income levels and ages. In some part of the globe a woman is physically abused, beaten, and even killed every 15 seconds by someone with whom she has an intimate relationship. Domestic violence is the leading cause of injury, more than accidents and rape combined. One-third of the perpetrators were not "alcoholics" or "psychopaths." They are benevolent, well-respected men in their communities: doctors, lawyers, psychologists, ministers, business executives and even philanthropists!!

Very often the charm and compassion they exhibit in their public lives adds to the incredulity of the stories of abuse and terrors their wives/partners reveal! The acts of violence include intimidation, threats, and submission to sexual demands by force, psychological abuse, isolation etc. to terrorize, control and coerce their spouses.

Alternately, batterers express contrition, eliciting sympathy and guilt from the women thus generating confirmation of being loving and affectionate men! This Jekyll–Hyde personality while adding to the terror and confusion deceives even the children who are witness to the shame and humiliation of their mothers. As adults, many children remember only the charm and affection their fathers were capable of! One child said: "My father only beat my mother because she did not cooperate and participate with him. He loved fun and parties!"

Research is increasingly revealing the incalculable socioeconomic, political, and psychological consequences of domestic violence. Domestic violence, child abuse, drug addiction and violence outside the family are inter-related. Like any other form of abuse, domestic violence is often a learned behavior. Children raised in homes where violence reigns suffer extreme emotional trauma. Exposed to shame and humiliation of their mothers at a very tender age they react with shock, fear, guilt manifested by withdrawal, poor performance in schools and aberrant behavior. As they grow older, embarrassed and frustrated they become disruptive or manipulative, searching for favors and attention as a way of coping with the situation.

Older children, especially girls assume parental responsibilities if the mother had to leave or is unable to do so because of physical and psychological injuries. Boys exhibit patterns of behavior modeled by their fathers, battering their siblings, and using violence to resolve conflict in their relationships inside and outside the family. Majority of these children develop a heightened sense of loyalty for the batterer they have grown up with. Through repeated reminders, they believe their mother has abandoned them, and "after all the father was mother and father to us." Denial is the strategy they adopt to cope with the complex emotions of abandonment and rejection they are engulfed in. In later life, most of them treat their mother with cold hostility, isolation, and rejection. Unable to heal, they are reluctant or unable to take responsibility for their own behavior in adult life. They perpetuate the vicious cycle of aggression, control, hostility and other destructive behaviors in public and private life.

Does one have to suffer the pain in order to realize that this is the story of every home? So often my own friends, countless parents express bewilderment and shock at the hostility and truant behaviors of their children. Working in a high school in the United States has helped me develop further insights from the tragic stories repeated over and over again.

Acquaintances and relatives, colleagues and parents whether in the west or the east, who had developed a "stony silence" as witnesses to domestic violence or, trivialized the incidents occurring in "other families" as *karmic*, or attributed "blame" to the victim, share their horror and disbelief that a grownup child of theirs is a victim now! Overprotective parents who were sure that such "disgrace," would never occur to their children are devastated by the announcement that their own daughters have been silent about being victims due to guilt and concern for "family honor."

A close family friend checked and re-checked an eligible young man to ensure a wonderful marriage for her only daughter. Neither she, nor her husband or close associates detected any problem when they visited their daughter after the marriage. Both the daughter and son-in-law put up their best appearances. Their daughter was convinced from her early socialization that once the parents had fulfilled their obligation to get her married to a desired match she was responsible for the success of the marriage!! For three years she lived in constant fear of her husband's uncontrollable temper. Within this short period she gave birth to two children. Every time she asked him why he was away on weekends, he beat her up. He accused her of not being supportive of the hard work he put in to maintain her in a state of luxury.

By coincidence a friend informed her that her husband was not at work, but seen in their locality with a woman on several occasions. Sensing there was something "fishy," further investigation revealed that the husband had a child out of wedlock, and was in an emotional quandary. His parents wanted a respectable daughter-in-law. He married this very naïve and protected young woman, but was threatened with dire consequences by his previous lover if he did not continue their relationship.

Once exposed, his temper knew no bounds! Bruised and severely traumatized, my friend's daughter managed to escape to this family friend's house. Her parents were summoned. And she returned to her maternal home. Despite the humiliation, the abuse their daughter had undergone, her parents persuaded the husband to leave the other woman and return to live with his "real" wife! The problem "out there" had unbelievably become theirs!! And of course there are enough statistics indicating that honor killings are justified in the name of family reputation!

A fisher woman's young daughter who was mutilated and burned in her husband's drunken rage has to return home, because the neighbors constantly blame her for provoking the husband! The mother and daughter leave the children unattended so that they can earn a living selling fish outside the house. Without a viable alternative she has no other option!

We warn her not to have any more children but she reminded us that, not having a male son was one of the reasons for being abused! These stories are endless. Evil does not exist in isolation. It is a product of amorality in consensus. The sense of absolute power, success in imposing visions that "sell," deadens the value of human lives. The tragic incidents of violence in schools in the US has heightened an international awareness of the corrosive influence of violence in the films and the electronic media which glorifies the acquisition of disposable consumer goods to attain a high standard of living, and other insidious messages through entertainment and advertisements which devalue human live, especially those of girls and women. Rapid globalization has exacerbated the interrelated problems.

Ignoring the enormity of the consequences of domestic violence in efforts to improve the quality of life in developed, or developing countries, is similar to discussing the elephant's tail and not realizing it is connected to the rest of the elephant!

International strategies for constructive change are increasingly aware that the global nature and effects of domestic violence dictates that, all agents of change, and Societal institutions engaged in dealing with different caveats of the problem should be cross-trained in excluding gender politics, to use "informed scientific judgment" which focus on a solution rather than to search for the "real victims." Sparked by a historic process of global activism and conferences, humanity is now recognizing that women's full equality and participation are pre-conditions to human progress.

Strategies and actions workable in other areas are now being piloted in many parts of the world. In India as in other developing countries the greatest obstacles to the implementation and acceleration of effective strategies is the dangerous notion that grinding poverty and economic injustices of the majority of people the concerns of survival needs is of greater priority than domestic violence. Stopping violence against women and girls is not just a matter of punishing individual acts. The issue is changing the perception—so deeply rooted hence often unconscious—that women are fundamentally of less value than men. Sustained multi-sectoral campaigns of action, heightened awareness through public education campaigns, and school programs, adult education in conjunction with gender sensitization, training every agent of change must focus on the fact that, violence against women is a shocking aberration rather than an invisible norm, without this fundamental change in perception, the harmful and deadly problem will continue to corrode the quality of life which technology claims to have improved. The choice is to sow the seeds of change and stem the violence, which threatens every living being, or to embark on the path of rapid destruction.

Chhaya Dey

Glossary

Abba—colloquial *Urdu* word for father.

Ai—vadil—mother and father, in colloquial Marathi.

Allahabad—once the capital city of UP in central India, famous for the *Kumbh Mela* and home town of India's first Prime Minister, Pandit Jawaharlal Nehru.

Amma—word for mother in several Indian languages.

Ashwini Jog—worked at the Special Cell for Women in Distress for three years, then as Lecturer at the Tata Institute for Social Sciences (TISS). Last known work as medical social worker at the Nagjee Memorial Hospital and Research Centre, Nasik.

Babus—Gentleman.

Bahu—daughter-in-law.

Bai—a term of respect for adult Women used in Maharashtra.

Baithaki—A classical style of the popular *Lavni* dance of Maharashtra.

Bandra—a Northern suburb in Mumbai city.

Barat—bridegroom's party.

Bihari—a man from the state of Bihar.

Bhabhi—Brother's wife.

Bhel puri—crunchy savouries, typical of Mumbai.

Chappatis—Handbaked wheat bread.

Chatra Andolan—student unrest.

Chawl—Small tenement.

Choli—short saree blouse.

Chawl—one room tenements, peculiar to Bombay.

chulha—Coal stove.

Chowkidar—Watchman.

Daal—Lentils, used at Indian homes to prepare a curry like dish.

Dadaji—paternal Grandfather.

Desh—Bengali literary Magazine from Anand Bazaar Group, Kolkata.

Devar—Husband's younger brother.

Dekho Natak Kar Rahi Hai—Watch how she is playing up.

Dhoti Diya, Kurta Nahin—given the trousers, not the shirt.

Dilasa—means assurence.

Ganapati—the name of Hindu God, Ganesh, or Siddhi Vinayak.

Gaud Saraswat Brahmin—A subcaste of Brahmins.

Gharana—Particular tradition of rendition.

Goa—a popular sea resort, once part of portuguese India.

Goonda—goons.

Gurusinghji—Guru Gobind Singh, the last of ten Gurus, revered by Sikhs.

Haveli—big mansion homes.

Iska ek pao ghar main to ek bahar—one foot in the home, the other out.

Isne to Itna Diya Shukar Hai—thankfully she has given a lot.

Jamun—Indian Black Berry.

Jethani—husband's elder brother's wife.

Juhu—a well know seaside in suburb of Santa Cruz, Mumbai.

Kangan—heavy bracelet.

Kayastha—in the caste hierarchy, Kayasthas rank third.

Khadi—Hand woven yarn, that Gandhiji advocated.

Kholi—local Marathi word for a room.

Khandan—full joint family, including cousins etc.

Khsatriya—the warrior Castes in Hindu.

Khala—mother's sister.

Kolatis—An encyclopedia meaning of Kolatis is a gypsy like community who sell odd items like bone comb, little rag dolls etc. Traditionally they do body tattoo work. This community is from Karnataka border. Girls are not forced to marry. Some of the girls who do not marry become prostitutes. The community also kidnaps young girls for prostitution.

Kothi—Big house, old style.

Kya lekar ayi hai baap ke ghar se—what have you got from your father's home.

Lathi—bamboo stick.

Lavni—erotic (sexual overtures are common features) style of performing arts where women dance and sing to please male cliental.

Lungi—Loin cloth; worn by men and women (mostly in south India/Assam).

Lord Vithoba—Hindu God Vishnu's nickname in Karnataka and Maharashtra. He is the Chief Deity in Pandharpur—a pilgrim town near Pune. Singers and poets of yore have worshipped *Vithoba*—the female Saint Poet Janabai considered Pandharpur her *maika*—mother's home.

MP—short for Madhya Pradesh, a large state in Central India.

Mada—Death ritual.

Mane muttva—ritual home coming.

Mangalsutra—Black beaded necklace, marriage symbol.

Main Kuch Bhi Nahin Layi—I brought nothing.

Maika—maternal home.

Matka—a gamble, illegal.

Marwari—a business community, originally from Rajasthan.

Memsaab—Madam; generally the illiterate maids call their matrons.

Mujhe kangan hi chahiye—I want a bracelet only.

Mujhe To Sone Main Tolke Diya Hai—I was weighed in gold.

Nari Kendra—Women's Centre in Vakola; activities, counseling, legal aid, campaigning, and providing resource.

Nikahnama—Muslim marriage document.

Nikah—Muslim Marriage.

Nanad—Husband's sister.

Neg—a demand of gift made by the husband's sister when the new bride enters her in-laws' home.

Natak—acting, here used in a derogatory way, i.e., first.

Nilgiris—The hills in Ootacamund (Tamil Nadu state).

Ozha—Village doctor-cum-priest.

Paan—beetul leaf.

Patil—The Head of the Village.

Panchayat—Village counsel who settle disputes etc.

Pandharpur—A popular pilgrimage in Maharashtra.

Padree—Christian Priest.

Pani Puree—Indian snacks also called *golgappa*.

Pao—small bread, popular in Bombay.

Phuga—baloon.

Phulkas—Hand baked fluffy bread.

Pitaji—Father.

Pujapath—Prayers.

Purda—Veil, also curtain.

Ragda pattice—spicy chick pea snack.

Rishta—marriage alliance, also means 'relationship'.

Roti—Same as chappati: hand baked bread.

Sardarji—used to describe a turbaned Sikh man.

Saree—six meter cloth worn by Indian women.

Sasubai—colloquial in Marathi for mother-in-law.

Satara—A small town in Maharashtra.

Sati-Savitri—Indian mythological female characters from the epic Ramayana and Mahabharat who reprsent idealized womanhood.

Satyagraha—Non-violent struggle against the British launched by Gandhiji.

Seva Dal—a social organization.

Shakti—female principle: meaning strength.

Shikari—Hunter.

Sindoor—red vermillion powder, put in the hair parting for married women.

Subhodrishti—The first glance at one's spouse during a Bengali marriage ceremony.

Suhag—Any auspicious marriage sign.

Talaq—Muslim divorce.

Tilak— Hindu ritual, before the wedding.

Tagore—Rabindranath Tagore, India's poet laureate awarded the Nobel Prize (1913) for his poetry collection, Geetanjali.

UP—abbreviation for Uttar Pradesh—the North Indian Hindi language State.

Tola—An Indian measure for gold, by weight approse. 10 gm

Usko Dena Parega—You must give her.

Vadas—spicy potato patties.

Yeh To Dena Hi Parega—Its obliged to be given.

Yeh Itna Has Rahi Hai—she laughs too much.

Yeh Sab Natak Hai—This is acting.

Yeh Dialogue Bolti Hai—She is delevering dialogues.

About the Editor and Contributors

Anwesha Arya is currently enrolled for her PhD in the Department of the Study of Religions, School of Oriental and African Studies (SOAS), University of London. She is researching the shift from bride-price practises to dowry in India and dowry related murder. Her Masters thesis, from SOAS, focused on dowry in ancient India. Her interests include legal reform, creative writing, and photography. She currently lives with her husband in London.

Rinki Bhattacharya is a well-known critic, columnist, writer, freelance journalist, and documentary film producer based in Mumbai, India. *CHAR DIWARI*, her documentary film on domestic violence received international acclaim. She has worked as a volunteer at Nari Kendra in Mumbai and started in 1989 a crisis hotline for battered women called HELP. Presently, she is Director, Bimal Roy Memorial and Film Society, Mumbai.

Chhaya Dey was born and brought up in India. She received her graduation and doctoral degrees from Columbia University, New York. She has won several scholarships and awards, as the Fullbright and the National endowment of the Humanities fellowships. She has written and published several personal and professional articles. Currently she is teaching in a High School in the United States. She hopes to continue her work as a bridge to transformation through her experiences. She hopes to return to India and make a difference in people's lives in her own way.

Sage 06157
18/1/14

Shirin Kudchedkar was the former Head of the Department of English at S. N. D. T. Women's University, Mumbai, for 14 years and Foreign Expert at Nanjing Normal University for a year. She retired as Director of the Canadian Studies Program at S. N. D. T. University in 1994. She has taught a course on Women Writing in India at the University of York, Toronto. She was the Gujrati Sectional Editor for the two volume publication *Women Writing in India: 600 BC to the Present* edited by Susie Tharu and K. Lalita, in which she translated Gujrati pieces into English. Dr Kudchedkar co-edited two books, *Violence Against Women: Women Against Violence* and *Canadian Voices: An Anthology of Canadian Poetry*. She has edited *Postmodernism and Feminism: Canadian Context*.

Kalindi Muzumdar retired as Vice-Principal of the College of Social Work, Nirmala Niketan. She is the coordinator of the Sakhya Anti-Dowry Guidance Cell which counsels dowry affected victims, assists in their rehabilitation, creates public awareness by conducting family-life education sessions and running a door-to-door campaign.

Mamta G Sagar Mamta G Sagar is a Kannada poet and play-wright. She has published two anthologies of poetry and three plays.

Sobha Venkatesh Ghosh Heads the Department of English at S.I.E.S. College, Mumbai. Her doctoral work was on feminist critical theory. She has published in the area of feminist theory and criticism.